Methods of Educational Measurement

Methods of Educational Measurement

D. Smith

Commonwealth

Methods of Educational Measurement

Edition : 2021

ISBN 81-7169-894-8

Published by :

COMMONWEALTH PUBLISHERS
4831/24, Prahlad Street,
Ansari Road, Darya Ganj,
New Delhi - 110002
Ph. : 23275511, 23257835
Fax : 91-011-23257835
e-mail : commonwealthbooks@gmail.com

Typesetting by :

Rishu Computers
Delhi - 110092

Printed at :
Roshan Offset Printers
Delhi

Preface

Basic to using the results of measurement is the interpretation of scores. A test score is merely a number, devoid of meaning in and by itself. Not until it is related to something does it become meaningful and thus useful. Before we proceed with a discussion of the various uses of test results, it would be well to take another look at a device which facilities interpretation. This is the *profile,* a graphic method of depicting the results of the testing of individuals and of groups. The profile typically shows the results of an achievement battery such as the *Stanford,* an aptitude battery such as the *Differential Aptitude Tests,* or scores on an interest inventory for various occupations such as the *Strong.* Although a profile actually adds nothing to the information given by scores, norms and statistical interpretations, it does facilitate comparisons and interpretations by presenting results graphically and all in one package for a given individual or a group.

The author is grateful to John E. Bell and K. Buros Oscar and specifically to the committees on test standards of the American Educational Research Association and the National Council on Measurements used in education for their most valuable contributions in this area.

D. Smith

Contents

1

Trying out and Evaluating the Teacher-made Test

Assembling the Test

When the teacher or test-maker has constructed the test items and edited and recorded them, either on cards or in some other manner, he is ready to arrange them preparatory to having the test reproduced. In the case of an essay test, the sequence of questions presents no problem since such a test usually involves writing the questions on the board at the time of the examination, although it is probably preferable to duplicate the set of essay questions and give each pupil a copy. For tests employing items of a more objective nature, however, the requirements are different. In the following section we shall discuss some of the problems relating to the organization of an objective test.

Arranging the Items

A number of factors have a bearing on the arrangement of items in an objective test. Among these are: (1) difficulty, (2) type of item, (3) content, and (4) anticipated use of the score. Ordinarily, in a standardised test the items are arranged is accordance with most or all of these criteria at the same time. For example, in nearly all such tests the items are arranged in order of difficulty, from the easiest to the most difficult. This system has two advantages. First, it encourages the person taking the test by starting him on items he can easily manage. Second, it tends to avoid the possibility of the student's getting stuck on a difficult item which might not leave him time enough to answer many easier ones that follow. Of course, the difficulty of individual test items is determined on the basis of responses by groups, and does not necessarily coincide with the item-difficulty pattern of any particular individual. The assumption which must be made is that the average difficulty based on responses of the group is the best available difficulty index for the individuals in the group.

It is customary to group items according to type—that is, to place true-false items in one group, multiple-choice in another, etc.—and then to arrange the items within each category according to difficulty, as just described. If there are a great many items of one kind, they may, of course, be divided into two or more groups according to some other criterion such as content. For example, if there are fifty multiple-choice items and fifty true-false items to be arranged, each type might be subdivided into two groups of twenty-five each, particularly, if there is some obvious and logical basis for such a division. If, in an arithmetic test, half of the true-false items deal with fractions and half with decimals, the items might be divided on that basis, and similarly the multiple-choice questions. In instances in which part scores on these aspects of arithmetic are desired, such an arrangement will make it easier to obtain them.

Basically then, in most objective tests items are arranged according to type and within the type groups, according to difficulty. The amateur test-maker, as distinguished from the professional, usually has no basis for determining the difficulty of individual test items except his personal judgment. Whereas the producer of standardised tests tries out the items in preliminary forms to determine difficulty, the classroom teacher almost never has the opportunity to do this. Therefore, he does the best he can by grouping the items according to his own estimate of their difficulty. Parenthetically, a word might be added here concerning the grouping of items according to type. This practice is now almost universal and the reasons are fairly obvious. In the first place, it facilitates scoring, since items all of the same type are easier to score than a mixture of various types. In the second place, a test in which items are grouped according to types of items is usually more agreeable to the examinee.

Arranging items within the type groups according to estimated difficulty cannot be a very exact process, and the test-maker will usually have to rely upon his own experience and judgment in this matter. It is sometimes quite satisfactory to arrange items according to length, placing the shortest first. Length is never a valid basis for judging difficulty, but an arrangement of this sort may encourage the examinee by leading him to assume that the hardest items will come at the end of the test.

Items may be arranged according to content, as in the example of the arithmetic test given above. In every field of concern to him, the teacher has certain ideas or plans for organisation of the subject-matter. Usually, subject-matter is organised by units and by areas within the units. For example, a unit on transportation may be organised according to historical periods or according to kinds of transportation—land, sea and air, or mechanical and animal. Items in such divisions as these may in turn be arranged according to type, difficulty, and content simultaneously, provided, of course, that there are enough items. For short tests of twenty-five items or less, the grouping of the items on any basis except type is not often practical or useful.

There is one other situation in which the grouping of items is important, namely, when diagnosis is the purpose of the test. Let us assume that in arithmetic, English, or reading, the examiner wishes to identify specific strengths and weaknesses in the pupils' grasp of fundamentals. The first step in constructing a test for diagnostic purposes is to make a careful analysis of the rules and skills that are basic to progress in the subject. The next step is to construct an adequate number of items on each rule or skill and then arrange them in the test so that each group constitutes a measure of understanding of one of these. Thus, when the test results are available the responses of each pupil, as well as of the entire class, to items testing a particular rule or skill will be easily determined. Advance arrangement of items for such purposes will facilitate diagnosis and remedial instruction. This will be discussed and illustrated in more detail in Chapter 9.

Preparing Directions

When the arrangement and grouping of the test items have been determined, the next step is to prepare directions. Before the test is duplicated, directions should be prepared for the test as a whole, as well as for the sub-tests or parts. If the test is to be used as a semester-or year-end final examination, a title page may be used. This gives the test a more finished appearance; also, if pupils are not to start work on it until preliminary directions have been given, a title page serves to cover the test proper until the directions have been read and the pupils told to begin. If there is to be a title page, it may be set up in a form similar to Figure 1.1.

If the examination is a cooperative effort and is given to classes under the supervision of several different teachers, there should be space for the pupil to indicate his section and his teacher's name, so that the papers can be readily sorted.

If a title page is not used, the essential information can be put at the top of the first page of the test.

Directions for each part should come at the beginning of the part, as follows:

> *Directions:* The statements in this part are either True or False. Read each one carefully. If you think it is *true,* place a + in the parentheses in front of the statement; if you think it is *false,* place a 0 in the parentheses.

If the scoring is to be on the basis of right answers minus wrong answers, the following should be added:

> If you are not sure of the correct answer, but can make an intelligent guess, mark the statement; if not, omit it. Your score on this part of the test will be the number of right answers minus the number of wrong answers.

If the scoring is to be based on the number of right answers only, the following should be added:

> Mark every statement. Your score will be the number right.

If locally duplicated answer sheets are used (see page 9), the directions given first above should be modified in part as follows:

> If you think it is *true,* place a + on the answer sheet opposite the number which corresponds to the number of the statement. If you think it is *false,* place a 0, etc.

If machine-scored or printed answer sheets are used, the directions should be:

> If you think it is *true*, make a heavy black mark between the dotted lines in Column 1 opposite the number which corresponds to the number of the statement. If you think it

is *false*, blacken the space between the pair of lines in Column 2. You should use only pencils provided or, if directed to do so, a soft lead pencil (No. 2 or No. 2½) to mark the answer sheet. Do *not* use a pen or coloured pencil.

Score	Name ....
Part 1	Date ....
Part 2	Section ....
Total	Teacher's Name ....

Final Examination

English 10A

Directions : Do not turn the page until you are told to do so. The examination consists of two parts. Part 1 is True-False and Part 2 is Multiple-Choice. Directions are given in the test for each part. Please read them carefully and follow them exactly. You will have forty minutes to work on the test. Try to answer every question, but if you do not know the answer to a question go on to the next ones and come back to it later. Do not "skip around". Begin at the beginning and work straight through. Your score on the test will be the number answered correctly.

Fig. 1.1 : Typical Title Page for a Teacher-Made Test.

In similar fashion, directions for multiple-choice, matching, or short-answers items should be worked out and reproduced on the test paper so that the directions will precede the part to which they apply.

With younger pupils especially, and in any case where pupils are not accustomed to objective-type tests, it is well to include a sample item with the directions. For example, the following could be used after the directions for matching items:

Example :

(*c*) paint	(*a*) compound
(*a*) water	(*b*) element
	(*c*) mixture

Paint is a mixture, so the letter *c* has been placed in the parentheses before *paint;* water is a compound, so the letter *a* has been placed in the parentheses before *water*. Mark the items below in the same way. Notice that there are more items in the right-hand column than in the left, so that after all the blanks have been filled you will have some on the right that you have not used. Some of the items in the right-hand column may be used more than once.

Directions for the test and the sub-tests or parts should be carefully worked out in advance and incorporated into the test. The ideal to strive for is to make the test as nearly self-administering as possible, so that the pupil understands what he is to do with a minimum of supplementary explanations. This is especially desirable if the test is to be used by more than one teacher, and it is advantageous in any case because a test which is nearly self-administering makes for uniformity and objectivity of administration. Otherwise, there is a danger that supplementary instructions will not be identical when given to various pupils or groups at different times.

Reproducing the Test

In most cases, teacher-made tests are duplicated in the school office. Copy is prepared by the teacher, often in handwritten form. It is important to make clear to the typist such matters as capitalisation, punctuation, spacing and provisions for marking answers. Capitalisation and punctuation generally do not cause any difficulty, provided the test-maker knows and indicates clearly what he wants. Words to be emphasised should be written in capitals, or underlined, or both.

The matter of spacing is important in setting up objective tests. All material on the page should be arranged and spaced in a manner which will make it as clear and legible as possible for the pupil. This procedure should be followed at all grade levels, and especially when preparing tests for younger children. If answers are to be written or marked on the test itself, sufficient space should be provided and it should be clear that the space left is for this purpose. For example, when answers are to be marked within parentheses they should be spaced thus (   ), not thus ( ). If words or phrases are to be written, ample space for writing them should be provided. This is usually accomplished by leaving a ruled space, thus, ——, as in short-answer or completion items. If the teacher desires to do so, he can give a clue to the length of the word by the amount of space provided. This is not generally recommended, however, since it provides what might be considered an irrelevant clue. If the size of the space is not intended to provide a clue, the directions should indicate this fact.

There should always be a double space between successive test items. It is poor economy to crowd them together; however, the statement of each item itself may be single-spaced. In the case of multiple-choice items, general practice favours setting them up in this manner:

( ) The study of living things is called

(a) physics

(b) chemistry

(c) biology

(d) geology

(e) astronomy

The latter method is generally preferred to the plan of listing choices thus:

( ) The study of living things is called (a) physics (b) chemistry (c) biology (d) geology (e) astronomy

Items should be numbered consecutively through the entire test rather than consecutively within each part. The latter procedure results in having two or more items with the same number, as two number 1's, two number 2's, etc. If there are several parts, there will, of course, be an item numbered *1* in each, and so on. This leads to confusion, particularly if locally made answer sheets are used. Most teacher-made answer sheets are set up with numbered spaces in columns, as shown in Figure 1.2.

Pupils will become confused if the numbers on the items do not correspond with the numbers on the answer sheet. When the numbering of items in different parts of the test begins in each case with number 1, no standard answer sheet can be used; instead, each test must have its own answer sheet with numbers coinciding with those on the test. The consecutive arrangement shown in Figure 1.2 is nearly always followed with answer sheets accompanying standardised tests.

Any study or analysis of individual test items is also facilitated by a consecutive numbering system, since each number quickly identifies a particular question and its corresponding answer and distinguishes that question and answer from all others on the test.

Tests may be reproduced by a number of different processes, each of which has some advantages. If more than one method is available, the choice will be determined by local needs and circumstances. Objective tests should *always* be duplicated. Although some attempts have been made to administer objective tests orally be reading the questions aloud, this method is not recommended. The pupil is entitled to have the test before him and should not be expected to keep the questions in mind or make snap decisions at the moment the questions are read aloud.

Tests reproduced by processes available in most schools should be duplicated on one side of the sheet only. It is generally not satisfactory to use both sides because unless extra-heavy paper—and extreme care—are used, some of the print will show through and the material will be difficult to read. Also, when a test consists of several pages fastened together, it is easier for the pupil to handle if print appears on only one side of each page. This is especially true when tablet-arm chairs are used and when answers are marked on the test itself rather than on a separate answer sheet.

For ease in scoring, the test should be set up and duplicated so that answer spaces appear in a straight line, all at the same margin. This is easily arranged for true-false, multiple-choice and matching items by placing parentheses before the number of each item. With short answer and completion questions a plan similar to the example below may be used:

(15) The surrender of (a) took place a. ---------------

----

at Yorktown in the year (b) b. ---------------

Here all answers are written in the lettered spaces at the right-hand margin. Also, since all the answer spaces are of the same length, there is no irrelevant clue to the length of the correct answer.

If answers are written on the test itself, enough copies of the test must be made so that there will be a new one for each examinee every time the test is administered. If separate answer sheets are used, the tests themselves can be used repeatedly. When the same test is used with several groups it is important to collect

Subject ---------------------------- Score ------------- Name --------------------

Instructor ------------------------ Date ----------------------

1. ---------------	26. -----------------	51. ---------------	76. ------------------
2. ---------------	27. -----------------	52. ---------------	77. ------------------
3. ---------------	28. -----------------	53. ---------------	78. ------------------
4. ---------------	29. -----------------	54. ---------------	79. ------------------
5. ---------------	30. -----------------	55. ---------------	80. ------------------
6. ---------------	31. -----------------	56. ---------------	81. ------------------
7. ---------------	32. -----------------	57. ---------------	82. ------------------
8. ---------------	33. -----------------	58. ---------------	83. ------------------
9. ---------------	34. -----------------	59. ---------------	84. ------------------
10. ---------------	35. -----------------	60. ---------------	85. ------------------
11. ---------------	36. -----------------	61. ---------------	86. ------------------
12. ---------------	37. -----------------	62. ---------------	87. ------------------
13. ---------------	38. -----------------	63. ---------------	88. ------------------
14. ---------------	39. -----------------	64. ---------------	89. ------------------
15. ---------------	40. -----------------	65. ---------------	90. ------------------
16. ---------------	41. -----------------	66. ---------------	91. ------------------
17. ---------------	42. -----------------	67. ---------------	92. ------------------
18. ---------------	43. -----------------	68. ---------------	93. ------------------
19. ---------------	44. -----------------	69. ---------------	94. ------------------
20. ---------------	45. -----------------	70. ---------------	95. ------------------
21. ---------------	46. -----------------	71. ---------------	96. ------------------
22. ---------------	47. -----------------	72. ---------------	97. ------------------
23. ---------------	48. -----------------	73. ---------------	98. ------------------
24. ---------------	49. -----------------	74. ---------------	99. ------------------
25. ---------------	50. -----------------	75. -------------	100. ------------------

Fig. 1.2 : Sample of a Teacher-made answer sheet.

all copies each time it is used, for if copies get into circulation the examination will obviously lose its usefulness as a testing or measuring instrument. It is helpful to number all copies and require each pupil to write the number of the copy he is using on the answer sheet, provided separate answer sheets are used. In this way, missing copies of the test can be traced and usually recovered. It is also necessary, if tests are used more than once, to scan them after each use and erase all marks made on them by the previous users.

In arranging objective tests for duplication it is not desirable to have a question continue from one page to the next; starting a question on a new page is preferable to dividing it. *This is particularly important with matching questions,* for the examinee would become justifiably annoyed if he constantly had to turn a page back and forth to consult the two parts of each list on two separate pages.

The Scoring Key

When answers are to be marked on the test proper and the blanks are spaced in the manner suggested above, the preparation of a scoring key is simple. The scoring key usually consists of a strip of heavy paper or cardboard about an inch and a half wide and as long as the answer column on the test page. The correct answers are entered on this strip, spaced to match exactly the spacing of the items on the test page. Then the strip is laid alongside the column of answers and the scorer checks the wrong or the right answers, whichever method he has decided to use in scoring. The answers on the key should be typed or printed near the edge of the strip so that when it is laid on the test the correct answers will be close to the answer spaces on the test.

When locally made answer sheets are used, the same type of scoring key is usable, since the spaces on these answer sheets are usually arranged in columns—usually four to the page—about an inch to an inch and a half wide. One hundred such spaces can easily be typed, double spaced, on an ordinary sheet of paper, with twenty-five items in each of the four columns, as shown in Figure 1.2.

When the machine-scorable type of answer sheet is scored by hand, the most convenient key is one made of a sheet of cardboard the same size as the answer sheet. At each place where a correct answer mark should appear on the answer sheet a small hole is punched in the cardboard. This makes a stencil which can be laid over the answer sheet. Scoring is then done by simply counting the number of marks that appear through the holes in the stencil. This type of scoring stencil is usually provided by publishers of standardised tests. It may be used for hand scoring as well as for machine scoring. When using such a scoring stencil, it is necessary to scan the answer sheet before covering it with the stencil to see that only one space is marked for each item. Where more than one space is marked, such items should be counted wrong unless, of course, there is more than one correct answer to the items in question.

Another type of locally produced answer sheet, shown in Figure 1.3, incorporates some features of the machine-scorable sheet. Rather than providing spaces in which short answers can be written, this sheet provides spaces corresponding to the answer alternatives only. Pupils indicate their answers either by blackening or crossing out the intended space. If the sheets are reproduced by Multilith or duplicating equipment, some copies can be run on heavy paper or cardboard for use in preparing keys. The example of a key in Figure 1.4 shows that spaces are punched to correspond to the correct answers.

If answers are marked on the test itself, spaces for recording scores should be provided either on the title page as shown on page 5 or at the top of page 1 of the test. If part-scores are determined, they should be recorded separately and added to obtain the total score. If derived scores of some type such as ranks or standard scores are calculated, they should also be recorded in additional spaces provided for the purpose. The same principles apply if separate answer sheets are used, but the scores are recorded on the answer sheets, not on the tests.

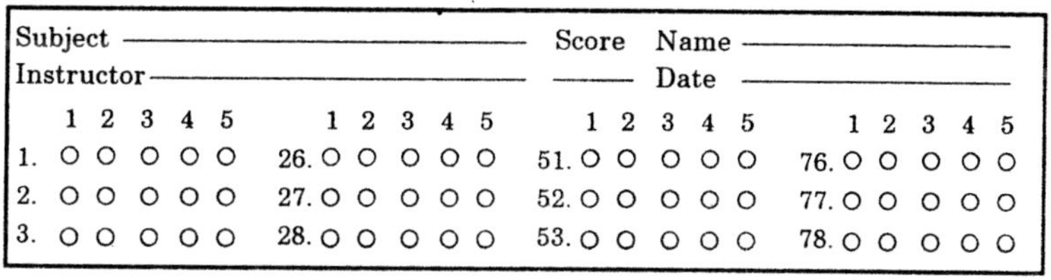

Fig. 1.3. : A locally prepared answer sheet with response positions.

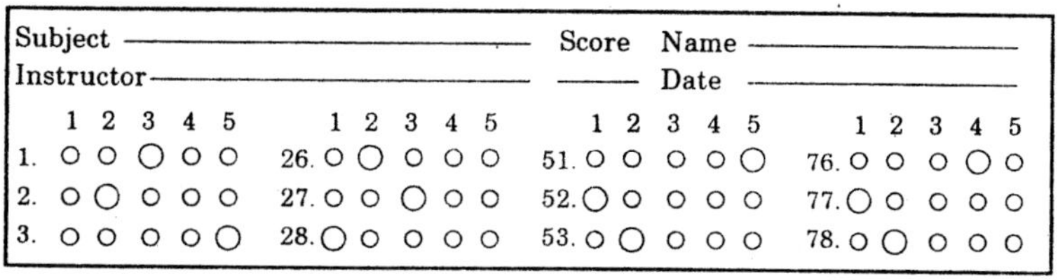

Fig. 1.4. : A key for a locally prepared answer sheet.

Analysing the Results

After a test has been tried out and scored the results may be analysed in two ways. One is from the standpoint of what the results reveal about the pupils' learning or how successful instruction has been. This means far more than simply tabulating total scores on the test, since high scores may result from an easy test as well as from good teaching, and conversely, low scores may be caused by a difficult test or by inferior teaching. Thorough analysis of test results involves some attempt at diagnosis, even though the test may not have been set up with this purpose clearly in mind. It is always desirable to formulate some kind of analysis showing the degree of success with specific items and parts of the test in order to appraise the efficacy of teaching and learning. Unless an attempt at such analysis is made, the results of the test cannot be put to maximum use.

A simple analysis of the results of a test for diagnostic purposes can be performed in two ways: (1) the teacher can tabulate the responses to each item, which will tell him how often each item was missed, or (2) he can return the scored tests or answer sheets to the students and ask for a show of hands on each item by those who missed it. (In either case, it should be noted, the scoring should be done by checking *wrong answers.*) In this way it is possible to analyse the performance of the students on the test and to identify individual points and areas of content or objectives that have not been well learned. The results of such analysis may provide a basis for re-teaching or remedial work with individual students.

Another type of analysis has for its purpose the evaluation of the test as a measuring instrument. How effective is the test and how well does it function? Although careful analytical appraisal is an essential part of the process of producing a standardised test, this is not generally practiced by classroom teachers in the test-making. Yet some evaluation of this sort might well be a part of every teacher's measurement programme. Unless teachers are willing to "test the test," the effectiveness of their measurement techniques cannot be satisfactorily determined.

The rest of this chapter will be devoted to the explanation of a few simple techniques which any test-maker can use with a test of his own construction to appraise its worth as a measuring instrument.

Validity

It will be remembered that validity refers to an degree to which a test measures what it is intended to measure. How can a teacher appraise the validity of his own tests? Obviously, curricular validity is one measure. If the teacher has constructed the test on the basis of his instructional objectives, and if the test covers or measures what he has been teaching, the test may be said to have a degree of curricular validity; that is, it is valid because it tests what the teacher has been teaching.

If the teacher wishes to go beyond curricular validity, he can compare the test scores with scores on other tests he has given, with marks based on class and laboratory work, and with other measures of achievement such as standardised tests in the same subject. Correlation is the usual method of determining the extent of such relationships.

The discrimination power of individual items on a test is a valuable index for evaluating their quality. It has been regarded by some authorities as an indicator of validity, or lack of it. The argument runs something like this: one must assume, first, that scores on the whole test have some validity and, second, that scores on a particular valid item should agree with scores on the whole test. Let us examine these assumptions. The first usually implies that the test has curricular validity. There may be other evidence of validity, but generally when item-discrimination is used as a means of establishing validity, the test, which is in this case the criterion of validity, is assumed to have curricular validity because it measures what has been taught. The second assumption is tested by comparing results on a given test item with score on the whole test. Since the test is assumed to have some validity, an item which agrees with the scores on the test also has some validity. That is, an item which is answered correctly by a higher proportion of those who make high scores on the test than of those who make low scores is functioning in a manner consistent with the scores on the whole test. Whether or not we accept this line of reasoning as justification for regarding the discrimination power of items as evidence of validity, the technique is a widely used an generally accepted method of identifying "good" items and culling out "poor" ones.

To consider how this is done, let us assume that a test has

been given and scored and that the papers have been arranged in order of score, from highest to lowest. We may call the highest one-fourth of these the "high group" and the lowest one-fourth the "low group". In a class of forty, the highest ten on the test would constitute the high group, and the lowest ten, the low group.

Now let us consider that the results of a hypothetical test item are as follows:

Item No. 15

	Answered correctly by
High Group	7 (of the top 10)
Low Group	3 (of the lowest 10)

We may conclude that this item discriminates as it should; that is, 70 per cent of the pupils in the high group get it right, while only 30 per cent in the low group do so. Such an item is said to have a positive discrimination value, or to discriminate positively. On the other hand, not every test item will discriminate positively. For example:

Item No. 16

	Answered correctly by
High Group	4 (of the top 10)
Low Group	7 (of the lowest 10)

This item is said to discriminate negatively because a higher proportion of the low group get it right than of the high group. Items showing negative discrimination are not common, but it should be the aim of the good test technician to identify and eliminate them whenever he can.

The following item is one that actually discriminated negatively in a national tryout:

(2) Temporary teeth in children do *not* include

(a) incisors

(b) bicuspids

(c) canines

(d) molars

In trying out this item with about fifteen hundred students in Grades 7, 8 and 9, it was found that (b), "bicuspids," the correct answer, was chosen by 11 per cent of the lowest fourth and by only 8 per cent of the highest fourth. Moreover, for some reason, 67 per cent of the top fourth and 42 per cent of the bottom chose (d), "molars," as the right answer. Of all the students tested, only about 10 per cent answered the item correctly. There is no factor here of ambiguity, since (b) is unquestionably the right choice. It is simply matter of difficulty. The item was not included in the final forms of the test because of its negative discrimination.

The usual explanation for negatively discriminating items is ambiguity in the statement of the item itself. In such items the abler, more thoughtful pupil may see some implications which the maker of the test himself overlooked, and may thus be led to choose an answer that has not been labelled as the correct one. The less able pupil, on the other hand, considering the item on a more superficial basis, arrives at the answer which has been keyed as correct.

Sometimes the maker of a test feels that a question missed by a substantial proportion of his class is a bad item or that it reflects on his teaching ability. Consider the following typical results:

Item No. 37

	Answered correctly by
High Group	30%
Low Group	10%

This item is answered correctly by less than one-third of the high-scoring pupils and by 10 per cent of the low scores. Of the class as a whole, probably about one-fifth would get it right. However, the item appears to be a good one since it discriminates clearly between the high and low groups in a positive direction. Some items of this difficulty level can be justifiably included on a test, but a test containing a large proportion of such items will not be maximally efficient.

It should be kept in mind that most item-discrimination techniques start with all the members of the group who have taken the test. Suppose, for example the teacher has given a test to four classes in first-year algebra. There are 120 students in the four classes. After scoring the test he arranges the test papers in order from highest score to lowest score. Then, starting at the top he takes off the first thirty (top 25 per cent), and starting with the paper having the lowest score he count off thirty (another 25 per cent) from the bottom. These are, respectively, the high and low fourths of all (120) who took the test. Now, beginning with item Number 1 he counts the number in the high group who answered it correctly and the number in the low group who answered it correctly. These two numbers are the basis for determining the discriminating power for that item.

A simple formula for determining the discriminating power of a test item is $d = \frac{n_H - n_L}{N}$, where d = the discrimination index, n_H = the number in the high group answering the item correctly, n_L = the number in the low group answering the item correctly, and N = the total number in either high or low group (N = 25 per cent of all who took the test). For example, if $n_H = 20$, $n_L = 10$ and N = 30, $d = \frac{20-10}{30} = \frac{10}{30} = .33$. This index has a possible range from +1 to –1. An item answered correctly by all the highs and missed by all the lows would have an index of +1. Conversely, an item answered correctly by all the lows and missed by all the highs would have an index of –1. An item answered correctly by equal numbers of highs and lows has an index of 0. A reasonable criterion in using this index would be a value of .25. An item having an index lower than this would be considered a poorly discriminating item.

Functioning of Choices

There is another type of analysis which professional test-makers apply to multiple-choice items, namely, the determination of how the choices in each such item function. A choice which no examinee chooses as the correct answer is simply filler or "deadwood". In determining the quality of multiple-choice items it is customary to determine how often each choice is marked as the correct answer. In the case of a positively discriminating item the *correct* answer must be chosen more often by the high group than by the low group; but each of the wrong choices, or distractors, should be chosen by some.

Thus, a complete analysis for a multiple-choice item might look like this:

Item No. 10 :

	Choices (Per cent)				
	1	2	3*	4	5
Highs	10	12	50	7	21
Lows	13	17	31	11	28

*Correct answer.

Here it can be seen that 50 per cent of the "highs" answered the item correctly as compared with 31 per cent of the "lows." All choice function, i.e., all were marked correct by some examinees. Consider, however, the following example:

Item No. 11 :

	Choices (Per cent)				
	1	2*	3	4	5
Highs	5	84	0	11	0
Lows	14	70	4	12	0

*Correct answer.

This item is also a "good" item in that it discriminates positively. However, note that choice 3 was marked correct by only 4 per cent of the lows and none of the highs and that choice 5 is chosen by none of either group. This item would probably be carefully studied and the third and fifth choices would be revised or replaced, since they are so obviously wrong that they are contributing little or nothing to the usefulness of the item.

The teacher who makes a test for repeated use can carry out a simple item analysis as explained here, and enter the results on the item card. Items which do not discriminate positively—that is, which are not answered correctly by a larger proportion of the best pupils than of the less able ones—should be studied for clues to the reason for the negative discrimination. Unless negatively discriminating items can be shown to have other important values, or can be made positively discriminating, there is little reason to retain them, for they will detract from the validity of the test as a whole.

Difficulty

Closely related to considerations of the discrimination values of test items is the question of difficulty. Except for special and unusual reasons, items which are answered correctly or which are missed by all pupils are not considered good, for such items make no discrimination whatever in the class or group being tested. A test made up entirely of such items would result in everyone's getting the same score, either perfect or zero. Obviously, such a result tells nothing about differences in achievement among members of the class. Rather, it demonstrates that the test was either entirely too easy or too difficult, and thus reflects unfavourably on the test-maker's ability.

The only exception to this position might occur if one were testing for mastery. That is, if the teacher had been drilling on certain combinations in addition or perhaps a spelling list, his goal might be complete mastery or 100 per cent accuracy. In such an instance he would expect most of his pupils eventually to achieve this goal. Ordinarily, however, we do not expect or get 100 per cent mastery or perfection on any educational objective; our tests are designed to challenge the best students and at the same time to provide ample opportunity for the poorest to show what they can do.

The simplest way for the teacher to determine whether his test is appropriate in difficulty for the group tested is to study the distribution of scores on the test. If the mean is at or near the middle of the range and if there are no perfect or zero scores, the teacher may be fairly certain that the test is suitable for that group. For example, on a test containing eighty questions it is found that the mean score is 42 and the range of scores is from 11 to 75. Such facts indicate that the test was suitable in range and difficulty for this class. Let us suppose, however, that with another class or grade the same test shows an average score of 69 and a range from 50 to 80; obviously the test was to easy for this group. If, on the other hand, the mean is 15 and the range from 0 to 40, the test would have been too difficult.

Thus, it may be inferred that difficulty has a bearing on the discrimination value of a test—that a test which is too hard or too easy will not discriminate between individuals of different levels of achievement as well as one which is more appropriate for the range of abilities in the group.

Though absolutely fixed points for acceptable averages or range can rarely be established, the following general principles may serve as a useful guide to the student.

(1) Items which are missed or answered correctly by every pupil are not discriminating in that group.

(2) On a test which is appropriate in difficulty for a given group, the mean should be near the middle of the range of possible scores.

(3) On a test suitable for a group of the usual variability, the range of scores should be as wide as possible, short of zero or perfect scores.

(4) If the number of pupils tested is fairly large (about 30 or more) and fairly heterogeneous, and the foregoing principles are met, the scores on a test should distribute themselves symmetrically around the average.

(5) Tests which give zero scores or perfect scores are not discriminating for the individuals who make such scores.

Reliability

Another characteristic of importance to the test-maker is reliability. This is a measure of the consistency with which a test measures whatever it is intended to measure. Various methods for determining reliability—the test-retest, equivalent forms, and the split-half methods. However, test reliability may be estimated by a shorter method which is accurate enough for classroom tests and other ordinary situations. It requires the calculation of only two measures, the mean and the standard deviation of the distribution of scores on the test. The formula follows:

$$r_t = \frac{n\sigma_t^2 - M(n-M)}{\sigma_t^2(n-1)}$$

where r_t = reliability of the test, n = number of items in the test, σ_t = standard deviation of the scores on the test, and M = mean of scores on the test.

An example will help to clarify the use of this formula. Suppose that a teacher has given a test of fifty items and has found the mean to be 30 and the standard deviation 6. Though circumstances make it inconvenient for him to use any of the usual methods of determining test reliability, he wants to estimate the reliability of this test. To do so, he uses the formula given above, substituting these values: $n = 50$, $M = 30$ and $\sigma_t = 6$:

$$r_t = \frac{\left[50 \times (6)^2\right] - [30(50-30)]}{(6)^2(50-1)}$$

$$= \frac{[50 \times 36] - [30 \times 20]}{36 \times 49}$$

$$= \frac{1800 - 600}{1764}$$

$$= \frac{1200}{1764}$$

$$= .68$$

Thus, the teacher finds that his test has a reliability of .68, which is not very high. However, he can take some comfort from the knowledge that this formula nearly always gives a lower estimate of reliability than most other approaches give, and that his test therefore probably has a reliability at least as high as .68. Knowing the reliability of his test enables the teacher to determine how much reliance he can place on the scores yielded by it.

There are many refinements and technical details of test analysis which, because they are beyond the scope of the usual first course in educational measurement, are not mentioned here. The average teacher or counsellor, however, should be able to follow the suggestions and procedures presented here; certainly if he does use such procedures he will achieve steady improvement in the construction of his tests and in his whole measurement programme, and will thus experience a sense of genuine satisfaction in this important part of his job.

2

Measuring Achievement in the Elementary Grades

In this chapter and the following one we shall discuss the measurement of achievement in the elementary and secondary grades and describe the types of instruments most commonly used. Since there are hundreds of standardised achievement tests available, it is obviously beyond the score of this book to attempt to describe all or even a substantial number of them. Nevertheless, we shall describe in some detail examples of each of the important types and list other major tests which are available in the same areas. No claim is made here that the tests or other measures chosen for detailed description in these chapters are necessarily the best of their respective types. Rather, an attempt has been made to select representative or typical instruments and avoid emphasising the product of any single publisher. Unquestionably, in many cases other equally good and equally representative samples might be chosen for illustration. Above all, it is the writers' intention to make the descriptions of the tests as instructive as possible by the selection of examples varying widely in organisation, approach, format, techniques, methods of scoring and interpretation, etc. It is hoped that those tests described, taken together, will constitute a reasonably representative sample of the better achievement tests available today.

A check list or schedule is followed in the test descriptions in this chapter and the next so that the descriptions will be systematic and comparable from test to test. The items or categories in the check list are as follows:

(1) Names of test and author(s).
(2) Nature and purpose of test.
(3) Grade level.
(4) Number of forms.
(5) Publisher and date of publication.
(6) Cost.
(7) Content: source, nature, types of sub-tests, types of items.
(8) Time required to administer.
(9) Directions for and ease of administering.
(10) Validity: nature of data.
(11) Reliability: nature of data.
(12) Manual: nature of, adequacy, clarity, simplicity.
(13) Scoring: methods, ease, objectivity, scores.
(14) Norms: type, adequacy, usability.
(15) Format: paper, printing, arrangement.

In addition to the information presented about a particular test in the check list, comments of a general nature will be made where it seems appropriate and wherever such comments will be helpful in giving the student a better understanding of the test being discussed.

Survey Batteries

Survey batteries have long been used for a number of purposes. When an overall measure of achievement in the common branches or subjects of instruction is needed for purposes of grade placement, promotion, or grouping, the survey battery is most often used. It is also useful in comparisons among classes, schools, or school systems, among individual pupils, or in comparisons of the individual pupil with norms for his age or grade. The survey battery may be employed to good advantage in analysing and comparing a pupil's achievement in the different subject-matter areas, thereby revealing his strengths and deficiencies. For example, a pupil may be at or above the grade norms in certain areas such as reading and social studies, but below the norms in certain others such as arithmetic. The survey battery is a convenient instrument for revealing such differences, and the deficient areas may be followed up with diagnostic tests to identify specific weaknesses. Survey batteries have a further advantage: the norms for the sub-tests are based on the same population sample and are therefore directly comparable. Generally speaking, the norms will not be comparable when separate tests are used in different subjects.

It is important to keep in mind that such comparisons, for example, by the use of individual profiles, must always be made and interpreted with caution. The sub-tests of a battery are often quite short, which means that the reliability of scores on them may be quite low. Consequently, differences between scores on sub-tests are often chance differences which have no statistical significance. Publishers of test batteries have the obligation to provide information on the reliability of sub-scores and to furnish the necessary data to determine the reliability of differences between them.

Survey batteries have found widest use in the elementary grades where there is much uniformity of objectives and content in fundamental areas. The makers of these tests have generally had to confine the scope of the test items to the knowledge and skills which are common to virtually all textbooks and courses of study in a particular subject for a given grade level in order to meet the practical limitations on time for the use of such tests. In spite of these restrictions, many survey batteries have found extensive use over a long period of time, which indicates that the tests have met the needs of many teachers and administrators.

Stanford Achievement Test

The first of its kind to be published, this test appeared in 1923. Revised editions appeared in 1929, 1940 and 1953, and the present edition was issued in 1964. It has held position of leadership in the field for nearly fifty years, and is still probably one of the best known and most widely used survey batteries in existence.

1. ***Name of test and authors*** **:** *Stanford Achievement Test.* Authors: Truman L. Kelley, formerly Harvard University; Richard Madden, Sonoma State College; Eric Gardner, Syracuse University; Herbert C. Rudman, Michigan State University.

2. ***Nature and purpose*** **:** Survey battery of achievement tests in common branches of the elementary curriculum. To provide dependable measures of knowledge, skills, and understanding commonly accepted as desirable outcomes.

3. ***Grade level*** : Kindergarten through grade 9. Early School Achievement Test, Grades K.1–1.1; Primary 1 Battery, Grades 1.5–2.4; Primary II Battery, Grades 2.5–3.9; Intermediate I Battery, Grades 4.0–5.4; Intermediate II Battery, Grades 5.5–6.9; Advanced Battery, Grades 7.0–9.9.

4. ***Number of forms*** : W, X and Y, except Early School Achievement–one form.

5. ***Publisher and date of publication*** : Harcourt Brace Jovanovich, Inc., 1964–1969.

6. ***Cost*** : Early School Achievement, $ 8.50 for a package of 35; Primary I Battery (Complete), $ 7.50 for a package of 35; Primary II Battery (Complete); $7.80 for a package of 35; Intermediate I or II Batteries (Complete), Advanced Battery (Complete), $12.50 for a package of 35; Intermediate I or II Batteries (Partial), Advanced Battery (Partial), $11.00 for a package of 35.

7. ***Content*** : The Early School Achievement Test is intended to be a measure of the child's cognitive abilities. It includes tests of the environment (social and natural), mathematics (number, space, volume, counting, measurement, etc.), letters and sounds (recognition of upper and lower case letters and beginning sounds), and aural comprehension (ability to pay attention to, organise, interpret, infer and retain what has been heard). The Primary I Battery (Complete) includes tests of *Word Reading, Paragraph Meaning, Vocabulary, Spelling, Word Study Skills* and *Arithmetic.*

The Primary II Battery (Complete) includes tests of *Word Meaning, Paragraph Meaning, Science and Social Studies Concepts, Spelling, Word Study Skills, Language, Arithmetic Computation* and *Arithmetic Concepts.*

The Intermediate I Battery (Complete) includes tests of *Word Meaning, Paragraph Meaning, Spelling, Word Study Skills, Language, Arithmetic Computation, Arithmetic Concepts, Arithmetic Applications, Social Studies* and *Science.*

The Intermediate II Battery (Complete) includes tests of *Word Meaning, Paragraph Meaning, Spelling, Language, Arithmetic*

Computation, Arithmetic Concepts, Arithmetic Applications, Social Studies and *Science.*

The Advanced Battery (Complete) includes tests of *Paragraph Meaning, Spelling, Language, Arithmetic Computation, Arithmetic Concepts, Arithmetic Applications, Social Studies* and *Science.*

The Intermediate and Advanced Partial Batteries contain all the tests included in the Complete Batteries except *Social Studies* and *Science.*

The following are examples of typical items from some of the tests in the Early School Achievement Test:

(a) *The Environment:*

Mark under the map of city.

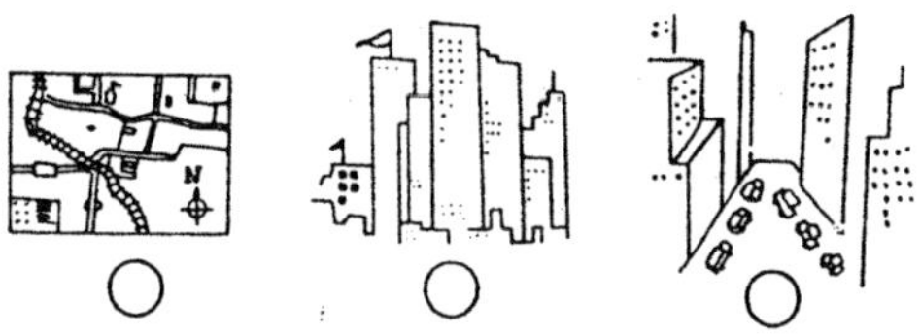

Mark under the girl who is doing something she must do to keep herself healthy.

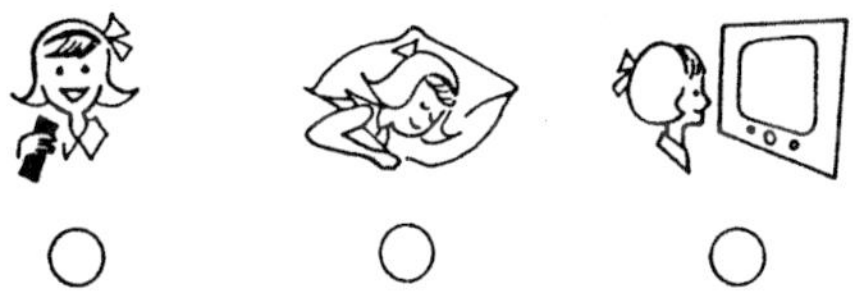

(b) *Mathematics:*

Mark under the star that will fit into the place that has been cut out.

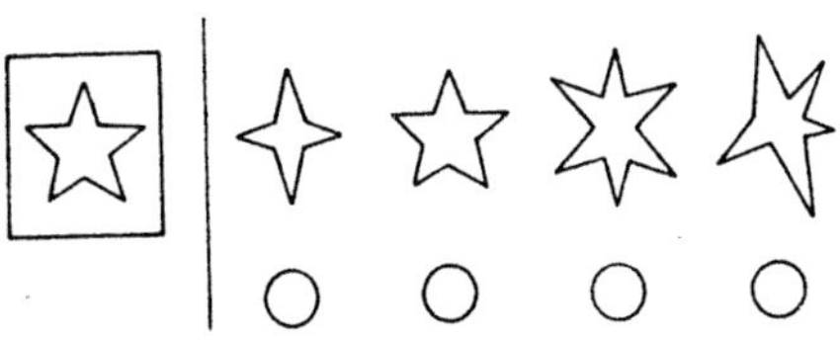

Mark under the pot that has one more flower than the first pot.

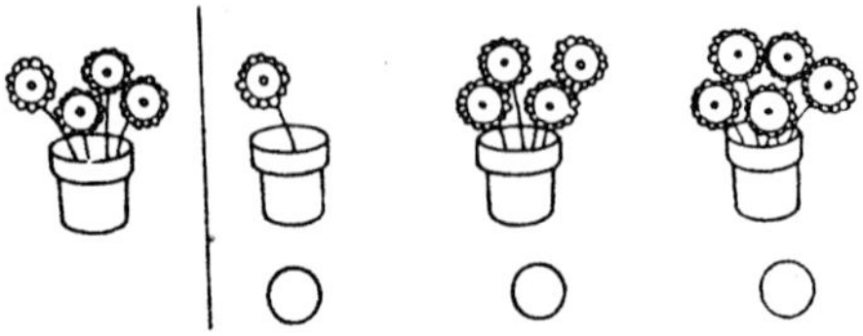

(c) *Letters and Sounds*

Mark under the letter B.

U M B D

You see a picture of a sock. The other pictures are leg, horn, saw. Mark under the one that starts with the same sound as sock. (Pause) Leg, horn, or saw.

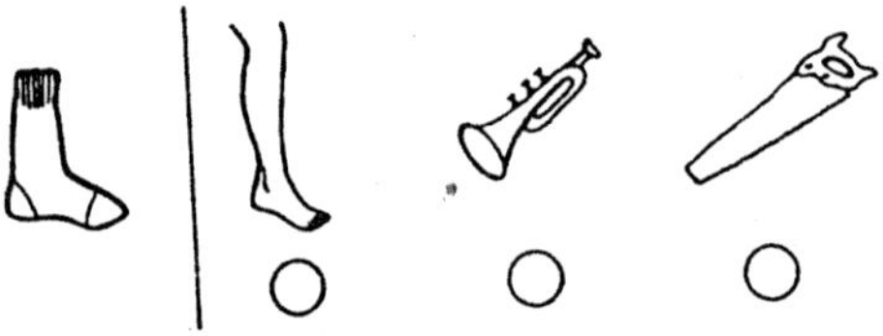

(d) *Aural Comprehension*:

You see birds sitting in a tree, a whistle, and birds flying away from a tree.

This is the story: A lot of birds were sitting in tree. Somebody scared them with a whistle.

Mark under the picture that shows what happened next. (Pause) Remember birds were sitting in a tree and someone scared them with a whistle. Mark under the picture that shows what happened next.

Doris, Sandy and Ann are sisters. Ann is taller than Sandy

and Sandy is taller than Doris. Mark under the picture of Doris.

The following are examples of typical items from some of the tests in the Primary I Battery:

(a) *Word Reading*:

Find the word that tells what the picture is.

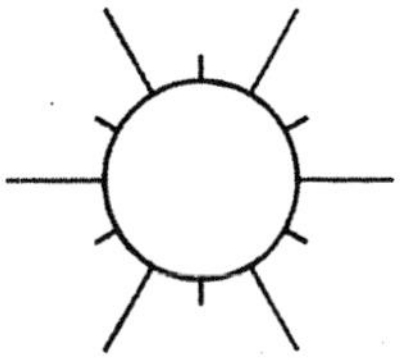

not o
him o
sun o
sit o

(b) *Vocabulary* :

Which of these three words means something to wear?

(1) picture o (2) coat o (3) dream o

(c) *Word Study Skills:*

Items measure the ability to recognise beginning and ending sounds of words, entire words spoken as part of a sentence and rhyming.

(d) *Arithmetic:*

(1) Concepts such as "nearest," "farthest," "most," numbers, and amounts, e.g., "Make a cross on the *tallest* flower" and (2) problem solving, including simple addition and subtraction and a bit of multiplication and/or division.

Items typical of some of the tests in the Primary II Battery are the following:

(a) *Paragraph Meaning*:

Billy did a trick.

He stood on his head.

His——went up in the air.

hands head ball feet

(b) *Spelling:*

In all forms of the Primary Batteries a word is pronounced, a sentence containing the word is read, and the word is pronounced again. The pupil writes the word:

fire The fire crackled cheerily. *fire*

(c) *Science and Social Studies Concepts*:

A large body of ice is

a planet O

the pole O

a glacier O

The Pilgrims came from

Europe O

Africa O

Asia O

(d) Language:

The pupils makes a cross (×) over the correct answer:

(1) *Capitalisation.*

mary and tom are going (T) (t)

(2) *Punctuation*

are you going to school (.) (?) (N)

(3) *Usage.*

1 set

Joe in the chair (1) (2) (N)

2 sat

Typical items from some of the tests in the Intermediate I Battery are:

(a) *Spelling:*

Finding the misspelled word:

1 this	2 kap	3 cold	4 tell	1	2	3	4
				O	O	O	O

(b) *Word Study Skills:*

(1) Finding the word that has the same sound:

ride

1 sick 2 fine 3 wish 1 2 3

O O O

(2) Syllabification:

kitten

1 ki tten 2 ki tt en 3 kit ten 4 kitten 1 2 3 4

O O O O

(c) Arithmetic Applications :

Joe, Fred and Don are saving money for a trip. Here are some of their problems:

(1) Joe has saved $ 2.50, Fred has saved $ 1.35 and Don has saved 900. How much have all three boys saved?

(a) $ 3.75 *(b)* $ 3.85 *(c)* $ 4.75 *(d)* $ 4.85 *(e)* NG

a b c d e

O O O O O

(d) Social Studies—Content

Money to pay the cost of a new public school comes from:

(1) dues (2) taxes (3) stamps (4) mints 1 2 3 4

O O O O

Columbus probably took with him on his trip to America a man who knew much about:

(1) stars (2) radio waves (3) motors (4) Indians

1 2 3 4

O O O O

Social Studies—Study Skills

Items based on graphs and maps, requiring their reading and interpretation:

Use the graph below in answering questions 25 - 29.

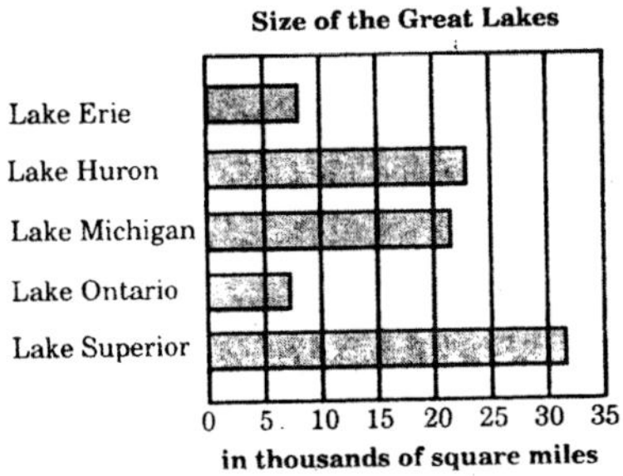

(26) Which lake is the smallest?

(1) Superior (3) Ontario

(2) Erie (4) Michagan

1	2	3	4
O	O	O	O

(e) Science:

As water boils, it changes to:

(1) ice (2) dew (3) steam (4) snow

1	2	3	4
O	O	O	O

The following are typical items from some of the tests in the Advanced Battery:

(a) Paragraph Meaning:

We went up in an airplane. At first we flew near the A where we could see people and animals. Later we could not see them. Our plane was too B.

A 1 houses 2 ground 3 town 4 hills

B. 5 high 6 low 7 far 8 fast

	1	2	3	4
A	O	O	O	O
	5	6	7	8
B	O	O	O	O

(b) Dictionary Skills:

Check (chek) 1. n. A pattern in squares of different colours. 2. v. To prove true or right. 3. n. A mark showing that something has been examined or compared. 4. v. To hold back or control.

A. Miss Jones made a check beside each sample.

	1	2	3	4
A	O	O	O	O

B. The word *check* in the sentence above is:

(a) a noun *(b)* a verb *(c)* an adjective *(d)* an adverb

	a	b	c	d
B	O	O	O	O

(c) Arithmetic Concepts:

Which number comes next in this set?

35 30 26 23

e 22 f 21 g 20 h 19

e	f	g	h
O	O	O	O

(*d*) *Arithmetic Applications*:

A box contains a black, a white, and a yellow marble. What are the chances that Jerry, without looking, will draw out the black marble first, then the yellow and finally the white one?

(*a*) 1/2 (*b*) 1/3 (*c*) 1/6 (*d*) 1/8 (*e*) NG

a	b	c	d	e
O	O	O	O	O

(*e*) *Social Studies—Content*:

Which of these four nations achieved the greatest increase in world influence following Word War II?

(1) England (2) Germany
(3) France (4) Russia

1	2	3	4
O	O	O	O

(*f*) *Science*:

If you want to know whether an animal is an insect, you look for:

(1) head, mouth and gills
(2) colour, size and sound
(3) mouth, feelers and gills
(4) head, thorax and abdomen

1	2	3	4
O	O	O	O

Sometimes telephone men string wire very loosely. They are *least* likely to do this when the air is:

1. warm 2. cold 3. humid 4. dry

1	2	3	4
O	O	O	O

The preceding examples are chosen essentially at random to give a picture of the nature of the items, their appropriateness for the different levels, and their content. It should be clear that not all tests in a battery for a given level have been sampled. Also, no items from Intermediate II were included, since Intermediate I and II are quite similar.

8. *Time required to administer* : The total time for each battery and recommended sittings are as follows:

Batteries	Total
Early School Achievement—Five sittings—25, 15, 15, 15, 20 minutes	90 min.

Primary I—Five sittings—22, 30, 40, 32, 36 minutes	2 hr. 40 min.
Primary II—Seven sittings—20, 33, 41, 35, 37, 33, 35 minutes	3 hr. 54 min.
Intermediate I Compete—Seven sittings—48, 41, 47, 38, 56, 41, 28 minutes	4 hr. 59 min.
Intermediate I Partial—Five sittings—48, 41, 47, 38, 56 minutes	3 hr. 50 min.
Intermediate II Complete—Seven sittings—18, 51, 54, 38, 58, 56, 28 minutes	5 hr. 3 min.
Intermediate II Partial–Five sittings—18, 51, 54, 38, 58 minutes	3 hr. 39 min.
Advanced Complete—Six sittings—53, 52, 35, 61, 58, 28 minutes	4 hr. 47 min.
Advanced Partial—Four sittings—53, 52, 35, 61 minutes	3 hr. 21 min.

Each test in each battery may be given at a separate sitting if desired, but the tests can be administered most efficiently by following the schedule outlined above. The tests are not speeded and time limits are considered ample for most classes.

9. *Directions for and ease of administering* : Directions are clear and complete, both as to general administration and specific directions for each sub-test. No special training or experience is required to administer the batteries. It is assumed that the examiner will become thoroughly familiar with the test and all directions and that he will follow them exactly. Directions to pupils are carefully worked out and include sample items and/ or practice items preceding each test in a battery.

10. *Validity* : The evidence on validity of the *Stanford Achievement Test* is largely curricular in nature. The manual states:

> A major goal in the preparation of this edition of the Stanford was to insure that the content of the test would be in harmony with present objectives and measure what is actually being taught in today's schools. To make certain that the test content would be valid in this sense, the construction of the new edition. . .was preceded by a thorough analysis of the

most widely used series of elementary textbooks in the various subjects, of a wide variety of courses of study, and of the research literature pertaining to children's concepts, experiences and vocabulary at successive ages or grades.

The tests were constructed according to outlines based on these analyses. Subject-matter specialists were consulted at each step in the development of the tests.

For each item in the experimental forms an item profile was constructed showing the per cent of pupils at each grade level answering the item correctly. The extent to which success on each item correlated with progress through school was regarded as an important index of item validity and was used as one basis for the selection of items for the final forms.

The authors of the battery believe that the *Stanford* measures a substantial sampling of the important outcomes or goals of instruction in the common branches at the elementary level. It would have been helpful if at least some of the sources used had been specifically named.

11. *Reliability* : Reliability data include odd-even split-half and Kuder-Richardson reliability coefficients, and standard errors of measurement by grades for each sub-test of each battery. The results are summarised below:

Battery	*Range of Coefficients*	*Trend*	*Range of S.E.*	*Trend*
Early School	High .70's to			
Achievement	.76-.89	Low .80's	2.0–2.8	±2.5
Primary I	.79-.95	High .80's	.5–2.5	±1
Primary II	.66-.94	Middle .80's	2.0–6.0	±3
Intermediate I	.86-.94	±.90	2.5–5.0	±4
Intermediate II	.77-.95	High .80's	4.0–6.0	±5
Advanced	.76-.94	High .80's	7th Gr. 5.0–9.0	
			8th Gr. 8.0–12.5	
			9th Gr. 8.0–13.0	

It is apparent that the great majority of reliability coefficients are in the .80's and .90's. The exceptions are those for *Aural Comprehension* in the Early School Achievement Test (.76 and

.77 for Kindergarten and Grade 1, respectively); *Science and Social Studies Concepts* in Primary II; *Arithmetic Concepts* in Intermediate II, Grade 5; and *Arithmetic Applications* in Advanced, Grades 7 and 9. These coefficients are in the high .60's and .70's.

Standard errors of measurement, expressed in grade score units (see number 13 below) increase from about 1 in Primary I to about 10 in Advanced, Grade 9.

On the whole, the reliabilities, except as noted, are entirely satisfactory, especially in view of the fact that each is calculated for a sub-test within a single grade, where both the shortness of the tests and their restricted range have a depressing effect on reliability coefficients. The reliability of any total battery would probably be in the area of .95.

12. *Manual* : There are separate manuals for each battery. All are clear and complete.

13. *Scoring* : Early School Achievement Tests and Primary Batteries are hand-scored. For Intermediate and Advanced Batteries a booklet may be hand-scored or be used with separate answer sheets for machine scoring. In the latter case, booklets are reusable. Directions for scoring are complete and not difficult to follow.

Scores are obtained as the number right on each sub-test. In all except Early School Achievement these are converted to "grade scores" by means of a table of equivalents at the end of each sub-test. Grade scores are grade equivalents without decimals. Thus, a grade score of 58 equals a grade equivalent of 5.8. Grade equivalents may be converted to percentiles and stanines. All three types of scores are recorded for each sub-test on the title page of the test booklet or the answer sheet if booklets are not consumed. A profile may be constructed for each pupil based on his stanine scores.

14. *Norms* : Three type of norms are provided, as indicated above—grade, percentile and stanine. "All norms are based on the total enrolment in regular classes at each grade level except for a small group markedly atypical as to age". The grade equivalents provided for all batteries except the Early School Achievement represent the average score made by pupils at a specified grade placement. Percentile ranks corresponding to grade scores are provided for beginning, middle and end-of-year testing. Finally, stanine equivalents are provided for defined ranges or bands of percentile ranks and grade scores.

15. *Format* : Paper, printing, and general organisation of tests and accessories are excellent. The use of coordinated colour for each battery and accessories is a new and attractive feature. In addition to manual and scoring key, accessories include a *Class Record* and *Analysis Chart.* These are useful for studying results of the testing for a class as a whole.

Other Survey Batteries

1. *American School Achievement Tests.* 1960. Forms D and E, all levels. Also F and G for Primary II, Intermediate and Advanced. Primary I, Grade 1. *Word Recognition, Word Meaning, Numbers.* $ 4.85 per 35. 35 (50) minutes.

Primary II, Grades 2-3. *Sentence and Word Meaning, Paragraph Meaning, Arithmetic Computation, Arithmetic Problems, Language* and *Spelling.* $ 7.20 per 35. 85 (105) minutes.

Intermediate Battery Complete. Grades 4–6. *Reading, Arithmetic, Language, Spelling, Social Studies, Science.* $11.50 per 35. 127 (147) minutes.

Advanced Battery Complete. Grades 7–9. *Reading, Arithmetic, Language, Spelling, Social Studies, Science.* $11.50 per 35. 147 (170) minutes.

Intermediate Battery Partial. Grades 4–6. *Reading, Arithmetic, Language, Spelling.* $ 8.10 per 35. 117 (137) minutes.

Advanced Battery Partial. Grades 7–9. *Reading, Arithmetic, Language, Spelling.* $ 8.10 per 35.137 (157) minutes.

All answers are marked on test booklets and hand-scored. The Bobbs-Merrill Company, Inc.

2. *California Achievement Tests.* 1957 Edition. 1963 Norms. *Reading Vocabulary, Reading Comprehension, Arithmetic Reasoning, Arithmetic Fundamentals, Mechanics of English, Spelling.*

Lower Primary. Grades 1-2. Areas same as above. Forms W ('57), X ('57). $ 6.50 per 35. 89 minutes.

Upper Primary. Grades H2-L4. Areas same as above. Forms W ('57), X ('57). $ 7.00 per 35. 178 minutes.

Elementary. Grades 4, 5, 6. Areas same as above. IBM. Forms W ('57), X ('57), Y ('57), Z ('57). $ 8.00 per 35. 178 minutes.

Junior High Level. Grades 7–9. Areas same as above. IBM. Forms W ('57), X ('57), Y ('57), Z ('57). $ 8.00 per 35. 178 minutes.

Advanced. Grades 9–14. Areas same as above. IBM. Forms W ('57), X ('57), Y ('57), $ 8.00 per 35. 178 minutes. California Test Bureau.

3. *Iowa Every-Pupil Tests of Basic Skills,* New Edition. 1940–50. Elementary, Grades 3-5; Advanced, Grades 5-9.

Form O consisting of Test A, *Silent Reading Comprehension;* Test B, *Work-Study Skills;* Test C, *Basic Language Skills,* Test D, *Basic Arithmetic Skills.* Elementary tests, $ 5.40 per 35; advanced tests, $ 5.40 per 35. Houghton Mifflin Company.

4. *Iowa Tests of Basic Skills.* 1956. Multi-level edition for Grades 3-9. *Vocabulary, Reading Comprehension, Language Skills, Work-Study Skills,* and *Arithmetic Skills.* Forms 1, 2, 3, 4, 5, 6. $.96 per copy. 4 hours, 39 minutes. Houghton Mifflin Company.

5. *Metropolitan Achievement Tests.* 1958–1962. Primary I, Grade 1. *Word Knowledge, Word Discrimination, Reading, Arithmetic.* Forms A, B, C. $ 8.00 per 35. 105 minutes.

Primary II, Grade 2. *Reading, Vocabulary, Arithmetic Fundamentals, Arithmetic Problems, Spelling.* Forms A, B, C. $10.00 per 35. 2 hours.

Elementary, Grades 3 and 4. *Reading, Vocabulary, Arithmetic Fundamentals, Arithmetic Problems, Language, Spelling.* Forms A, B, C, D. $ 10.40 per 35. 2 hours, 45 minutes.

Intermediate, Grades 5-6. Complete: *Reading, Vocabulary, Arithmetic Fundamentals, Arithmetic Problems, English, Literature, Geography, History, Civics, Science, Spelling.* Forms A, B, C, D. $ 13.50 per 35. 3 hours, 30 minutes.

Intermediate, Grades 5-6. Partial: *Reading, Vocabulary, Arithmetic Fundamentals, Arithmetic Problems, English, Spelling.* Forms A, B, C, D. $11.50 per 35. 3 hours, 30 minutes.

Advanced, Grades 7–9. Complete: areas same as intermediate complete. $13.50 per 35. 4 hours, 15 minutes. Partial: Same as intermediate partial. $11.50 per 35. 3 hours, 45 minutes. Harcourt Brace Jovanovich, Inc.

6. *Sequential Tests of Educational Progress*. Series II, 1970-1971. Grades 4–6, 7–9, 10–12, 13–14. *Mechanics of Expression, Reading, Writing, Mathematics, Science, Social Studies*. Four levels in each subject area.

Forms 1A and 1B for each level. $7.00 per 20. 60 minutes, Levels 1 and 2; 45 minutes, Levels 3 and 4. Educational Testing Service.

7. *S.R.A. Achievement Series*. New edition. 1954–1964. First level, Grades 1-2. *Reading, Arithmetic*. Forms C and D. $ 4.25 per 20 booklets. Approximately 4 hours.

Second, third, and fourth levels, Grades 2–4, 4–6 and 6–9. *Reading, Arithmetic, Language Arts*. Forms C and D. $ 6.30 and $17.35 per 20 booklets. Batteries 2-4 and 4-6, 4 hours; battery 4-9, 6 hours. Science Research Associates, Inc.

Measurement of the Three R's

Traditionally, the Three R's have meant reading, writing and arithmetic. At one time these subjects constituted the curriculum in the grammar school, and the curriculum was unadorned and unhampered by any "fads and frills". In a very real sense they are still the backbone or basic core of all instruction, not only in the elementary grades, but also at higher levels. They represent the means of communicating ideas and concepts without which such exchange is limited to word-of-mouth expression. In primitive societies transmission by word of mouth is used to convey folklore and some rudiments of culture from generation to generation, but no society has ever achieved a high degree of civilisation without having first progressed beyond oral communication.

It is not surprising, therefore, that schools everywhere place great emphasis on the development of these skills. In the kindergarten an attempt is made to develop reading readiness, number concepts, and skill in using crude writing tools such as chalk and crayon. If the child does not attend kindergarten, but has his first school experience in first grade he still, as a rule, has opportunities to develop some of these rudimentary but important skills and concepts through children's story books, games and toys. He learns to associate words with objects and pictures, orally at first by naming them, and later by recognising the printed word; he learns to count blocks, or kittens, or soldiers;

and he learns to hold and use crayons or other writing tools by colouring, copying, or drawing pictures.

The concept of the Three R's has broadened somewhat to include more than reading, writing, and arithmetic. What are now considered basic tool-subjects, include, in addition to these three, spelling and language arts (capitalisation, punctuation, grammar, and sentence structure), as well as oral communication. To be sure, instruction in most of these other subjects was a related part of the Three R's in earlier days, but the others were not generally regarded as separate subjects or areas of instruction. In the section which follows, consideration will be given to measurement practices and techniques in reading, writing, arithmetic, spelling, and the language arts, where these have resulted in some generally accepted and widely used instrument, e.g., standardised tests.

Reading and Reading Readiness

Reading is perhaps the most important of the tool-subjects mentioned above, for it comes close to being the basis of our civilisation. Illiterate persons cannot progress far in our society, nor can they be effective citizens. It is not surprising, therefore, that reading is the first accomplishment the school attempts to give the child. Until he can read, the child cannot become educated according to our concepts of education. If he does not learn to read well he is constantly handicapped in his progress through the schools. Because of the importance accorded to reading, much research and study have been done on the nature of the reading process, on methods of teaching reading, on the causes and remedies for reading disabilities, and, together with all of these, on the development of tests and techniques for measuring reading ability and skill. Literature in educational research contains a wealth of material on this subject. Much of this material is of interest and concern to every teacher, from the kindergarten to the university level.

Reading tests have been mainly concerned with three areas of measurement. One of these area is reading readiness. It has become pretty generally accepted that readiness to learn to read is, at least in part, a maturational process. That is, a child is ready to learn to read when he has developed intellectually and in other ways to a given level of maturity. Authorities differ on the exact level required, but it is generally agreed that it is not much below the mental age or maturity of the average six-year-old. Some place the minimum a half year or so lower. Whatever the minimum is and it probably varies somewhat under different circumstances—it seems clear that it is very difficult and possibly even useless to try to teach a child to read before he has reached this minimum maturity level. A good deal of work has been done to develop tests which will give a fairly accurate measure of a child's readiness in a short time.

Another area of measurement in reading concerns achievement. Reading achievement tests are available for use at all levels from first grade upwards. They generally are directed toward the measurement of vocabulary, reading comprehension and speed of reading. Reading comprehension is usually thought of as the power to understand and remember what is read, while speed of reading refers to the amount that is read in a given time without measurable loss in comprehension. These, plus vocabulary, are important reading skills, and most reading achievement tests are designed to measure all three, either directly or indirectly.

The third area of measurement in reading involves diagnostic testing. This is most useful with the slow reader or the reader who has difficulties of one sort or another. The diagnostic reading test is designed to identify such difficulties or weaknesses and to suggest ways of overcoming them. One approach to this—more in the nature of a tool than a test—involves a machine that photographs the eye movements of the reader as he reads. This device has made it very clear that one demonstrable and consistent difference between good and poor readers is in the number of pauses the eye makes. The good reader makes relatively few pauses and his eyes take in long fragments without stopping; the poor reader, on the other hand, reads jerkily, his eyes pause much more often and take in only a word or, at best, a few words between pauses. While the apparatus for photographing eye movements is not a test in the usual sense, it is a measuring instrument that yields information which has been found very useful in helping poor readers to improve.

Gates-MacGinitie Testing Programme in Reading

In order to orient the student to the area of measurement in reading, we shall describe in detail a comprehensive testing programme by Gates and MacGinitie. This programme is unique in that it provides a continuous and related series of reading tests from kindergarten to twelfth grade. It includes tests of every type found in this area, with the possible exception of study skills. The student who gains some familiarity with and understanding of these tests will have a good orientation not only to the types of tests commonly used but also to a wide variety of techniques of measurement in reading. The first tests in the *Gates-MacGinitie Testing Programme* are the *Reading Readiness Tests.*

1. ***Name of tests and authors*** : *Gates-MacGinitie Reading Readiness Skills.* Arthur I. Gates and Walter H. MacGinitie, Teachers College, Columbia University.

2. ***Purpose*** : To determine which children are ready to begin reading; how rapid their progress is likely to be; what specific abilities required in learning to read need development.

3. ***Grade level*** : End of kindergarten and beginning of first grade.

4. ***Number of forms*** : One.

5. ***Publisher and date of publication*** : Bureau of Publications, Teachers College, Columbia University, 1966.

6. ***Cost*** : $ 4.25 per 35.

7. ***Content*** : *Listening Comprehension* measures the child's ability to understand the total thought of a simple story. The teacher reads a story aloud, asks a question, and the child marks one of three pictures that best answers it.

Auditory Discrimination measures skill in distinguishing two words of similar sound by marking one of two pictures.

Visual Discrimination uses printed forms of four words, three alike and one different. The child marks the one that is different.

Following Directions measures the child's skill in following increasingly complex directions for marking panels of four pictures.

Letter Recognition consists of items of four letters of the alphabet in each. The child marks the one named by the examiner in each set of four.

Visual-Motor Coordination measures ability to complete incomplete printed letters using the complete letter as a model.

Auditory Blending provides information about the child's ability to join the parts of a word, presented orally, into a whole word.

Word Recognition measures ability to recognise whole words. The examiner pronounces one word in each set of three and the child marks that word.

8. *Time required* : The tests are to be given in four sittings requiring approximately one-half hour each.

9. *Directions for and ease of administering* : The tests are easily and simply administered.

10. *Validity* : It seems obvious that these tests measure what they are said to measure—Listening Comprehension, Auditory Discrimination, etc., as described above. Whether these have validity as measures of Reading Readiness Skills is not so obvious. Essentially, their validity for this purpose is construct in nature since they are the skills which fit the authors' theory of what constitutes the equipment necessary to success in learning to read. It is interesting to note that the term "validity" does not appear in any of the materials relating to the test.

11. *Reliability* : A few cautions are given pertaining to interpretation of scores on sub-tests, scores at the extremes of the distribution, and differences between scores on two sub-tests. However, no information is given on reliability in terms such as reliability coefficients or standard errors of measurement.

12. *Manual* : The Teacher's Manual contains a description of the test, directions for administering, scoring, interpreting scores and tables of norms. There are also suggestions for observing traits or characteristics not measured by the tests but which may have a bearing on reading readiness.

13. *Scoring* : All sub-tests are scored one point for each correct answer except Visual-Motor Coordination in which each exercise is scored 0–3 depending on the quality of the response of the child. The score on each sub-test (except Word Recognition) is weighted by a factor of 1, 2 or 3 to obtain a Total Weighted Score. All scoring is done by hand with printed keys.

14. *Norms* : Stanine, percentile and standard score norms are provided for kindergarten and Grade 1 separately. The stanine norms are provided for sub-test scores; total weighted scores are used for percentile and standard score norms. No information is provided regarding the normative population for these tests.

15. *Format* : The tests are printed on good quality paper in an 8½″ × 11″ booklet of 8 pages. The Teacher's Manual is a 20-page booklet of the same format.

The next tests in the series are the *Primary Reading Tests.* A description of these tests follows.

1. *Name of tests and authors* : *Gates-MacGinitie Primary A Reading Tests.* Arthur I. Gates and Walter H. MacGinitie.

2. *Purpose* : These tests are intended to measure level and range of ability in Vocabulary and Comprehension.

3. *Grade level* : Grade 1.

4. *Number of forms* : Forms 1 and 2.

5. *Publisher and date of publication* : Bureau of Publications, Teachers College, Columbia University, 1965.

6. *Cost* : $ 3.60 per 35 copies.

7. *Content* : The Vocabulary Test consists of forty-eight exercises, each of which is made up of a picture followed by four words. The task is to select the one word in each exercise that "tells the most about the picture." For example:

(B)

bed swim

milk fly

The Comprehension Test consists of thirty-four exercises, each containing four drawings followed by a sentence or a short paragraph directing the child to do something with the drawings. For example:

Where is the baby

The hardest exercises contain paragraphs consisting of several sentences, usually describing the drawings or telling a little story. Following the directions requires an understanding of the sense of the paragraph.

8. *Time required* : Vocabulary, 15 minutes; Comprehension, 25 minutes.

9. *Directions for and ease of administering* : These are simple and easily followed. Mainly, the task is to make sure that pupils understand what they are to do and do their best. The teacher is encouraged to do anything that helps to achieve this purpose, short of telling anyone the answer to any exercise. Also, no deviation from the established time limits is permitted if norms are to apply.

10. *Validity* : The validity of the *Gates-MacGinitie Reading Tests* appears to rest chiefly on the assumption of validity of their parent tests, the earlier *Gates* series, the validity of which was primarily construct in nature. The term "validity" appears in neither the Teacher's Manual nor in the Technical Manual. A table of correlations between sub-test scores on Levels D and E and *Lorge-Thorndike Verbal I.Q.* shows a range from .51 to .86 with a median of .74. No relationships between scores on the tests at the various levels and other reading tests or other measures of achievement are provided.

For *Primary A,* median discrimination indices are .64 and .66 for Vocabulary and .66 and .66 for Comprehension, Form 1 and Form 2, respectively.

11. *Reliability* : Extensive data on reliability are given. Alternate form reliability coefficient between two forms range from .67 to .89 with most in the .70's and .80's. Split-half reliability coefficients are also given for vocabulary and comprehension measures. They range from .88 to .96. The two types of coefficients are based on the same individuals in five communities, using for the split-half results the odd-even scores on the test form taken first by each child. Primary A alternate form reliabilities are .86 and .83 for Vocabulary and Comprehension, respectively. Split-half reliabilities are .91 and .94.

12. *Manual* : The Teacher's Manual contains a description of the tests, directions for administering, scoring and interpreting, and tables of norms. The Technical Manual includes descriptions of procedures for selection of items, establishing norms, reliability, interpreting differences between test scores, conversion of scores on the 1958 *Gates* series to comparable scores on the *Gates-MacGinitie* series, and for averaging scores. The necessary statistical data for carrying out these procedures are presented in a series of tables.

13. *Scoring* : The score is the number right and the tests are scored by hand with printed keys. Raw scores may be converted to grade, percentile, or normalised standard scores.

14. *Norms* : Norms are based on a nationwide sampling of approximately 40,000 pupils in thirty-eight communities selected on the basis of size, geographical location, average educational level and average family income. No details on these criteria are provided nor on the numbers tested per grade or per form.

15. *Format* : The format of the tests is very good. Printing and pictures are excellent.

The third set of tests in the *Gates* series are the *Primary B Reading Tests*. These are similar in organisation and content to the *Primary A Reading Tests*. They are designed for Grade 2.

The fourth test in the *Gates-MacGinitie Reading Test* series is *Primary C*. It is similar to *Primary A* and *Primary B* but at a more advanced level for Grade 3. It also consists of two parts, Vocabulary and Comprehension, both of which now include reading. Only the first twelve items of Vocabulary out of 52 are pictorial; the rest are four-response multiple-choice items. Comprehension consists of 24 short stories, each followed by two questions, the answers to which are in four-response multiple-choice form. There are no pictorial items in this part.

The next test in the *Gates-MacGinitie* series is a speed of reading test.

1. *Name of test and authors* : *Primary CS–Speed and Accuracy*. Arthur I. Gates and Walter H. MacGinitie.

2. *Purpose* : To measure objectively how rapidly children can read with understanding.

3. *Grade level* : Grades 2 and 3.

4. *Number of forms* : Forms 1, 2 and 3.

5. *Publisher and date of publication* : Bureau of Publications, Teachers College, Columbia University, 1964-65.

6. *Cost* : $ 2.25 per 35.

7. *Content* : Speed and accuracy are measured by 32 short paragraphs of a relatively uniform difficulty written in a primary vocabulary. Each paragraph ends in a question or an incomplete statement followed by a choice of four words from which the child selects the best answer. The number of paragraphs completed in the time allowed provides a measure of speed. The number of items answered correctly measures accuracy.

8. *Time required* : Seven minutes accurately timed.

9. *Directions for and ease of administering* : The tests are easily administered. Directions and timing must be followed exactly.

10. *Validity* : Median item discrimination indices are .76, .74, and .76 for Forms 1, 2 and 3 respectively.

11. *Reliability* : Alternate form reliability for speed is .72; for accuracy, .86.

12. *Manual* : The manual for this test follows closely in content and organisation those for the other *Primary* tests.

13. *Scoring* : The test is scored manually with a printed key. The speed score is the number of items attempted; the accuracy score is the number of items answered correctly.

14. *Norms* : Normalised standard score, percentile and grade norms are provided for speed and accuracy separately.

15. *Format* : The tests and manual are identical in appearance and organisation to the others in the series.

The next test in this series is the *Survey D.*

1. *Name of test and authors* : *Survey D.* Arthur I. Gates and Walter H. MacGinitie.

2. *Nature and purpose* : Three-part test to measure Speed and Accuracy, Vocabulary and Comprehension.

3. *Grade level* : Grades 4 through 6.

4. *Number of forms* : 1, 2 and 3 and 1M, 2M and 3M.

5. *Publisher and date of publication* : Teachers College Press, 1965.

6. *Cost* : $ 3.25 for 35. Answer sheets, $1.50 to $ 2.50 for 35. Scoring templates (IBM 805 only), $1.50 per set for each form.

7. *Content* : Speed and Accuracy—thirty-six paragraphs of relatively uniform difficulty. Each paragraph ends in a question or incomplete statement followed by four choices. Vocabulary—fifty items consisting of a test word followed by five other words, one of which is similar in meaning to the first word. Comprehension—twenty-one passages in which a total of fifty-two blank spaces have been introduced. For each blank space five choices are provided.

8. *Time required* : Speed and Accuracy—5 minutes; Vocabulary—15 minutes; Comprehension—25 minutes. Tests are timed exactly.

9. *Directions for and ease of administering* : Directions are clear and complete. Tests are not difficult to administer with sample exercises for each part.

10. *Validity* : Correlations of Lorge-Thorndike Verbal I.Q.'s with scores on Speed range from .18 to .44; with Accuracy, from .51 to .64; with scores on Vocabulary, from .60 to .77; and with scores on Comprehension, from .60 to .72. Correlations increase in every case from Grade 4 to Grade 6. Median discrimination indices range from .54 to .72.

11. *Reliability* : Alternate form reliability coefficients range from .67 to .89. All but one are over .72. Split-half reliability coefficients for Vocabulary are .88, .92, and .89 respectively for Grades 4, 5 and 6; for Comprehension these are .94, .96 and .95 respectively.

12. *Manual* : The Teacher's Manual is similar in content and format to those accompanying the other tests in the series. The Technical Manual is the same one for the entire series.

13. *Scoring* : The *Survey D* comes in two editions, one for hand-scoring with consumable booklets, the other for use with separate answer sheets. Templates for IBM 805 answer sheets may also be used for manual scoring.

14. *Norms* : Standard score and percentile norms are provided for October, February and May testing for each grade (4, 5, and 6) on Speed and Accuracy, Vocabulary and Comprehension. In addition, grade norm equivalents for raw scores on each test are also given.

15. *Format* : All tests and manuals in the *Gates-MacGinitie* series are alike in format.

Survey E is the next test in the *Gates-MacGinitie* series. It is similar in all respects to *Survey D* but is designed for use in Grades 7 through 9.

The last test in this series is *Survey F.* It is similar in all respects to *Survey D* and *Survey E* but is designed for use in Grades 10 through 12.

The last tests to be described in the *Gates* series are the *Gates-McKillop Reading Diagnostic Tests.*

1. *Name of tests and authors* : *Gates-McKillop Reading Diagnostic Tests.* Arthur I. Gates and Anne S. McKillop.

2. *Purpose* : This is an individual test designed to identify specific strengths and weaknesses in a child's reading skills.

3. *Grade level* : No grade limits are set for the usefulness of this test. However, it probably is most appropriate in the primary grades when a child's reading skills are being developed.

4. *Number of forms* : Forms 1 and 2.

5. *Publisher and date of publication* : Bureau of Publications, Teachers College, Columbia University, 1962.

6. *Cost* : Pupil Record Booklet, $.20 per copy. Test Materials, $1.50 per set (reusable). Manual, including tachistoscope, $.25 per copy.

7. *Content* : The tests included are (I) *Oral Reading;* (II) *Word Pronunciation: Flash Presentation;* (III) *Word Pronunciation: Untimed Presentation;* (IV) *Phrases: Flash Presentation;* (V) *Knowledge of Word Parts: Word Attack;* (V-1) *Recognising and Blending Common Word Parts;* (V-2) *Giving Letter Sounds;* (V-3) *Naming Capital Letters;* (V-4) *Naming Lower Case Letters;* (VI) *Recognising the Visual Form or Word Equivalents of Sounds:* (VI-1) *Nonsense Words;* (VI-2) *Initial Letters;* (VI-3) *Final Letters;* (VI-4) *Vowels;* (VII) *Auditory Blending;* (VIII) *Supplementary Tests:* (VIII-1) *Spelling;* (VIII-2) *Oral Vocabulary;* (VIII-3) *Syllabification;* (VIII-4) *Auditory Discrimination.*

8. *Time required* : The only tests in which time is a factor are the two flash presentation tests. In these, the words or phrases are flashed at a speed of two per second. In all others the test proceeds at the speed at which the child can work. It is estimated that to give all tests in the battery would require several hours. They would not be given all at one sitting, however, especially with younger pupils, nor would all the tests necessarily be used. The important thing is to use the tests according to their appropriateness for individual diagnosis.

9. *Directions for and ease of administering* : The directions are probably as clear and complete as they can be. The tests are numerous and varied; their administration is necessarily complicated, resembling in some respects the administration of a *Binet* or *Wechsler* individual intelligence examination. Anyone using them will need first, careful study and preparation and second, some practice.

10. *Validity* : For a battery such as this the question of validity in the usual sense is not easily answered. The authors have developed a series of measures in accordance with a logical plan (construct) of the basic elements of reading ability. That these tests do differentiate between individual children with respect to the abilities measured seems evident. Whether the results of the tests agree with other criteria of reading ability (or disability) such as teachers' judgments, other tests, or grade progress, etc., the manual does not say. On the whole, the validation of a battery such as this must rest primarily on evidence of how well it serves its purpose, and such evidence is not provided in the manual.

11. *Reliability* : No information was found in the manual or elsewhere on this point.

12. *Manual* : The manual is a twenty-page booklet giving the rationale of the battery, detailed directions for administering the tests, and for recording results, and tables of norms and directions for scoring and interpreting results. It is detailed and complete.

13. *Scoring* : The recording of a child's responses in the *Pupil Record Booklet* is an important part of the use of the battery, essential to accurate scoring and meaningful interpretation. This record is the basis for determining a score but, more important, it is carefully studied to determine types of errors made. The manual gives clues and suggestions regarding the most common types of errors in the various tests. In almost all instances the raw score is the number correct.

$$\left(\textit{Oral Vocabulary} - \text{Raw Score} = R - \frac{\text{Errors}}{3} \right).$$

14. *Norms* : For all tests, grade score norms are provided. These are further classified as normal progress, low and very low for most tests.

15. *Format* : All materials are well designed, and they are printed on good paper and durably bound. In this respect, they are the equal of any other tests.

Other Reading and Reading Readiness Tests

Reading Tests

(1) *Durrell Analysis of Reading Difficulty.* 1956. Grades 1-6. *Silent and Oral Reading, Listening Comprehension, Word Analysis, Phonetics, Faulty Pronunciation, Writing* and *Spelling.* One form: individual. $ 6.50 per examiner's kit. Additional forms and record blanks, $ 6.50 per 35. 30-45 minutes. Harcourt Brace Jovanovich, Inc.

(2) *Durrell-Sullivan Reading Capacity and Achievement Tests.* 1955. Primary, Grades 2.5—4.5; Intermediate, Grades 3–6. Capacity: *Pictorial—Word Meaning* and *Paragraph Meaning*—measured by *Oral Language,* Achievement: *Word Meaning, Paragraph Meaning, Spelling* and *Written Recall.* Primary, $ 7.70 per 35; Intermediate, Capacity, $ 5.70 per 35; Achievement, $ 6.70 per 35. Harcourt Brace Jovanovich, Inc.

(3) *Gray Oral Reading Tests.* 1963. Grades 1–12. *Standardised Oral Reading Paragraphs.* Forms A, B, C, D. Reading Passages—each form—$ 2.00; record booklets—$ 3.90 per 35. The Bobbs-Merrill Company, Inc.

(4) *Iowa Silent Reading Tests.* 1956. Elementary, Grades 4–8; Advanced, high school, and college. *Rate of Reading, Comprehension,* and *Skills in Locating Information.* Forms AM, BM, CM and DM. Elementary, $ 6.40 per 35; Advanced, $7.50 per 35. Elementary, 49 minutes; Advanced, 45 minutes. Harcourt Brace Jovanovich, Inc.

(5) *Kelley-Greene Reading Comprehension Test.* 1952. Grades 9–13. *Reading Comprehension, Directed Reading* and *Retentior of details.* Forms AM and BM. $7.50 per 35. 63 minutes. Harcout Brace Jovanovich, Inc.

(6) *Lee-Clark Reading Test, First Reader.* 1962. Grades K, 1. *Vocabulary, Following Directions, Sentence Completion, Inference.* Form A. $ 5.00 per 35. 25 minutes. California Test Bureau.

(7) *Nelson-Denny Reading Test.* 1960. Grades 9–16. *Vocabulary* and *Reading Comprehension.* Forms A and B. $ 5.40 per 35 tests. 30 minutes. Houghton Mifflin Company.

(8) *Nelson Reading Test.* 1962. Grades 3–9. *Vocabulary, Reading Comprehension, Ability to Note Details, Ability to Predict Outcomes.* Forms A and B. $ 5.40 per 35 tests; $ 3.60 per 35 self-marking answer booklets. 30 minutes. Houghton Mifflin Company.

(9) *Traxler High School Reading Test.* 1967. Grades 10, 11 and 12. Part I, *Rate of Reading and Comprehension at That Rate;* Part II, *Finding Main Ideas in a Paragraph.* Forms A and B. 45 minutes. $ 4.60 per 35. Manual, $.35. The Bobbs-Merrill Company, Inc.

(10) *Traxler Silent Reading Test.* 1969. Grades 7 to 10. *Rate of Reading; Story Comprehension; Word Meaning; Power of Comprehension.* Forms 1, 2, 3 and 4. 46 minutes. $ 4.60 per 35. Manual, $.35. The Bobbs-Merrill Company, Inc.

Readiness Tests

(1) *American School Reading Readiness Test.* 1964. Kindergarten, Grade 1. *Vocabulary, Discrimination of Letter Forms and Letter Combinations, Recognition of Words, Discrimination of Geometric Forms, Following Directions, Memory of Geometric Forms.* Form X. $ 4.40 per 35. The Bobbs-Merrill Company, Inc.

(2) *Harrison-Stroud Reading Readiness Profiles.* 1950, 1956. Kindergarten, Grade 1. *Visual Discrimination, Using the Context, Auditory Discrimination, Using Context and Auditory Clues, Using Symbols.* One form. $ 4.50 per 35. 79 minutes. Houghton Mifflin Company.

(3) *Lee-Clark Reading Readiness Test.* 1962. Kindergarten, Grade 1. *Visual Discrimination in Letters, Conceptual Maturity, Vocabulary, Following Instructions, Word Forms.* One form. $ 5.00 per 35. 20 minutes. California Test Bureau.

(4) *Metropolitan Readiness Tests.* 1965. Kindergarten, Grade 1. *Word Meaning, Listening, Matching, Alphabet, Numbers,*

Copying. Forms A and B. $ 7.90 per 35. 60 minutes. Harcourt Brace Jovanovich, Inc.

Handwriting

Writing and speech are sometimes referred to as the "expressive language arts", as contrasted with reading and listening, which are called the "receptive language arts". Of these, reading and writing are the ones considered here. Although tests measuring reading ability are extensive—as we have learned in the preceding section—few tests for the measurement of speech or listening abilities have been published.

There has been considerable change in emphasis in the teaching of writing in recent years. Attention and effort in teaching have shifted from mechanics to function. That is, in the teaching of handwriting a generation ago considerable attention was devoted to the pupil's development of a beautiful script. Much time was spent on practice from copy and on imitation of symmetrical handwriting. More recently, interest has shifted to the development of speed with legibility, and emphasis has been placed on handwriting as a means of communication and self-expression. Writing is regarded as a developmental process which presupposes the ability to think clearly. The objective is the ability to express ideas clearly and legibly; little attention is given now to the artistic qualities of handwriting. This is not to say that inartistic writing is encouraged or condoned; indeed, those who insist upon expressing their individuality through their handwriting—to the point where their writing is practically illegible—should be discouraged from this practice.

In measuring handwriting we find a number of attempts to produce what is sometimes referred to as a *product scale*. One of the earliest of these was the *Thorndike Scale for Hand-Writing of Children*.

The scale reproduces samples of writing varying from Quality 4 (the worst writing of fourth-grade children) to Quality 18 (nearly the best writing of eighth-grade children). Each level of quality differs from the next higher or lower by one-tenth of the difference between the best and the worst of the formal writings of one thousand children in Grades 5 to 8, as ranked by competent judges. A few samples follow:

Quality 6:

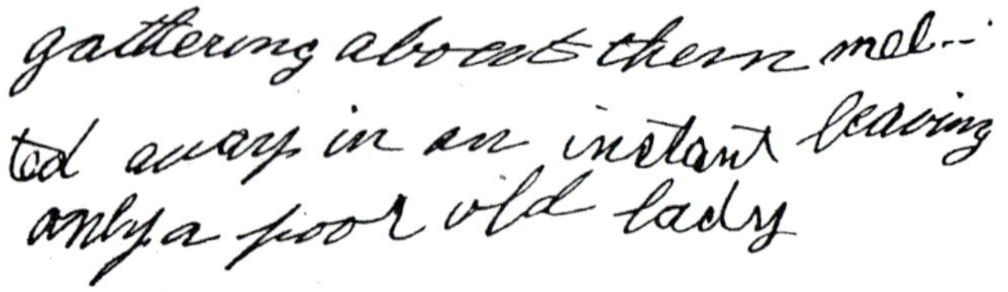

Quality 11:

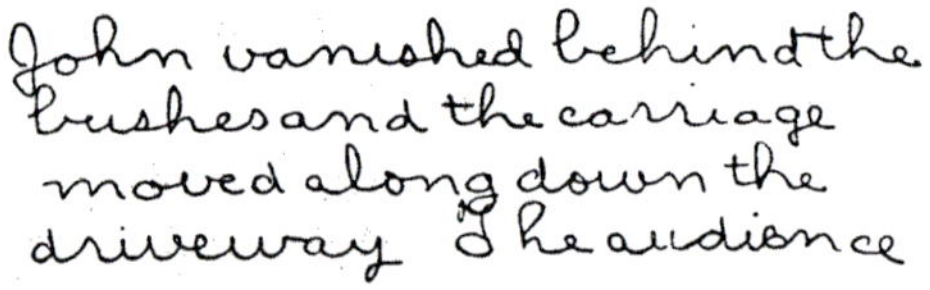

Quality 16:

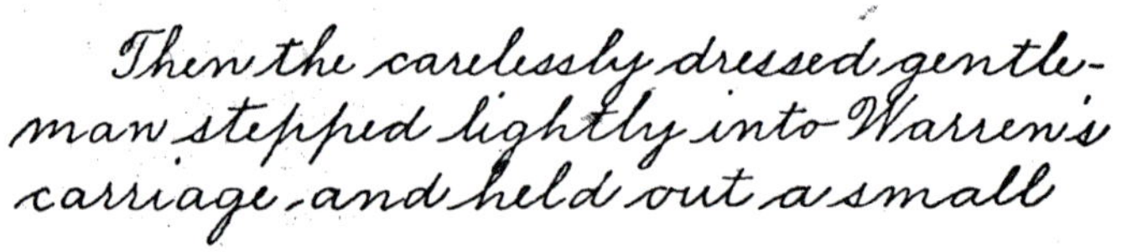

Standards are given in terms of the number of letters (of familiar material)– written per minute without substantial loss of quality, for not more than three minutes; the quality of writing when the pupil is writing naturally; and the quality of writing when the instructions are to write as well as possible. The pupil's samples of handwriting are compared with the scale to find that level of quality in the scale which his writing most closely resembles.

Another scale similar to that of the Thorndike is the *Ayres Scale,* often referred to as the *Gettysburg Edition.* This was one of the most widely used scales ever devised, more than six hundred thousand copies having been printed between 1917 and 1935. It derives its name from the fact that the opening lines of Lincoln's "Gettysburg Address" are used as the subject-matter. The teacher writes on the board the first three sentences of this address and instructs his pupils to read and copy until familiar with it. They then copy it, writing with ink on lined paper for exactly two minutes. The scale includes eight samples of levels of quality, graded from 20 to 90. The pupil's writing is compared with the samples for quality, and the total number of letters written in the two minutes is counted.

Norms are given for both speed and quality for Grades 2 to 8. There are also distributions of quality and rate scores for each grade from 5 to 8, inclusive. The norms show a relatively constant and substantial relationship between speed and quality, and steady progression in both from grade to grade.

Other scales for measuring handwriting are those by Freeman and Hildreth. The Freeman scale may be used for diagnostic purposes to identify handwriting faults in the areas of slantedness or straightness (too slanted or too straight), weight (too heavy or too light), regularity (too much variation in letter forms), and spacing (too much or too little space between letters or words). The Hildreth scale measures the quality of manuscript writing, i.e., printing, on a scale of ten to seventy. The quality of fifty is shown below:

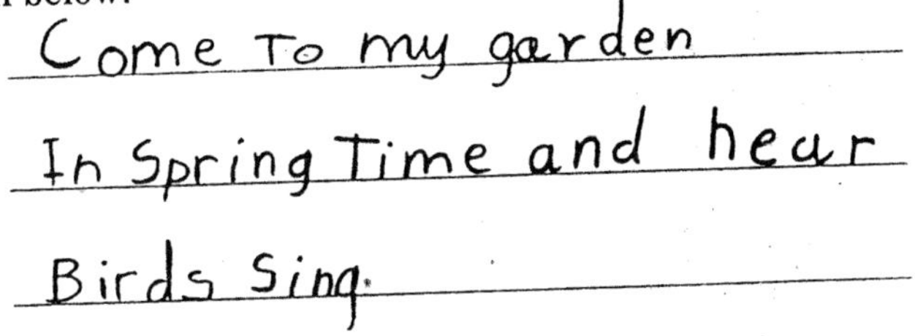

Lateral dominance or handedness may affect a child's ability to learn to write. It is a rather common observation that left-handed children have more difficulty in learning to write and in actual writing than right-handed children. Sometimes the difficulty results from the fact that the teacher is right-handed, and consequently, she and the left-handed pupils have a different orientation and approach to the task. Another source of difficulty grows out of attempts to change the left-handed to right-handed. The effects of such pressures, psychologically speaking, are not completely understood. Emotional difficulties often seem to be associated with them, and handwriting, a finely organised and complex sensory-motor skill, often seems adversely affected.

Teaching a left-handed child to write with his right hand should be undertaken only after a careful study of the individual concerned reveals that such a course would be desirable and wise from a psychological point of view. In any case, tests of lateral dominance should be given to determine the status of the child in this trait before any decisions are made about changing his handedness.

Arithmetic

Except for reading, probably no subject in the elementary curriculum has been studied and investigated more than the teaching of arithmetic. Many books and articles have been written about it. Perhaps a few almost axiomatic observations about arithmetic will be useful before considering problems of measurement in this subject. In the first place, it is quite generally agreed that arithmetic is a comparatively difficult subject. It calls for thinking of a rigorously exact nature, understanding rather than memory, and the ability to apply principles in different though analogous situations. These objectives are not easily attained, and most pupils do not seem to come by them naturally.

In the second place, arithmetic is not a popular subject, partly because it is difficult. Pupils do not generally elect courses in mathematics, once they pass the required ones, unless they have a special interest in it or unless their educational or vocational objectives require it.

The above statements might be interpreted to mean that arithmetic is inherently difficult and distasteful to many. This may be a safe assumption, yet it should be remembered that through improved teaching it may be possible to make arithmetic better liked and less difficult. Many students of the problem maintain that arithmetic has been poorly taught. It is said that the emphasis has been on memorising and mechanical learning rather than on functional use and understanding. The problems and activities used in the teaching of arithmetic have often had little relationship to the lives and activities of people. It is believed that a reorientation and reorganisation of the teaching of arithmetic to emphasise meaning, understanding, and applications would do much to make it more functional, less difficult, and consequently less distasteful. Many of the more recent textbooks and courses of study show evidences of thought and effort in this direction.

Much has happened in the teaching of arithmetic in the grades during recent years. The curricular changes are such that it may be inappropriate to use the term "arithmetic". As in other areas of instruction, the past decade has been one of innovation and break with tradition. Concepts formerly introduced only at secondary school levels have been incorporated in the "new math" for elementary grades. Simpler phases of algebra and geometry are now often included in the subject-matter of mathematics taught below the junior high school.

Challenging as these new developments have been to both pupil and teacher, they pose a problem to the maker of standardised tests. On the one hand, there is the continuing need for measures of the basic fundamentals without mastery of which it is impossible to perform successfully at more advanced levels. On the other hand, there is a need for tests that adequately reflect the modern curriculum. To accomplish both objectives in one measuring instrument, though perhaps not impossible, is seemingly impractical. Either the test would have to be too long for use in most situations, or so thin in its treatment of many topics as to yield unreliable results.

The test chosen to be described is an example of an instrument designed to measure achievement, primarily in the "new math". Many items in it require competence in the "fundamental operations" but measurement of this outcome is not its major purpose. It is the result of careful planning and development by experienced teachers of mathematics and specialists in the teaching of the subject.

1. *Name of test and authors* : *Wisconsin Contemporary Test of Elementary Mathematics.* M. Vere DeVault, Elizabeth Fennema, K. Allen Neufeled, and Lewis B. Smith.

2. *Nature and purposes* : A test whose content focuses on those mathematical facts and concepts which have been introduced into elementary mathematics primarily since 1962. It is designed to measure achievement in contemporary elementary mathematics.

3. *Grade level* : Grades 3–7: Level 1, end of Grade 3 and Grade 4; Level 2, Grades 5, 6, and beginning Grade 7.

4. *Number of forms* : A and B.

5. *Publisher and date of publication* : Personnel Press, Inc., 1967.

6. Cost : $ 4.50 per 25.

7. Content : Each form of Level 1 contains 52 four-response multiple-choice items; each form of Level 2 contains 60 four-response multiple-choice items. The items in each form are equally divided between those designed to measure Facts and those designed to measure Concept. These two categories are further subdivided into Fundamentals, Operations, and Measurement and Geometry. A few sample items follow:

Level 1—Facts-Fundamentals

Which word is missing?

first, second, __?__, fourth, fifth

a. third
b. sixth
c, tenth
d. eighth

Concepts-Operations:

Which number makes the statement true?

271 × _?_ = 271

a. 1
b. 0
c. 10
d. ½

Level 2—Facts-Operations

Which answer is correct?

$$\begin{array}{r} 2{,}011 \\ \underline{-1{,}919} \end{array}$$

a. 192
b. 102
c. 92
d. 1,102

Concepts-Measurement

Given the length and width of a rectangle one can find:

a. perimeter and radius
b. volume and area
c. area and perimeter
d. radiùs and volume

8. *Time required* : Fifty minutes per form actual working time in one sitting (60–75 minute overall).

9. *Directions for and ease of administering* : The directions are clear and complete. The test is designed to be administered in the classroom by teachers, and administration is simple and uncomplicated provided the examiner has acquainted himself thoroughly with the test and the directions beforehand. There are two sets of directions, one for use if students write answers on test booklets, and one set to be followed if separate answer sheets are used.

10. *Validity* : The validity of the *Wisconsin Contemporary Test of Elementary Mathematics* is primarily content in nature. The authors based their selection of content upon careful examination of major commercial mathematics textbooks series published since 1962. These ranged from "Slightly Modern" to "Extremely Modern". Most were judged to fall in the range of "Modern". The tests were planned to measure the common elements in this range excluding only the most Extremely Modern. Experience of the authors had shown that teachers generally make moderate or slight changes in what they teach regardless of the nature of their texts. Also it was found that test items based upon Extremely Modern content were so difficult for pupils that their test scores tended toward chance results.

Under "Construct Validity" the authors submit the information already presented above on classification of items into the six cells resulting from the major categories, Facts and Concepts, each subdivided into Fundamentals, Operations and Measurement-Geometry. Fact items are said to require the recall of a single definition, term, or basic number combination; concept items to require recall of several facts and the ability to comprehend relationships between them. Approximately 40 per cent of items in Level 1 are categorised as operations; 30 per cent as fundamentals and 30 per cent as measurement-geometry. The items in fifth and sixth grade tests are divided equally among the three categories. All items were classified by the four authors independently and only those whose placement was agreed on by three of the four authors were used.

Data on criterion related validity are presented in the form of correlations between WCTEM and Arithmetic Concepts and Problem Solving sections of the Iowa Tests of Basic Skills. The mean of the correlations between total scores of WCTEM and the two sections of ITBS is .74. The mean correlations of WCTEM

Facts and WCTEM Concepts scores with ITBS Arithmetic Concepts scores are both .69. With ITBS Problem Solving they are .62 and .61 respectively.

11. *Reliability* : Extensive data on reliability are presented. Kuder-Richardson coefficients for Facts and Concepts scores are around .80. For total scores they are close to .90. Standard errors of measurement average about 2 points for part scores and about 3 for total scores. Test-retest coefficients with over five months intervening averaged about .68 for Facts, about .64 for Concepts and .72 for total scores. Between form reliability coefficients ranged from .85 to .89 for total scores, from .70 to .81 for Fact scores and from .72 to .81 for Concept scores. Standard errors of measurement were practically identical with those based upon split-half coefficients.

12. *Manual* : The manual is comprehensive and complete. It is an excellent example of adherence to the Standards for Educational and Psychological Tests and Manuals.

13. *Scoring* : Tests may be scored by hand or machine. If answers are written in test booklets, strip keys for hand scoring must be used. Digitek-IBM 805 answer sheets may be scored manually or by machine. Digitek and IBM 1230 answer sheets must be scored by optical scanning.

Two scores, Facts and Concepts, are easily obtained by hand or machine scoring. Correlations between these two scores are generally in the .70's, raising the possibility that the two parts of the test may be measuring nearly the same traits. Further data on this point are being collected.

Scores on subdivisions Fundamentals, Operations and Measurement-Geometry for research purposes may be determined by manual scoring but are best obtained by machine scoring.

14. *Norms* : Since the WCTEM is somewhat different in purpose and content from conventional tests of achievement in mathematics, a rather unusual procedure for establishing norms was used. It was decided that norms should be based on users of the test rather than on a carefully selected sample. Therefore, norms are based on results from 10,403 pupils in 73 schools in 21 states tested in the spring of 1967, and from 7,334 pupils in 71 schools in 19 states tested in the fall of 1967. Between 85 per cent and 89 per cent of the schools were public, the rest were nonpublic, church-related. Of the communities tested slightly over 40 per cent described themselves as above average in socioeconomic level; over 40 per cent, average; and less than 15 per cent as below average. Over one-half were suburban, two-fifths were urban, and less than 10 per cent rural. About 20 per cent of the schools were in systems enrolling more than 75,000; about 25 per cent from 2-10,000; and 2,000 or less, 7 per cent. These schools were largely those who had ordered tests, supplemented by some additional schools whose cooperation was solicited. The number of pupils tested in spring and fall was approximately 2,500 in each of Grades 3 to 6 inclusive.

Norms are provided for Grades 3, 4, 5 and 6 for spring testing and for Grades 4, 5 and 6 based on fall testing. Norms are in the form of percentile ranks and stanines.

15. *Format* : Tests and accessories are attractive and efficient in composition and organisation. Colour coordination is used effectively.

Arithmetic Tests

(1) *Brief Survey of Arithmetic Skills.* 1947–53. Grades 5–12. *Computation, Reasoning.* Forms A and B. $ 3.50 per 35. 20 (25) minutes. The Bobbs-Merrill Company, Inc.

(2) *Diagnostic Tests and Self-Helps.* 1955. Grades 3–12. Screening tests in *whole numbers, fractions, decimals* and *arithmetic,* plus twenty-three tests covering *addition, subtraction, multiplication, division,* and all the major areas (*fractions, decimals, per cent,* etc.) diagnostically, with self-helps on the back of each test. One form. $ 2.00 per 50. Untimed; complete set would require several hours. California Test Bureau.

(3) *Number Fact Check Test.* 1946. Grades 5–8. *Addition, Subtraction, Multiplication and Division Facts.* Forms A and B $ .05 per copy, plus $ .60 for scoring stencil. 25 minutes. California Test Bureau.

(4) *American School Achievement-Arithmetic Readiness Test.* 1941–55. Grade 1. *Numbers.* One Form. $ 4.00 per 35. The Bobbs-Merrill Company, Inc.

Spelling

The process of spelling seems not to be fully understood from a psychological point of view. It involves memory, sensorimotor functions including vision, hearing, and muscular coordination, intelligence, phonics, and perhaps an indefinable (or at least a not-well-defined) sense of letter and word combinations, to name only the more obvious factors. It is intimately associated with reading and writing, both of which depend in part on the ability to spell and at the same time contribute to this ability. Individuals differ widely in spelling ability within the same grade, the same I.O. group, and the same age level.

The measurement of spelling ability raises such questions as what words to test, how many, how to choose them, etc. Usually, words for this purpose are chosen from lists such as Thorndike's *The Teacher's Word Book,* a compilation from many sources of words found most frequently in running discourse, classified by frequency into the first, second and third thousands, etc., up to ten thousand. Other lists of a similar nature are also available. The assumption is that an educated person's needs in spelling are related to the frequency with which words are found in English usage, and that the more difficult words are found, by and large, in the less frequently occurring groups.

In setting up tests of spelling, a random sample of words or even a dictionary will generally provide a list which covers a wide range of difficulty and frequency of use. The difficulty can be determined by trying out the words with pupils of varying ages and levels of development. After difficulty has been determined, the words are arranged in order of difficulty in what is usually called a *spelling scale.* In testing, the words are presented in this order, proceeding from easiest to hardest. The scale may be segmented so that a list of one hundred words is divided into a number of overlapping groups of perhaps twenty words each, the first twenty constituting the test for the lowest level, those from the eleventh to the thirtieth word, the next level, and so on to the highest level, the eighty-first to the hundredth.

Various methods are employed to make the testing of spelling ability more objective than simply having the person write the word as it is pronounced. One method is to present groups of four or five different words, one of which may be misspelled; another is to present several spellings of the same word, from which the correct one is chosen. A less objective though possibly more common practice is to pronounce the word, use it in a sentence, pronounce it again, and then have the pupils write it. For example :

crowd—There was a large *crowd* at the game.—crowd

Since a spelling test was described in the earlier part of this chapter in the discussion of survey tests, and since spelling tests do not occupy a particularly important place among standardised tests and are all essentially the same, at least for the elementary grades, no further detailed description of such tests will be given. The following list may be useful for reference purposes, however.

Spelling Tests

(1) *The New Iowa Spelling Scale.* Grades 2–8. Contains 5,507 words chosen from the writings of children and adults or from the Thorndike-Lorge *Teacher's Word Book.* All words are said to be of high social utility. One form. $. 65 per copy. Bureau of Educational Research and Service.

(2) *Lincoln Diagnostic Spelling Tests.* 1942–57. Advanced. Grades 8–12. *Pronunciation, Enunciation,* and *Use of Rules in Spelling.* Forms A and B. $ 3.15 per 35. 50 minutes. The Bobbs-Merrill Company, Inc.

Language Arts

The concept of the language arts generally includes language skills other than reading, handwriting, and spelling, although the latter is often included in tests labelled "language arts". Broadly speaking, the concept may also include oral expression and listening comprehension as expressive and receptive language arts.

Since a conventional test measuring skills in spelling, punctuation, capitalisation, phonics, syllabification, usage, dictionary skills, and sentence sense has already been described as part of the *Stanford Achievement Test,* another test of communication skills will be described below. This is the test of Listening, a part of the *Cooperative Primary Tests.* This type of test is somewhat different from the usual test of language arts in that it attempts to measure what might be referred to as a receptive skill.

1. ***Name of tests and authors*** : *Cooperative Primary Tests: Listening.* Staff of the Cooperative Test Division, Educational Testing Service and lay committees and consultants.

2. ***Nature and purposes*** : The tests were designed to measure verbal and quantitative understanding, skills and concepts basic to future development in reading, writing listening and mathematics. The Listening Test was designed to measure comprehension, recall, interpretation, evaluation of, and inference from the spoken word.

3. ***Grade level*** : Grades 1 through 3.

4. ***Number of forms*** : 12A and B, 23A and B.

5. ***Publisher and date of publication.*** Cooperative Test Division, Educational Testing Service. 1965.

6. ***Cost*** : Pilot test—$ 2.00 per 20. Separate booklets—$ 3.25 per 20. Combined booklets containing tests at both levels—$ 5.00 per 20. Handbook—$ 3.00.

7. ***Content*** : The administrator reads a word or a sentence and the pupils mark one of three pictures that "goes best with it". The teacher reads a sentence or a short story and then asks questions about it which the pupils again answer by marking one of three pictures. There are 50 questions in each form.

8. ***Time required*** : Approximately 35 minutes.

9. ***Directions for and ease of administering*** : Directions are clear and complete. A Pilot Test is used to give pupils practice in making the types of responses called for by the test, in this case, marking pictures with a large X. In the Listening Test it is very important that the teacher read clearly and distinctly.

10. ***Validity*** : The tests are designed to measure "developed abilities", and their validity is based on the judgment of persons well qualified to know the relationship of test content to teaching objectives. Each user of the test is encouraged to make his own judgment of content validity.

11. ***Reliability*** : Internal consistency coefficients average about .80. Standard errors of measurement are approximately 3

points of raw score. Alternate form correlations are reported between 12A and 12B as .82 and .75.

12. *Manual* : The Handbook is a complete manual including a description of the construction of the tests, instructions for administering, scoring, interpreting test results and their use and technical data.

13. *Scoring* : Score is the number right. Strip keys are provided. Raw scores are recorded on the backs of the test booklets.

14. *Norms* : The national norms are based upon carefully chosen probability samples of school districts in states representing all sections of the country. Samples were tested in spring and fall from Grade 1, spring, to Grade 3, fall. Each sample included approximately 1,800 pupils in some 180 schools chosen in about 150 school districts. The pupils in fall and spring samples were chosen from different sets of schools. Norms are provided in the forms of scaled scores and mid-percentile ranks. The scaled scores have a mean of 150 and standard deviation of 5.

15. *Format* : The format of the test is excellent and is designed to be attractive to children at the grade levels for which the test is appropriate.

Other Tests of Language Arts

(1) *Essentials of English Test,* Revised. Grades 7–12. *Punctuation, Capitalisation, Sentence Structure, Correct Usage, Spelling.* Forms A and B. $ 2.60 per 25. 45 minutes. American Guidance Service.

(2) *Hoyum-Schrammel English Essentials Tests.* 1955-56. Grades 3-4, 5-6, 7-8. *Sentence Recognition, Capitalisation, Punctuation, Correct Usage, Alphabetisation* (or *Reference Materials*). Forms A, B, C, D. $1.25 per 25. 40 (50) minutes. Bureau of Educational Measurements.

(3) *Language Skills.* Sub-test of *Iowa Every-Pupil Test of Basic Skills.* 1943–47. Grades 3–5. *Punctuation, Capitalisation, Usage, Spelling, Sentence-Sense.* Form O. $ 5.40 per 35. 46 minutes. Houghton Mifflin Company.

Measurement in Social Studies and Science

In addition to the fundamental tool-subjects taught in all

elementary grades, there is always some instruction in social studies and, to a growing extent, in natural science. Social studies has long been an important part of the elementary curriculum, but elementary science, as it is understood today, is relatively new—at least under that name. Its predecessor, nature study, had a long period of usefulness, but has now been largely replaced by a more systematic and scientific type of instruction concerned with helping the child to understand the natural world, and giving him an understanding of the methods by which science has advanced and improved human living.

Social Studies

Recent emphases in the social studies have been on (1) world geography and a world point of view, (2) social studies as a means of interpreting the past and understanding current events, (3) citizenship in a democracy, its responsibilities as well as its privileges, and (4) the scientific study of man and his civilisation. As in the case of the other subjects already discussed, these trends represent departures from the history and geography that emphasised learning facts about dates, discoveries, battles, boundaries, capitals, seaports, exports imports, and memorising speeches, parts of the branches of government, etc. Not that a knowledge of such matters is unimportant; but it is most important that the process does not stop with the learning of facts. To be useful, such learning must proceed to the interpretation, integration and application of these facts. Of what value is it if a pupil knows many facts about the organisation of government, has memorised the Constitution and the Bill of Rights, but fails to vote at elections, or violates one of the articles in the Bill of Rights without ever relating his actions to the meaning of that article?

Present-day textbooks and courses of study reflect the trends listed above to a greater or lesser degree. Certainly no modern textbook in history, geography, or civics ignores them. Today's pupils seem increasingly to get out of the classroom and into the community to see how governments actually work. The greater mobility of our age makes geography and history much more real and meaningful. Standardised tests reflect to some extent the trends in social studies, although tests tend to be somewhat more conservative than the best teaching—a fact that is also true of other areas, as has been noted. The tests to be described as examples are probably typical of many others in the field.

California Tests in Social and Related Sciences: Social Sciences

1. ***Name of tests and authors*** : *California Tests in Social and Related Sciences: Social Studies I and Social Studies II.* Georgia Sachs Adams and John A. Sexson.

2. ***Nature and purposes*** : *Social Studies I* includes Test 1, *The American Heritage,* and Test 2, *People of Other Lands and Times. Social Studies II* includes Test 3, *Geography,* and Test 4, *Basic Social Processes.*

Test 1 deals with (A) Exploration and Colonisation of America, (B) The Westward Movement, (C) Later Development of the Nation, and (D) Understanding of Democracy.

Test 2 deals with (A) People of Other Lands (Latin America, and Orient, and European countries commonly studied in elementary grades), and (B) People of Other Times (early civilisations of China, Egypt and Greece), with emphasis on their contributions to the culture of today.

Test 3 deals with (A) Geography of the U.S., (B) World geography, (C) Map Reading and Knowledge of Geographical Terms and (D) Effects of Geography on the Life of Man.

Test 4 deals with (A) Food, Clothing and Shelter, (B) Transportation and Communication.

3. ***Grade level*** : The Elementary Test is designed for use in Grades 4-8.

4. ***Forms*** : AA and BB.

5. ***Publisher and date*** : California Test Bureau. 1946–1955.

6. ***Cost*** : Part I, Tests 1 and 2, or Part II, Tests 3 and 4. $ 4.50 per 35.

7. ***Content*** : Test 1, Section A, consists of twenty-two multiple-choice items.

Sample :

The first President of the United States was

(a) Lincoln *(b)* Washington

(c) Jackson *(d)* Wilson

Test 1, Section B, consists of eight true-false items and twenty multiple-choice items.

Samples:

Many of the pioneers built small houses
or shelters on their flat boats. T F

When the pioneers camped at night on their trail to the West, they arranged their wagons in a circle. Their chief reason for doing this was to provide :

(a) a central place for eating, singing and dancing

(b) better protection against Indians

(c) heat from a central fire

(d) protection against rain

Test 1, Section C, consists of five true-false items, and fifteen multiple-choice items dealing with the Civil War and more recent events, including World War I.

Test 1, Section D, consists of twelve true-false items, seven multiple-choice items similar to the samples already given, but dealing with democracy and its principles. In addition to these nineteen items, there are six items to be marked "U.S.," if the item is more often found in the United States: "D," if found more often in dictatorships; and "O," if the pupil thinks it is found in neither.

Sample:

Studying the laws of a city in order to suggest improvements..

Test 2, Section A, consists of fourteen true-false and sixteen multiple-choice items dealing with life and conditions in other countries today.

Test 2, Section B, consists of ten true-false and ten multiple-choice items dealing with the civilisations of ancient times and the Middle Ages.

Test 3, Section A, consists of thirty-five multiple-choice items dealing with geography of the United States. The last fifteen items are based on a map of the United States and deal with the location of large cities, certain states and some important bodies of water.

Test 3, Section B, consists of six true-false and twenty-four multiple-choice items dealing primarily with the geography of regions other than the United States. The last twelve of the multiple-choice items are based on a Mercator projection of the world and test for knowledge of location of larger cities, certain countries and bodies of water.

Test 3, Section C, consists of twenty three response multiple-choice items testing knowledge of terms such as weather, longitude, etc. and the ability to read a map with symbols for capital cities, distances, etc.

Test 3, Section D, consists of twenty three- or four-response multiple-choice items testing knowledge and understanding of the effects of altitude, latitude, etc. on climate, crops, location of cities, etc. The first six items are based on the same map used in Section C.

Test 4, Section B, includes eighteen true-false and fourteen multiple-choice items dealing with food, how and where it is grown, and clothing and shelter under different conditions and times.

Test 4, Section B, includes eighteen true-false and fourteen multiple-choice items on transportation and communication in modern times and their importance.

In all, Test 1 consists of twenty-five true-false and sixty-four multiple-choice items; Test 2, of twenty-four true-false and twenty-six multiple-choice items; Test 3, of six true-false and ninety-nine multiple-choice items; Test 4, of twenty-six true-false and thirty-four multiple-choice items.

8. *Time required* : If answers are marked on test booklets: Test 1, 33 minutes; Test 2, 17 minutes; Test 3, 32 minutes; Test 4, 18 minutes. When separate answer sheets are used: Test 1, 40 minutes; Test 2, 20 minutes; Test 3, 38 minutes; Test 4, 22 minutes. These are suggested actual working times; they do not include time for passing out and collecting materials, reading directions, or answering questions.

9. *Directions for and ease of administering* : Directions are complete and clear.

10. *Validity* : Evidence of the validity of the tests rests on three bases:

(*a*) Analysis of course of study and textbooks for content to be used in making preliminary test items.

(*b*) Try-out and statistical analysis of preliminary items

(*c*) Rating of items by teachers and supervisors as to degree of importance of the information or concept tested.

Items were selected for the tests on the bases of statistical criteria and ratings.

11. *Reliability* : Reliabilities (Kuder-Richardson) were computed for each of Grades 4–8 and for each part of each test. They are given in terms of correlation coefficients and standard errors of measurement. The reliability coefficients are generally in the .80's, and, in the seventh and eighth grades, mostly in the .90's. Considering the restricted range, the method used for calculating the correlation coefficient, and the standard errors of measurement, these values are quite satisfactory for scores on the four tests. The user is cautioned not to place much reliance on scores on the sub-tests or parts of each test, since their reliabilities are often below the level necessary for use in individual diagnosis.

12. *Manual* : The manual for the *Tests in Social and Related Sciences* is excellent. It provides the information needed to administer and score the tests and to interpret the results. This includes the completion, on each test booklet, of a diagnostic profile for that pupil, based on the scores on each of twelve parts or sub-tests of the four tests in social science. Suggestions are given in the manual for use of the test results in appraising needs of an entire class or grade and the needs of pupils transferring from another school.

13. *Scoring* : The tests may be scored in three ways. If the pupil marks his answers on the test booklet, the scoring is done by hand with a printed strip scoring key. Machine-scorable answer sheets may be used and scored by machine or by hand.

The score throughout is the number right. No correction is made for chance, even though true-false and some three-response multiple-choice items are used.

14. *Norms* : The normative population for the tests came from eleven states in the northern half of the United States. The population was selected to give a median I.Q. of 100 with a standard deviation of 16; 70 per cent of the pupils were making normal progress, 20 per cent were retarded a half year or more, and 10 per cent were accelerated a half year or more. About 85 per cent were white and the remainder consisted of Mexicans, Negroes, and members of other minority groups.

Percentile norms are provided for each sub-test or part of the four tests in Social Science. There are also grade equivalents and age norms for each of the four tests.

15. *Format* : The physical appearance, printing, arrangement and general organisation of these tests leave little to be desired. The booklets are attractive and convenient in size. Accessories include a class record sheet.

Other Tests in Social Studies

(1) *Emporia Geography Test.* 1937. Grades 4–7. Part I: Knowledge of *U.S. geography,* tested by reference to a map. Part II: Sixty true-false items on *world geography.* Part III: Forty multiple-choice items on *world geography.* Forms A and B. $1.20 per 25. 30 minutes. Bureau of Educational Measurement.

(2) *Emporia United States History Tests.* 1937. Test I, Grades 5 and 6; Test II, Grades 7 and 8. Test I consists of thirty-four true–false and twenty-six multiple-choice items on *U.S. History.* Test II consists of sixty-four true-false, twenty-five multiple-choice, a set of twenty-six matching, and five *historical sequence* items. Forms A and B. $1.20 per 25. 40 minutes. Bureau of Educational Measurement.

(3) Primary Social Studies Test. Grades 1–3. *Social Studies content most commonly taught in the primary grades.* Form A. $ 6.00 per 35. 30 minutes. Houghton Mifflin Company.

Natural Science

Since elementary science is comparatively new and not as completely established in the curriculum as reading or arithmetic, for example, few standardised tests have been developed. This is not entirely surprising, for not all elementary schools offer science; it is not widely taught in every grade, and not always as a regular subject where it is taught. It is still offered in many schools on an incidental and irregular basis. Under such conditions, it is very difficult to develop tests that will meet with the approval, and fit the needs, of many teachers. The content must be either quite general and therefore weak, or extremely limited, in order to satisfy and substantial number of situations. Nevertheless, a few standardised tests are on the market. Most of them are sub-tests or tests drawn from parts of elementary batteries, but a few are published independently. Part III of the *California Tests in Social and Related Sciences* is described below. Parts I and II have been described in the preceding section.

California Tests in Social and Related Sciences: Related Sciences

1. ***Name of tests and authors*** : *California Tests in Social and Related Sciences*. Georgia Sachs Adams and John A. Sexson.

2. ***Nature and purposes*** : *Related Sciences* includes Test 5, *Health and Safety,* and Test 6, *Elementary Science.*

Test 5 deals with (A) Eating for Health, (B) Other Health Information, and (C) Safety Information.

Test 6 deals with (A) The World About Us, and (B) Man's Conquest of Nature.

3. ***Grade level*** : The Elementary Test is designed for use in Grades 4–8.

4. ***Forms*** : AA and BB.

5. ***Publisher and date*** : California Test Bureau. 1946–1955.

6. ***Cost*** : Test booklets, $ 4.50 per 35.

7. ***Content*** : Test 5, Section A, consists of nine true-false and sixteen multiple-choice items.

Samples:

A camel makes long journeys on the desert without stopping for water. T F

One of the best sources of calcium is—

(*a*) white bread (*b*) milk

(*c*) oatmeal (*d*) raisins

Test 5, Section B, includes thirteen true-false and seventeen multiple-choice items dealing with teeth, disease, health habits, alcohol and tobacco.

Test 5, Section C, consists of thirteen true-false and seven multiple-choice items dealing with safety practices and first aid.

Test 6, Section A, consists of fifteen true-false and twenty-five multiple-choice items measuring knowledge and understanding about plant and animal life and the solar system.

Test 6, Section B, is made up of ten true-false and fifteen multiple-choice items concerned with man's early efforts to control nature and modern means of conserving and developing resources and power.

8. *Time required* : If answers are marked on test booklets: Test 5, 21 minutes; Test 6, 19 minutes. If separate answer sheets are used: Test 5, 27 minutes; Test 6, 23 minute. These suggested times are actual working times only. Both tests—Social Studies and Related Sciences—require a total time of three hours.

9. *Directions for and ease of administering* : Directions are complete and clear.

10. *Validity* : See page 68.

11. *Reliability* : See page 68.

12. *Manual* : See page 68.

13. *Scoring* : See page 68.

14. *Norms* : See page 69.

15. *Format* : See page 69.

Other Tests in Elementary Science

(1) *Metropolitan Science Tests.* 1959. Grades 5–9. *Science Information, Generalisations* and *Understandings.* Intermediate and Advanced. Forms AM, BM, CM. $ 5.20 per 35. 20 minutes. Harcourt Brace Jovanovich, Inc.

(2) *Sequential Tests of Educational Progress: Science.* 1957. Grades 4–6. *Applications of Scientific Knowledge.* Forms A and B. $ 5.00 per 20. 70 minutes. Educational Testing Service.

3

Measuring Achievement in the Secondary Grades

The problems of producing standardised achievement tests in secondary school subjects are somewhat different from those encountered by the makers of tests for the elementary grades. In the first place, there is not such a well-established core in the high school programme as there is at the elementary level. The most common areas of study in high school are English, Social Studies, Science and Mathematics. Almost all high school pupils take courses in English and Social Studies, but content and emphases vary widely. For instance, Social Studies courses may include anything from civics to ancient history and may be taught in a year's time or over a period of four years.

Prior to Sputnik it could be said that perhaps half the secondary school population took some kind of a course in science before graduation, usually as an elective, and a similar situation held in the field of mathematics. Many graduated from high school without having taken any mathematics at all in the secondary grades. In recent years the situation has changed. Today there is a greatly increased emphasis on science and mathematics in secondary schools, largely as a reflection of a drive for more technically trained persons, but also as a result of a reaction against so-called "Mickey Mouse" courses.

No other academic subjects in the high school curriculum are as common as those mentioned, yet there is a great variety of other subjects offered in most schools; all of these subjects provide an opportunity to produce many different tests. Nor does the diversity in high school subject areas end with the names of courses; it extends also to objectives and content. Here again, there is a contrast with the situation in the elementary grades, where objectives and content are much more standardised. An extreme example of such diversity in secondary school subjects is in the field of literature, where it is practically impossible to construct a test whose content will satisfy all or a majority of English teachers. In varying degrees, this same principle applies in other subject-matter areas.

Makers of achievement tests for the secondary grades usually attempt to solve this problem in one or both of two ways. The first and more usual practice is to base the tests on the common essentials as determined by an analysis of leading textbooks and courses of study, putting into the tests only such content and skills as are found in all or nearly all such curricular material. The second approach is to make a test that measures the ability to use the knowledge and skills learned, rather than just knowledge and skills, *per se*. A test of this sort might include measures of a wide variety of objectives besides knowledge, such as study skills, or the ability to apply or generalise knowledge.

While no sharp line of demarcation can be drawn to identify all current standardised tests with one type or the other, the tendency is away from the currently predominant first type, and toward the second, which may be called by functional approach. Most modern tests for high school subjects lean in this direction, though they nearly always have a definite content orientation as well. This combination is certainly not undesirable and is probably necessary, for it is difficult to conceive of anyone interpreting and applying knowledge which he does not possess. On the other hand, it seems entirely reasonable to assume that if one is successful on a test of applications, one would also do well on a test of knowledge. Both types of objectives are valuable, and an ideal test should attempt to measure both.

Time is another factor which complicates the situation for the maker and user of standardised tests in high schools. The elementary school programme is much more flexible in this respect than that of the high school. Usually, the elementary teacher remains all day in the same room with the same pupils, and if she wishes to devote several hours of one day to a particular activity, whether this be testing, classwork, or a field trip, the matter of scheduling presents no serious problems. There are no fixed periods and no rigid schedules, generally speaking, no other teachers must be consulted about a change in procedure for the day. The high school programme, on the other hand, is nearly always on a fixed schedule of class periods, averaging perhaps forty-five minutes in length. To detain a given group or class for more than one period for testing or other reasons on any given day nearly always requires consultation with others, adjustment in schedules, and approval of arrangements by several persons. As a result, high school tests sometimes seem to be constructed to fit a time schedule rather than to adequately measure important instructional goals. Most batteries, of course, are designed so that they can be given in several sittings, and this arrangement makes possible adherence to a school schedule and yet provides reasonably adequate measurement in each subject.

Finally, since there is such a wide variety of individual study patterns and subjects in the high school, most standardised achievement tests must include items covering a wide range of difficulty and content in order to satisfy a majority. To formulate a test which is inclusive and which samples an area adequately poses difficult problems for those who construct or use standardised tests at the secondary level. The situation is reflected by high school teachers in their most frequently voiced criticism of standardised tests, namely, that "they don't measure what I teach".

In this chapter, as in the preceding one, the study of the types of achievement tests will depend principally on prototypes or examples. There are so many standardised tests for high school subjects, especially in the common or core subjects, that it would be impossible to describe and discuss even a substantial proportion of them in a volume such as this. However, lists of tests will be found at the end of each section, briefly noting such matters as date of publication, cost, content, publisher, number of forms and time required.

Survey batteries are discussed in the first section, then tests in the specific subject areas of English, Social Studies, Science and Mathematics. The annotated bibliography at the end of the book lists a number of books which include discussions and descriptions of tests in many other fields.

Survey Batteries

The problems that have just been discussed are of particular importance to teachers and to those who construct survey batteries for use in the high school grades. The variety of courses, the fixed schedules, and the wide range in content and difficulty all affect the survey battery even more than they affect a test in a single subject, and these factors provoke such questions as the following: Which fields or subject-matter areas should such a battery include? How extensively can the battery sample each area, and how simple must some of the exercises be so that every pupil may find something at which he can succeed? How wide an area can the battery cover before it becomes so thin and superficial that its users will have no confidence in it? Above all, how can an adequate job of measurement be done in a time short enough to enable schools to use the instrument?

The authors of most high school survey batteries meet these questions and situations by confining the tests to the subjects of English, Social Studies, Science and Mathematics. When they venture beyond these areas of knowledge, it is usually to measure interpretive and applicative abilities related to the content areas. Also, test authors usually attempt to include a wide enough range of difficulty in each subject to measure achievement of those pupils who have had from one to eight or more semesters in that area. As a result, the tests are sometimes too difficult for the beginners, or too easy for the bright twelfth-graders.

While conditions and needs at the secondary level vary greatly, they have enough in common to make the survey battery useful for certain purposes. As a measure of a pupil's basic orientation in the broad fields already mentioned, the survey battery is rapid and fairly accurate. Obviously, it does not give adequate measurement in any one subject such as American history or trigonometry. Yet it does reveal inequalities in a pupil's background and achievement among the fields covered and provides a basis for comparison of the achievement of individuals and groups with that of other secondary school pupils. The survey battery is also a useful tool for the guidance worker seeking to assist pupils in making decisions about courses and curriculums. It should be remembered that test batteries differentiate only roughly and should always be used with full regard for their limitations and in conjunction with other more sensitive measuring instruments.

Iowa Tests of Educational Development

The high school survey battery to be described here as an example was first published in 1942. In this first edition, the tests were rented and not sold, and no separate forms of the individual tests were available. This survey battery represents an outstanding example of an attempt to use the functional rather than the content-centered approach. Other survey batteries for high school use, some of equal quality, are listed at the end of this section.

1. *Names of tests and authors* : *Iowa Tests of Educational Development (ITED).* E.F. Lindquist and Leonard S. Feldt, with the assistance of Robert A. Forsyth and Esther D. Neckere.

2. *Nature and purposes* : The battery requires the student to interpret and analyse new material and to apply broad concepts and skills to situations not generally encountered in the classroom. The tests are designed to measure not so much what a student knows as what he can do with what he knows or with what is provided for him.

3. *Grade* : Grades 9–12 inclusive.

4. *Number of forms* : X-5 and Y-5.

5. *Publisher and date of publication* : Science Research Associates, Inc., 1970.

6. *Cost* : Test booklets, either form, $19.25 per 25. Booklets may be rented and scoring service provided, $1.05 to $1.35 per student, depending on types of reports requested. If booklets are owned or purchased the cost of scoring and reports varies from $.72 to $1.02 per student.

7. *Content* : Test 1, *Reading: Comprehension,* consists of fifty-four multiple-choice items based upon five prose passages and one poem Actual working time, 40 minutes.

Reading: Vocabulary, consists of forty items, each consisting of one word followed by five choices, one of which has most nearly the same meaning as the key word. Actual working time, 15 minutes.

Test 2. *Language Arts, Part I: Usage,* consists of fifty-four items designed to measure punctuation, capitalisation, manner of expression, word and sentence order and organisation of ideas.

Sample item:

My friend is a terrible poor	S1.	A (No change)
S1		B awful
		C very
student. I tried to help her	S2.	A (No change)
S2		B student,
		C student—
		D student:

with her French yesterday.

Language Arts, Part II: Spelling. Consists of forty multiple-choice items consisting of four words and a "none wrong" response. The task is to find a misspelled word if one is present.

The two Language Arts sub-tests are combined into a single 40-minutes test.

Test 3. *Mathematics.* Consists of thirty-six multiple-choice items designed to measure ability to apply useful mathematical concepts and to demonstrate an understanding of number systems and other advanced mathematical ideas. Actual working time, 40 minutes.

Test 4. *Social Studies: Background.* There are thirty multiple-choice items, requiring 20 minutes' working time, designed to measure the student's knowledge and understanding of social institutions, the economy, and world developments. The score on this test is combined with that on two of the passages in *Reading. Comprehension* to obtain a total social studies score.

Test 5. *Science: Background.* Consists of two parts: two science passages in *Reading Comprehension* and thirty multiple-choice items designed to measure the student's understanding of facts, principles, applications and generalisations in biological, physical and earth sciences. Actual working time on *Science: Background* is 20 minutes.

Test 6. *Use of Sources.* There are forty-six multiple-choice items purporting to measure familiarity with, and ability to use, important library references and other sources. Actual working time, 20 minutes.

8. *Time required* : Total actual working time required for the entire battery is 3¼ hours. Estimated total time required for administration is 4½ hours including 10–15 minutes for a break between first three tests and last three. It is recommended, however, that the first five tests be given in one session with a break between the Reading test and the Language Arts and Mathematics tests, and that the remaining three be given in another session.

9. *Directions for and ease of administering* : The tests are easily administered. Directions are clear and complete. However, since electronically scored answer sheets are used, considerable care must be exercised in seeing that spaces for name blocks, etc., are properly filled in.

10. *Validity* : No conventional validity data such as correlations of scores with teachers' marks or scores on other standardised tests are presented. The content is said to be based on an "introspective analysis of the skills used by educated people in reading for information and pleasure, in expressing their thoughts in writing, and in handling quantitative concepts". In addition, the tests in social studies and science are intended to measure important concepts and their applications. The last test purports to measure knowledge and use of sources of information to which a student or adult might have to refer.

11. *Reliability* : Reliability coefficients ($K\text{–}R_{20}$) and standard errors of measurement are provided by grade and form. The coefficients range from .81 to .94 for the separate sub-tests. For groups of sub-tests (Reading, Language Arts) they range from .92 to .96. For the composite for the battery they vary from .95 in Grade 9 to .99 in Grade 10. Except for rather low values for mathematics in Grade 9 (.81 for Y-5 and .82 for X-5) the reliability coefficients are quite satisfactory.

12. *Manuals* : Two manuals are provided, one for teachers and examiners, and one for test coordinators. The former contains instructions for preparation for testing; for administering the tests; an analysis of each sub-test indicating the content categories covered and the items allocated to each category; for interpretation of scores and score reports; and suggestions for use of test results. The manual for test coordinators includes sections on the nature and purposes of the battery, directions for administering the battery, and for administrative follow-up of the testing programme. The latter also contains suggestions regarding such matters as assisting teachers in interpretation of test results, informing parents and pupils of test results, and administrative use of test results.

13. *Scoring* : Either Digitek, IBM 1230, or SRA-type answer sheets may be used with the 1970 edition of *ITED*. Scores are reported in the form of standard scores, national percentile ranks, and national statnies for each test and sub-test, and for a so-called 3R core (a combination of scores on Reading, Language Arts, and Mathematics taken together). In addition, there is a Growth Scale intended to provide a continuous measure of growth rates from Grades 1–12 based on the SRA Achievement Series and the *Iowa Tests of Educational Development.*

14. *Norms* : National per centile norms are provided for each grade (9-12) and for each sub-test of the battery and the Reading, Language arts, and Mathematics composite. These norms are based on the 1971 standardisation of Forms X-5 and Y-5.

15. *Format* : The material and workmanship of the *Iowa Tests of Educational Development* are of high quality.

Other Survey Batteries

(1) *Adult Basic Learning Examination.* Grades 5–8. 1967. *Reading, Spelling, Arithmetic Computation, Problem Solving.* Forms A and B. $16.00 per 35. Specimen set, $ 2.00. 2 hours. Harcourt Brace Jovanovich, Inc.

(2) *California Achievement Tests.* Grades 7–9, 9–14. Junior High School and Advanced Batteries. 1957, 1963. *Reading Vocabulary, Reading Comprehension, Arithmetical Reasoning, Arithmetic Fundamentals, Mechanics of English* and *Spelling.* Forms W, X, Y and Z. $ 8.00 per 35; $1.25 per specimen set. Approximately 3 hours. California Test Bureau.

(3) *Comprehensive Tests of Basic Skills.* Grades 8–12. 1968. *Reading, Language, Arithmetic, Study Skills.* Forms Q and R. $11.00 per 35. $1.50 per specimen set. 2 hours and 50 minutes. California Test Bureau.

(4) *Metropolitan Achievement Tests: High School Battery.* 1962. Grades 9–12. *Reading, Spelling, Language, Language Study Skills, Social Studies Study Skills, Social Studies Vocabulary and Information, Mathematical Computation and Concepts, Mathematical Analysis and Problem Solving, Scientific Concepts, Understandings and Information.* Forms AM and BM. $13.50 per 35. $ 2.00 per specimen set. 5 hours, 15 minute. Harcourt Brace Jovanovich, Inc.

(5) *Sequential Tests of Educational Progress, Series II.* Grades 7–9, 10–12, 13–14. 1969. *English Expression, Reading, Mechanics of Writing, Mathematics Computation, Mathematics Basic Concepts, Science, Social Studies.* Forms A and B. Separate booklets, $7.00 per 20. Combined Booklets, $ 35.00 per 20. Specimen set, $ 5.00. Actual working time, seven tests, 5 hours, 10 minutes. Educational Testing Service.

(6) *Stanford Achievement Test: High School Battery.* Grades 9–12. 1966. *English, Numerical Competence, Mathematics, Reading, Science, Social Studies, Spelling.* (Supplementary tests in *Arts* and *Humanities, Business and Economics,* and *Technical Comprehension* available). Forms W and X. $15.90 per 35. Specimen set, $2.75. 5 hours, 20 minutes. Harcourt Brace Jovanovich, Inc.

(7) *Tests of Academic Progress.* Grades 9–12. 1970. *Social Studies, Composition, Science, Reading, Mathematics, Literature.* Forms 1 and 2. Booklets containing all six tests, $.96 per copy. Separate test booklets (single copy), $.30. 50–60 minutes per test. Houghton Mifflin Company.

Achievement Tests in Specific Subjects

Many standardised tests in English are available for junior and senior high school grades. There are tests in the fundamentals of English grammar, sentence structure, capitalisation and punctuation; tests to measure knowledge and appreciation of literature; scales to measure composition or writing ability; and tests of vocabulary and spelling ability. As before, only one test will be described in detail as an example in its field, but others will be listed for reference. This list is not complete or exhaustive, but it includes representative examples of the variety of tests available in this broad field.

Cooperative English Tests

1. ***Name of tests and authors*** : *Cooperative English Tests.* Clearance Derrick, David P. Harris and Biron Walker.

2. ***Nature and purposes*** : These tests are designed to measure competence in reading and written expression. *Reading Comprehension* consists of two parts, *vocabulary* and *comprehension,* and yields four scores: *Vocabulary; Level of Comprehension; Speed of Comprehension;* and *Total Reading Comprehension. English Expression* is in two parts, *effectiveness* and *mechanics,* but yields a single *English Expression* score.

3. ***Grade level*** : Level 1 is for college freshmen and sophomores. Level 2 is for Grades 9 through 12.

4. ***Number of forms*** : Forms 1A, 1B and 1C for college students. Forms 2A, 2B and 2C for high school students.

5. ***Publisher and date of publication*** : Cooperative Test Division, Educational Testing Service. 1960.

6. ***Cost*** : Separate booklets, *Reading Comprehension* or *English Expression,* $ 6.00 per 20. Combined booklet edition, $ 8.50 per 20. Answer sheets, $ 4.00 per 100 (SCRIBE, IBM, or Digitek).

7. ***Content*** : Test 1, *Reading Comprehension, Part I: Vocabulary,* consists of sixty multiple-choice items such as:

Boast

(A) sew *(C)* brag

(B) suffer *(D)* lift

Part II: Reading, consists of sixty multiple-choice items based on selected reading passages. The score on the first thirty item is called *Level of Comprehension,* since experience has shown that most students have time to try all of them. The score on all sixty items is called *Speed of Comprehension,* since it depends on speed as well as accuracy of performance.

Test 2, *English Expression, Part I: Effectiveness,* consists of thirty items testing the ability to recognise and select the word or phrase which precisely conveys the intended meaning of a sentence.

Example:

As far as his spending of money is concerned, his acquaintances consider him (   ).

(A) shabby	*(C)* stingy
(B) ignoble	*(D)* contemptible

Part II: Mechanics, consists of sixty items testing the ability to recognise errors is usage, spelling, punctuation and capitalisation.

Examples :

(A) When all the marks were	A	B	C	O
(B) Added together, his standing	o	o	o	o
(C) Was forth in the class				

The letter "C" is marked on the answer sheet.

(E) He had not known	E	F	G	O
(F) That she lived in	o	o	o	o
(G) Topeka, Kansas				

Here the fourth space, "O", is marked to indicate no error.

8. *Time required* : Test 1, *Reading Comprehension, Part I: Vocabulary,* 15 minutes; *Part II: Reading (Level of Comprehension* and *Speed of Comprehension* combined), 25 minutes.

Test 2, *English Expression, Part I: Effectiveness,* 15 minutes; *Part II: Mechanics,* 25 minutes.

9. *Directions for and ease of administering* : Directions are concise and clear. Tests are simple and easy to administer, with a minimum of participation by the examiner.

10. *Validity* : The validity of the *Cooperative English Tests* rests on the judgment and skill of the persons who planned and produced it. Well-qualified secondary school and college teachers were called on to prepare the test specifications and to write the test items. No claim is made that the tests will be suitable in all situations, but it is believed that they will be valid measures of the skills tested. It is suggested that the prospective user study the tests carefully to judge their appropriateness for his teaching objectives. It is also recommended that if the tests are to be used for predictive purposes, each institution conduct local validity studies.

11. *Reliability* : Alternate form reliability coefficients for the sub-tests of *Reading* based on combined groups of schools range from .71 to .89, with a median of approximately .83. The coefficients for total score on *Reading* range from .91 to .94. Standard errors of measurement range from 2.64 to 6.18 with a median of approximately 4. Alternate form reliabilities for *English Expression,* total scores, range from .81 to .86 with standard errors of measurement of about 4. Standard errors are in converted-score units. It is estimated that the reliability coefficients are from .03 to .10 higher than if they were based on cases within one average school. Although alternate form reliability coefficients are usually lower than corrected split-half coefficients, those reported here, particularly for part scores on Test 1 and total scores on Test 2, leave something to be desired.

12. *Manual* : The manuals for the *Cooperative English Tests* are excellent. There is one entitled *Directions for Administering and Scoring,* one called *Interpreting Scores,* and a *Technical Report.* Each is complete for its purpose. There is also a form called the *Student Report Profile.*

13. *Scoring* : Four types of answer sheets may be used with these tests, namely, standard IBM 805's, 1230's, Digitek, and the ETS SCRIBE. The IBM 805's may be hand- or machine-scored. The SCRIBE is the ETS version of the electronic scoring process, which does not require an electrographic or mark-sensing pencil and which is much faster and more complete than the IBM 805 process.

14. *Norms* : Raw scores are converted to standard scores, with a mean of 150 and a standard deviation of 10 for the eleventh-grade population. Percentile rank equivalents for "converted scores" are also provided. Percentile bands provide a useful means of estimating the accuracy of individual percentile ranks. A per centile band is the range of one standard error on each side of a given score. Thus a teacher or counsellor may interpret a student's score in relation to his most probable "true score."

Norms for the college level tests are based on scores of 751 freshmen enrolled in 105 colleges widely distributed geographically and representative of different types of higher institutions. Sophomore norms are based on 558 students enrolled in seventy-eight of the same colleges.

High school norms are based on scores of 8,839 ninth-graders, 8,327 tenth-graders, 7,041 eleventh-graders and 5,341 twelfth-graders. These students were enrolled in ninety-five schools located in all parts of the country.

For those who wish to equate scores on the 1960 tests with those on earlier editions, a table of equivalents is provided for each sub-test on *Reading* and between the 1960 *English Expression* score and *Mechanics of Expression* score on earlier forms.

15. *Format* : In appearance, quality of materials, and printing, these tests and accessories are the equal of any on the market and superior in many ways to most competing tests.

Other Tests in English

(1) *A Look at Literature.* 1968. Grades 4–6. *Perception of literary qualities and devices, comprehension of meaning,* and *extension and application of meaning.* Forms A and B. $ 7.00 per 20. 60 to 70 minutes. Educational Testing Service.

(2) *Campbell-Guiler Test in English Fundamentals.* 1957. Grades 9–12. *Spelling, punctuation, capitalisation, sentence organisation and structure, grammatical usage and terminology.* Forms 3 and 4. $ 3.50 per 35. 33 minutes. The Bobbs-Merrill Company, Inc.

(3) *Cooperative English Test. (Usage, spelling, vocabulary.)* 1938, 1939. Grades 7–12, and college. *Grammar, punctuation, capitalisation, sentence structure, spelling* and *word knowledge* are tested. Forms OM and PM. $ 6.00 per 20. 70 minutes. Educational Testing Service.

(4) *Essentials of English Tests.* 1939. Grades 7–13. *Spelling, grammatical usage, word usage, sentence structure, punctuation,* and *capitalisation.* Forms A and B. $ 2.60 per 25. 45 minutes. American Guidance Service.

(5) *Greene-Stapp Language Abilities Test.* 1951. Grades 9–13. *Capitalisation, spelling, punctuation, sentence structure and applied grammar,* and *usage and applied grammar.* Forms AM and BM. $7.50 per 35. 120 minute. Harcourt Brace Jovanovich, Inc.

(6) *Pressey Diagnostic Tests in English Composition.* Junior and Senior High School Grades. *Capitalisation, punctuation, grammar, sentence structure.* Forms 1, 2, 3 and 4 of each test. $ 2.80 per 35. 15 minutes. The Bobbs-Merrill Company, Inc.

(7) *Purdue High School English Test.* 1962. Grades 9–12. *Grammar, punctuation, effective expression, vocabulary, spelling.* Forms 1 and 2. $ 4.50 per 35. 36 minutes. Houghton Mifflin Company.

(8) *Rinsland-Beck Natural Tests of English Usage.* 1957. Grades 9-13. *Mechanics of English, Grammar, Rhetoric.* Forms C and D of each test. $ 4.55 per 35. The Bobbs-Merrill Company, Inc.

(9) *Test of English Usage.* 1950. Grades 10–13. *Capitalisation, use of apostrophe* and *punctuation; word usage, building sentences and paragraphs.* Forms A and B. $ 3.85 per 35. 100 minutes. California Test Bureau.

(10) *Tressler English Minimum Essentials Test.* 1932–1956. Grades 8-12. *Grammatical correctness, vocabulary, punctuation and capitalisation, sentence structure, sentence sense, inflection and accent spelling.* Forms A, B, C. $ 3.20 per 35. 40–50 minutes. The Bobbs-Merrill Company, Inc.

Social Studies

The field of social studies at the secondary level generally includes civics, ancient history, modern European history, world history, United States history, and a course often called Problems of Democracy or American Government. Standardised tests are available in each of these subjects, and most leading publishers have offerings in at least several. One standardised test in American history will be described in detail, and others in the various subjects will be listed for reference.

Carry American History Test

1. ***Name of test and author*** **:** *Crary American History Test, Revised Edition.* Ryland W. Crary.

2. ***Nature and purposes*** **:** The test is intended to measure the achievement of pupils with respect to the important objectives of a high school course in American history. The objectives and the number and proportion of items emphasising each are as follows:

	Knowledge (47 items) Percentages	*Understanding (29 items) Percentages*
Politico-National	39	17
Socio-Economic	8	4
Cultural-Scientific	8	5
Foreign Relations	3	7
Study Skills	4	5
	62	38

The above data are for Form E. Those for Form F are very similar.

3. ***Grade level*** **:** No particular grade level is specified but the test is intended to be given at the end of a year's course in American history in the high school, typically taught in the 11th grade.

4. ***Number of forms*** **:** E and F.

5. ***Publisher and date of publication*** **:** Harcourt Brace Jovanovich, Inc., 1965.

6. ***Cost*** **:** $ 8.50 per 35. Separate answer sheets at additional cost.

7. ***Content*** **:** The content of the test as outlined above is planned to deal with two major categories, factual knowledge and conceptual understanding. Approximately three-fifths of the seventy-six multiple-choice items are intended to measure achievement in the first category and the remaining two-fifths, achievement in the second. Knowledge of basic historical facts, fundamental concepts, time sequences, biographical information, and details of events is considered to be a necessary foundation for interpreting facts and ideas, making intelligent inferences and comparisons, recognising trends, and seeing cause and effect relationships.

Under Politico-National are included such topics as Expansion, Independence, Democratic Processes and Time-Event Comparisons; under Socio-Economic—Labour, Industry, Agriculture; under Cultural-Scientific—Literature, Technology,

Education; under Foreign Relations—Defence, Treaties, Trade; and under Study Skills—Reading, Interpretation, Source Location. Nearly all items (except those dealing with Study Skills and a few others) are categorised according to five time periods, 1450–1787, 1788–1865, 1866–1918, 1919–1945 and 1945–1963.

8. *Time required* : 40 minutes actual working time.

9. *Directions for and ease of administering* : The test is easy to administer, requiring no interruptions for sub-parts. There are four brief sets of directions for use when answers are marked on test booklets and for each of three different types of answer sheets. All are clear and adequate.

10. *Validity* : Evidence for the validity of the *Crary* test is largely curricular or content in nature. The test is intended "to provide a representative coverage of the important outcomes of American history instruction as attested to by authoritative judgments and by a consensus of current practices." Objectives and topics to be measured were determined according to frequency of inclusion in current instructional materials.

11. *Reliability* : Corrected split-half reliability coefficients and standard errors of measurement are reported for each form. Reliability coefficients range from .88 to .92. Standard errors of measurement range from 4.1 to 4.8 standard score units with an average of approximately 4.5.

12. *Manual* : The manual is clear and complete. It contains the necessary information for understanding, using and applying results of the test.

13. *Scoring* : The test may be either hand- or machine-scored. When answers are marked on test booklets, keys for each page of the test are used. For separate answer sheets, scoring stencils which may be used for either hand or machine scoring are provided. The score is the number of right answers. Raw scores are convertible into normalised standard scores, percentile ranks and stanines.

14. *Norms* : For high school students enrolled in American history, norms are based upon the total group tested, consisting of 9,523 students in 24 public high schools representing various sections of the country. Norms for two sub-groups, college prep and all others, are also provided. Presumably these sub-groups are the same students constituting the basis for the total group norms. Norms are normalised standard scores, percentile ranks and stanines.

It is important to note that the same population was used for norming and for item analysis, thus combining in one operation what has generally been carried out in two steps with different populations.

15. *Format* : The test, manual and other materials are of high quality in appearance and composition.

Other Tests in Social Studies

(1) *California Tests in Social and Related Sciences.* 1946–53. Advanced, Grades 9–12. *Creating a New Nation* (to 1789). 2. *Nationalism, Sectionalism and Conflict* (1790–1876). 3. *Emergence of Modern America* (1877–1918). 4. *The United States in Transition* (since 1918). Forms AA and BB. 1 and 2 in a booklet, 3 and 4 in a booklet, $ 4.50 per 35. 1 and 2, 45 minutes; 3 and 4, 45 minutes. California Test Bureau.

(2) *Cooperative Social Studies Tests.* 1964. Junior and senior high school grade. *American History,* Grades 7–8; *Civics,* Grades 8–9; *American History; Problems of Democracy; American Government; Modern European History; World History,* Grades 10–12. Forms A and B of each subject test. $ 6.00 per 20. 40 minutes. Educational Testing Service.

Natural Science

The commonly taught science subjects in junior and senior high schools are general science, biology, chemistry and physics. Another course, variously named—Senior Science, Consumer Science, Advanced General Science—has also found a place in the high school curriculum. These are, and have been for many years, the courses usually offered. However, as in the case of mathematics, profound changes have been taking place in their content and organisation since World War II. The developments in nuclear fission and fusion; the recent growth of space science and technology; and the new discoveries in biochemistry, biophysics and medicine have had a profound effect on high school science courses. National committees, including the Biological Science Curriculum Study, the Chem-Bond and Chem-Study groups, and the Physical Science Study Committee, have produced courses of study that represent significant changes, both in content and emphasis, in the traditional high school courses in science.

The committees responsible for the development of the new courses of study have had tests constructed to be used by teachers with their instructional materials. These are not usually suitable for use elsewhere, however. Nor are existing tests appropriate evaluative instruments with classes using the new materials. The tendency at present seems to be to revise existing tests or to produce new tests in the sciences which are a compromise between the traditional and the more recent. This will probably continue for some time to come until the changes in science courses become stabilised. Indeed, the content and organisation of the courses as they develop will almost certainly represent such a compromise.

One quite recent standardised test in general science is described in detail below.

Read General Science Test

1. ***Name of test and author*** : *Read General Science Test,* Revised Edition. John G. Read.

2. ***Nature and purposes*** : The objectives of the test are to measure the degree to which the following objectives have been attained:

(a) Knowledge of important facts, concepts and principles of science.

(b) Understanding of such facts, concepts and principles.

(c) Ability to apply such knowledge and understanding in the solution of new or unfamiliar problems.

(d) Ability to interpret data or situations which are new but to which such knowledge and understanding are relevant.

3. ***Grade level*** : Seventh, eighth and ninth grades.

4. ***Number of forms*** : E and F.

5. ***Publisher and date of publication*** : Harcourt Brace Jovanovich, Inc., 1964.

6. ***Cost*** : $ 8.20 per 35. Answer sheets at additional cost.

7. *Content* : Solids, liquids, work and machines, gases, heat, light, sound, electricity, magnetism, electronics, communication—21.3 per cent; properties and uses of familiar substances, chemical change—8.0 per cent; characteristics of living organisms, plants, animals, human biology, heredity, conservation, ecology—32.0 per cent; weather, climate, geology, exploration of space—28.0 per cent; solar system, stars, galaxies—5.3 per cent; scientific method, scientific attitudes—5.3 per cent. The test consists of two forms of seventy-five multiple-choice items each.

Samples :

The basic substance of all plant and animal life is:

1. lymph
2. protoplasm
3. serum
4. connective tissue
5. Don't Know

A recent discovery which allows many more television programmes and telephone messages to be sent at the same time is the:

1. transistor
2. transformer
3. Q-tube
4. laser
5. Don't Know

The response, "Don't Know," is used as a possible fifth choice on the theory that it reduces guessing by students who have no sound basis for answering. The validity of this assumption does not appear to have been established, however.

8. *Time required* : 40 minutes.

9. *Direction for and ease of administering* : The test is not difficult to administer. Directions are clear and complete. It may be used as a consumable booklet (the student marks his choices on the test booklet) or with separate answer sheets. The variety of answer media requires several sets of directions to the student, all clear and concise.

10. *Validity* : The test is designed to reflect current teaching of general science in junior high school Grades 7–9. It is based upon analysis of current instructional materials, pronouncements of national committees, such as BSCS. Chem-Bond, Chem-Study and PSSC, and research studies on the teaching of general science. It is, therefore, held to have a high degree of content or curricular validity.

Students in the standardisation population took the *Otis Gamma Mental Ability Test* along with the experimental forms of the revised *Read.* The correlations between *Otis* I.Q.'s and scores on the *Read* range from .645 to .709. These may be interpreted as indication of concurrent validity in that they show a marked tendency for brighter students to make higher scores on the science test than the less able. At the same time, the correlation is not high enough to suggest that the two tests are measures of the same thing.

Another indication of the validity of the revised *Read* is to be found in the consistent differences between the mean scores of grades 7, 8 and 9. The means are as follows:

Grade 7	*Grade 8*	*Grade 9*
32.69	38.11	40.53

Taking all these data into account, the *Read General Science Test* would appear to have a satisfactory degree of validity as a measure of current objectives and content of general science as taught in junior high school grades.

11. *Reliability* : Split-half reliability coefficients for each form by grades are as follows:

	Grade 7	*Grade 8*	*Grade 9*
Form E	.896	.908	.908
Form F	.903	.919	.914

The standard error of measurement for both forms and all three grade levels is approximately 4 raw score points.

12. *Manual* : The manual for the test is quite adequate. It contains information on the development of the test, its validity and reliability, equivalence of forms and norms. Directions for administering, scoring and interpreting are clear and complete. It also contains some suggestions for the use of test results.

13. *Scoring* : The *Read* test may be scored by hand or machine. When answers are marked on the test booklet, scoring must be done by hand. Answer sheets may be scored either way.

14. *Norms* : Percentile, scaled score and stanine norms are provided by grade level. The norms are based upon a sampling of 17,958 students enrolled in twenty-seven schools in seventeen states distributed in all sections of the country. Included were 6,172 pupils in Grade 7, 5,779 in Grade 8 and 6,007 in Grade 9.

15. *Format* : The appearance of the revised *Read General Science Test* has been improved by the use of colour and better typography and paper. The over-all format is pleasing.

Other Tests in Natural Science

(1) *Anderson-Fisk Chemistry Test.* 1966. Grades 10–13. End-of-course test for high school chemistry. *Understanding of facts and concepts; understanding and application of functional principles; understanding and application of scientific method; ability to use basic skills in chemistry.* Forms E and F. $ 8.20 per 35. 40 minutes. Harcourt Brace Jovanovich, Inc.

(2) *Cooperative Science Tests.* 1963. *General Science,* Grades 7–9. *Advanced General Science,* Grades 8–9. *Biology,* Grades 10–12. *Chemistry,* Grades 10–12. *Physics,* Grades 10–12. Forms A and B. $ 6.00 per 20. 40 minutes for *General Science;* 40 minutes for each of two parts in the other tests. Educational Testing Service.

(3) *Dubins Earth Science Test.* 1969. Grades 8–12. End-of-course test of student mastery of earth science in conventional and ESCP curriculums. Forms A and B. $ 8.20 per 35. 40 minutes. Harcourt Brace Jovanovich, Inc.

(4) *Dunning-Abeles Physics Test.* 1967. Grades 11 and 12. End-of-course test for high school physics. *Knowledge and understanding of basic facts, principles and laws; mechanics, heat, sound, light, electricity, and modern physics.* Forms E and F. $ 8.20 per 35. 40 minutes. Harcourt Brace Jovanovich, Inc.

(5) *Tests of the Physical Science Study Committee.* 1959–1967. Ten tests covering sections of the basic textbook. Also an end-of-course test and an advanced topics test. Series O, S, and N, $ 2.50 per 10; Form F, $ 6.00 per 20. Advanced topics test, $ 2.50 per 10. 45 minutes. Educational Testing Service.

Mathematics

Since World War II significant changes have been taking place in the mathematics curriculum. The traditional titles of courses—arithmetic, algebra, plane geometry, solid geometry and trigonometry are still in general use. However, the content of these courses has been undergoing continuous study and revision. Concepts new to high school courses have been introduced. More recently, the development of computers and programming has also begun to have an effect on the content of courses in mathematics.

Also significant is the trend toward moving downward in the mathematics curriculum content which had been traditionally reserved for college and university courses. Analytic geometry and calculus, for example, are being taught in high school mathematics classes, and, as mentioned in Chapter 2, much experimentation has been carried out in teaching the simpler or basic concepts of algebra and geometry in elementary schools. The entire mathematics programme below the college level is in a state of flux.

These changes are not yet stabilised or standardised Textbooks of the more traditional type are still widely used, although many are now available that reflect some of the "new mathematics". Of course, many teachers are neither prepared nor willing to change to the new mathematics, and it will take some time before the content of high school mathematics courses is firmly established and generally accepted.

The trends in the mathematics curriculum will eventually be reflected in standardised tests, but this will also take time. At present, a few tests are appearing that incorporate some of the changes, but they represent essentially a compromise between the old and the new. The tests described below are of this type.

New Cooperative Mathematics Tests

1. ***Name of tests and authors*** : *Cooperative Mathematics Tests* in Arithmetic, Structure of the Number System, Algebra I, Algebra II, Geometry, Trigonometry, Algebra III, Analytic Geometry and Calculus. Cooperative Test Division.

2. ***Nature and purposes*** : A series of tests for junior and senior high school grades and college reflecting a blend of some

of the newer content and terminology with important aspects of traditional mathematics courses.

3. *Grade level* **:** Grade 7-college.

4. *Number of forms* **:** *Arithmetic*—A, B, C; all others—A and B.

5. *Publisher and date of publication* **:** Educational Testing Service, 1961, 1963.

6. *Cost* **:** $ 6.00 per 20. Answer sheets, $ 4.00 per 20.

7. *Content* **:** Arithmetic: *Number concepts, fractions, decimals, ratio and proportion, percentage, graphs.* Algebra I: *Equations, inequalities, binomials, factoring, coordinates.* Algebra II: Same as Algebra I plus *linear and quadratic equations, logarithms, powers.* Geometry: *Angles, plane figures, theorems, intuitive solid geometry, rectangular coordinates.*

Samples

Arithmetic

Which of the following will never change the value of a number?

(i) Multiplying it by 1.

(ii) Dividing it by 1.

(iii) Multiplying it by its reciprocal.

(A) I only.

(B) II only.

(C) III only.

(D) I and II only.

(E) I and III only.

Algebra I:

What number must be added to $x^2 - 6x + 4$ in order to make it a perfect square?

A. –4

B. 0

C. 2

D. 5

E. 32

Algebra II

The graphs of two linear equations are distinct and do *not* intersect. How many solutions do these two equations have in common?

A. None.

B. One.

C. Two.

D. An unlimited number.

E. It cannot be determined from the information given.

Geometry:

The figure is a circle with center at O. The path once completely around the circle from P back to P is about how many times the path from P straight across through O to Q?

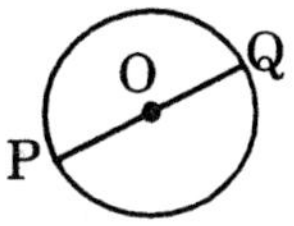

A. 1

B. 4/3

C. 3/2

D. 5/2

E. 22/7

For examples from other tests in this series see specimen sets.

8. *Time required* : 40 minutes (Geometry, two parts—40 minutes each.)

9. *Directions for and ease of administering* : Directions for administering are clear and complete. The tests themselves are practically self-administering. All answers are marked on answer sheets.

10. *Validity* : Content outlines for the tests were reviewed by a committee of mathematics educators and curriculum specialists. Outstanding classroom teachers and mathematicians participated in the preparation of test items. Validity must therefore rest on the judgment of persons involved in the production of the tests.

11. *Reliability* : Kuder-Richardson Formula 20 was used to determine estimates of reliability and standard errors of measurement. For *Arithmetic* single-grade coefficients range from .80 to .91; S.E. measurement is approximately 3 raw score points. For *Algebra I,* K–R_{20} reliability coefficients range from .82 to .85; S.E. measurement, about 2.65. For *Algebra II,* K–R_{20} coefficients range from .80 to .85; S.E. measurement, about 2.70. For *Geometry, Part I,* K–R_{20} coefficients range from .79 to .84; S.E. measurement, about 2.50. For *Geometry, Part I* and *Part II,* K–R_{20} coefficients range from .82 to .85; S.E. measurement, about 3.65.

12. *Manual* : Directions for administering and scoring are printed in one booklet and preliminary interpretive data, including information on reliability and norms, in another. A handbook with data on all tests in the series is available.

13. *Scoring* : Stencils are used for hand or machine scoring. Score is the number right.

14. *Norms* : Percentile rank and scaled score norms are available for each test in the series. Norms are interpreted by use of percentile bands.

15. *Format* : Tests in this edition are less attractive than other *Co-operative* tests. The format, although fairly good, is not up to the best standards.

Other Tests in Mathematics

(1) *Blyth Second-Year Algebra Test.* 1966. End of second-year algebra course in high schools. *Symbolic expression, factoring, radicals, exponents, logarithms, simple progressions, linear and quadratic equations* and *graphic methods.* Forms E and F. $ 8.20 per 35. 45 minutes. Harcourt Brace Jovanovich, Inc.

(2) *Howell Geometry Test.* 1969. Grades 9–12. End-of-course test in plane geometry suitable for students in both modern and traditional programmes. Forms A and B. $ 8.20 per 35. 40 minutes. Harcourt Brace Jovanovich, Inc.

(3) *Illinois Algebra Test.* 1956–58. Test I, first semester; Test II, second semester; Test III, one year's work. *Manipulative and mechanical skills.* One form. $ 2.80 per 35 of each test. 37 minutes. The Bobbs-Merrill Company, Inc.

(4) *Illinois Plane Geometry Test.* 1957. Tests 1–4 for one semester mid-term and final, second semester mid-term and final. One form. $ 3.15 per 35 of each test. 37 minutes. The Bobbs-Merrill Company, Inc.

(5) *Lankton First-Year Algebra Test.* 1965. End-of-course test in first-year algebra. *Vocabulary, meaning and use of symbols, fundamental operations, formulas, equations, simple algebraic fractions, radicals, ratio, proportion, variation, graphs, trigonometric functions* and *algebraic solution of problems.* Forms E and F. $ 8.20 per 35. 40 minutes. Harcourt Brace Jovanovich, Inc.

4

The Measurement of Capacity : General Intelligence

The term "capacity" as used here includes both intelligence and aptitude. This chapter deals with the measurement of intelligence, and the following one deals with the measurement of aptitude.

Numerous attempts have been made to define intelligence, yet educators and psychologists have never been able to come to complete agreement on the term or on the concepts which it involves. Substantial progress has been made in the measurement of intelligence, however; such progress has resulted from attempts to find measures that would differentiate feeble-minded from normal children, or pupils successful in school work from those who are less successful, as judged by their teachers. Actually, our definition of intelligence is circular, since we are in effect saying that intelligence is what intelligence tests measure, and that it is what makes for success in academic work. This is true, at least insofar as the schools are concerned.

A second type of capacity to be considered in Chapter 5, is often referred to as "aptitude". As used here, the meaning of the term differs from intelligence in one important respect. Aptitude refers to capacities in special fields, such as music, art, or mechanics. Intelligence tests have sometimes been referred to as tests of "scholastic aptitude," but the term "aptitude" is probably more applicable to tests that are narrower in scope and more specialised. In this chapter intelligence tests will be described and illustrated, and their theoretical bases and uses will be discussed briefly.

For a long time psychologists have been interested in the measurement of intelligence, and the history of the development of intelligence tests closely parallels the development of psychology as a science. Moreover, intelligence measurement is an area of study that is not without its controversial aspects. Also, it must be recognised that the use of intelligence tests requires in many instances a considerable amount of technical knowledge and training, and in no instance can one expect to use such tests properly without at least some preparation. The first part of this chapter treats three aspects of intelligence testing: the background of the movement, its associated problems, and its current procedures.

Historical Backgrounds of Intelligence Measurement

Present-day intelligence tests are based on the work of the French psychologist, Alfred Binet. Associated with him were, first, V. Henri, and later, Théodore Simon. There can be no doubt that Binet was the shining light and genius of this most important contribution to modern psychological methods, even though many others contributed to the developments which culminated in and have grown out of his work.

For instance, the work of Francis Galton (1822–1911), an English scientist, did much to stimulate interest in individual differences and their measurement. He devised various tests of sensory discrimination involving weights, tones, and mental imagery, and made important contributions to the advancement of statistical methods. He is generally regarded as having been the first to use standard scores and correlation.

In the United States a number of psychologists became interested in the possibility of measuring intelligence. At this point it must suffice to mention only one, James McKeen Cattell, who had more to do with early developments along these lines than anyone else in this country. Cattell studied psychology under the famous German, Wilhelm Wundt, who was not very favourably disposed toward the "new psychology"—that is, the measurement of mental abilities. However, Cattell became actively interested in the measurement of intelligence, and when he returned to this country he did much to stimulate interest in it. In 1896 he devised and administered to students at Columbia University a series of tests largely of the sensory-motor type.

These tests measured such traits or abilities as keenness of vision and hearing, reaction time, mental imagery, and perception of differences in weights, colours and tones. For the most part, the tests were simple, objective and easily administered. Almost without exception, however, the results showed little relation to teachers' estimates of their students' intelligence, or to the students' success in school work as measured by marks or other means.

Binet also experimented with most such tests and dozens of others with similarly unsatisfactory results. He and his co-workers became convinced that the value of such tests for measuring intelligence was extremely limited. Gradually, however, he developed a new approach to the problem, and began to make real progress. Binet based his theory on the assumption that success would depend on the measurement of complex mental processes rather than specific traits. In 1905, after years of research and experimentation, he published his first scale of intelligence developed primarily for the purpose of identifying subnormal children in the schools of Paris. This scale represented a distinct departure from previous efforts. In the first place, Binet's tests were arranged in order of increasing difficulty, and thus they constituted a scale for measuring the individual's level of mental development. In the second place, although the tests were of considerable variety, they were intended to measure a complex, central factor in intelligence which Binet called "judgment". Of course, Binet recognised that the thirty tests in the scale could not all be shown to measure this one factor; nevertheless, the originality and purpose of the tests were clearly evident. Some of the items required the student to execute simple orders such as "Close the door," to name objects designated in a picture, to cite from memory the differences between pairs of familiar objects or materials such as wood and glass, and to construct a sentence embodying three given words such as "Paris, gutter, fortune".

This first scale was followed in 1908 by a revision in which the tests were grouped at ages or levels, a marked improvement over the serial order of the original scale. In 1911 a second revision was published. This was the culmination of Binet's work, since he died in the same year at the age of fifty-four. This third scale was more complete, more carefully standardised, and more systematically scored than either of its predecessors.

During Binet's lifetime several psychologists, most of whom were Americans, translated and used the first and the second scales, and criticised them, largely to Binet's benefit. However, the basic principles were established by Binet, and it was clearly demonstrated that the third scale in particular was an instrument superior in usefulness, accuracy, and scope to anything that had preceded it. The need now was for further translations and adaptations of the scale for use with children of different nationalities, cultures and languages, this need was soon fulfilled, at least in the United States.

Three Americans are most closely associated with the development of the Binet tests. Henry Goddard translated both the 1905 and the 1908 scales into English and used them in his work at the Vineland, New Jersey, Training School for the Feeble-minded. In a similar way, Fred Kuhlmann used the early scales at an institution for feeble-minded at Faribault, Minnesota. He published the first translation and thoroughgoing revision of Binet's scales for use with American children in 1912. This edition has been revised several times subsequently, and still finds some use in certain sections of this country.

The major work in adapting the Binet scales for use with English-speaking subjects was done by Lewis M. Terman, who had carried on some experimentation with tests independently, but had not gone very far when the Binet scales appeared. He set to work at once on these, and in 1916 published what became the most widely used and accepted intelligence test, known as the *Stanford Revision of the Binet Scale.* This was a careful translation and revision, involving a complete standardisation on American children and adults. There were tests at Years III, IV, V, VI, VII, VIII, IX, X, XII, XIV, and for levels called Average Adult and Superior Adult. Terman rearranged many of the tests from the positions established by Binet, added new tests, especially at the upper end of the scale, and eliminated others. This became the standard instrument for the measurement of intelligence in the United States and other English-speaking countries for more than twenty years.

In time, certain shortcomings and weaknesses in Terman's scale became apparent, and in 1937 he and Maud A. Merrill published their revision of the *Stanford-Binet Scale* which remedied most, if not all, of these faults. The chief faults were a lack of equivalent forms, gaps in the scale, notably at Years XI and XIII, and incompleteness at both ends of the scale. The 1937 Revision appeared in two equivalent forms; it provided tests for the missing years, it extended downward to age two, with tests at half-year intervals from age two to age six, thus providing a far more thorough testing at these levels; and it extended upward to a much higher level by adding three sets of tests, Superior Adult I, II and III, giving the scale more "top" or "ceiling" for use with adults. Also, the normative population was more adequate and more carefully selected than in the earlier scale. A few samples from Form L of the *Revised Stanford-Binet Tests of Intelligence* will serve to show its nature.

Year III-6. Drawing Designs : Cross

Procedure: Give the child a pencil and as you draw a cross making diagonal lines about two inches in length (X) say to him, "You make one just like this." Illustrate once only. Give one trial.

Score: "Requirement is that child shall make two lines that cross each other. We disregard the angle of crossing and the straightness and length of the lines."

Year VIII. Comprehension IV

Procedure: Ask

(*a*) "What makes a sailboat move?"

(*b*) "What should you say when you are in a strange city and someone asks you how to find a certain address?"

(*c*) "What should you do if you found on the streets of a city a three-year-old baby that was lost from its parents?"

Score: 2 plus. Sample answers are given. In (*a*) for instance, "wind," "wind and water," "wind and sails," are acceptable; "water," "the motor" are not.

Superior Adult III. Repeating 9 Digits

Procedure: Say, "I am going to say some numbers and when I am through I want you to say them just the way I do. Listen carefully, and get them just right." Before each series repeat, "Listen carefully, and get them just right." Rate, one per second. Avoid accent and rhythm.

(*a*) 3 – 7 – 1, etc.
(*b*) 7 – 3 – 9, etc.
(*c*) 8 – 5 – 2, etc.

Score: 1 plus. The series must be repeated in correct order without error after a single reading.

The administration of this scale requires training, practice and skill. No one should attempt it except as a learner under expert supervision until he has all three requisites. The examiner should be so thoroughly familiar with the procedure that he can give major attention to the presentation of the tasks, recording of responses, and legitimate encouragement of the subject. Assuming that the user has attained satisfactory skill and has established rapport with the subject, the procedure for administering the scale is as follows:

1. Establish the basal mental age. This is the highest level on the scale at which the subject passes all the tests.
2. Proceed to give all the tests at successively higher levels, recording successes and failures at each level.
3. Stop at the level at which the subject fails all the tests.
4. Calculate the intelligence quotient.

The procedure may be illustrated with the example of Mary, aged eight years and six months. The examiner starts at the seven-year level at which he finds she passes all the tests; she does the same at eight; at the nine-year level she passes five out of six; at ten, three out of six; at eleven, two out of six; at twelve, one out of six; and none at the thirteen-year level. To summarise:

Mary, Age 8–6

Basal M.A., 8 years

Nine year level passes	5×2	=	10 months
Ten year level passes	3×2	=	6 months
Eleven year level passes	2×2	=	4 months
Twelve year level passes	1×2	=	2 months
			22 months

Mental Age: 8 years + 22 mos. = 9-10

$$\text{I.Q.} = \frac{\text{M.A}}{\text{C.A}} \times 100 = \frac{9-10}{8-6} \times 100 = \frac{118}{102} \times 100 = 116$$

The tests are placed at age levels such that the standardisation population yields an I.Q. of very close to 100 at each level. Assuming the sample to be representative of the total population, this is as it should be. Earlier, Binet and others had placed tests at age levels where approximately three-fourths of the standardisation population of a given age passed the test. This method was not entirely satisfactory and has been superseded by the method mentioned above. Under ideal circumstances, however, the two methods yield about the same results.

After nearly a quarter-century of use of Forms L and M of the 1937 scale, still another revision was published in 1960. It was made up of those items of Forms L and M which had proved to be most reliable and valid and whose content had not become out of date. Items which met these criteria were given a final tryout with several thousand cases and the best ones were combined into Form L-M. The 1937 Forms L and M are still available and widely used, but the best of them have been put into the new form. Since this is so, Form L-M is superior in certain respects to its predecessors, though there is no equivalent form to go with it.

The new scale also provides tables of deviation I.Q.'s, which can be read directly without calculations when the chronological age is known and the mental age has been established by administering either form of the 1937 scale or the 1960 L-M scale.

The Binet scales and their counterparts in other countries had one limitation, the significance of which was that only one person could be tested at a time by a trained examiner. This is a time-consuming procedure, although it has, nevertheless, certain desirable features, including the opportunity to establish rapport between subject and examiner and to observe the subject while being tested; also, when properly administered, it yields a very dependable appraisal. However, some American psychologists, notably Arthur S. Otis of The World Book Company, W. S. Miller of the University of Minnesota, Rudolf Pintner and E.L. Thorndike of Columbia University, and Terman himself, soon began experimenting with the adaptation of certain types of tests to group testing. In 1917, the entry of the United States into World War I gave this movement the impetus it required for success. Large numbers of men were being inducted into military service and the need for and potential usefulness of some kind of rapid, accurate, mental measurement of men soon became apparent. The government asked a number of psychologists to develop a test for this purpose. The result was *Army Alpha,* the first single, unified group test of intelligence. Its counterpart, *Army Beta,* was also constructed for use with illiterates and those who could not read well enough for *Army Alpha,* which presupposed about sixth-grade reading ability. Nearly two million men were tested by *Alpha* during the war, and in subsequent years it was widely used in schools and colleges.

Soon after *Army Alpha* and *Beta* were produced, many group tests were published, some very closely patterned after the army tests, and none differing materially from them. *Alpha* had been designed for use with adults; most of the new tests were adaptations for use with children and adolescents.

Although *Army Alpha* is rarely used today, it will be interesting and revealing to examine it a little more closely. It consisted of eight sub-tests or parts, each closely timed. The working time for the entire test was forty minutes. Some samples follow:

Army Alpha—Form 6

Test 3 : This is a test of common sense. Below are sixteen questions. Three answers are given to each question. You are to look at the answers carefully; then make a cross in the square before the best answer to each question, as in the sample:

Sample : Why do we use stoves? Because

☐ they look well

☒ they keep us warm

☐ they are black

Here the second answer is the best and is marked with a cross. Begin with No. 1 and keep on until time is called. Time: 1½ minutes.

Test 7.

Sample : sky—blue: : grass—table green warm big

fish—swims: : man—paper time walks girl

day—night: : white—red black clear pure

In each of the lines above, the first two words are related to each other in some way. What you are to do in each line is to see what the relation is between the first two words, and underline the word in heavy type that is related in the same way to the third word. Begin with No. 1 and mark as many sets as you can before time is called. Time: 3 minutes (for 40 analogies).

The other tests in *Army Alpha* were *Following Directions, Arithmetic, Opposites, Scrambled or Disarranged Sentences, Number Series Completion* and *General Information*. The items in each test were arranged in order of difficulty, closely timed, and speeded—that is, speed was strongly emphasised.

Army Beta was designed as a counterpart to *Army Alpha*, but it did not require the ability to read. It could be given without spoken or written directions, so it was strictly a no-verbal examination. It had the same number of parts as *Alpha* and was designed to parallel in purpose, but pictorially, most of the parts or sub-tests of *Alpha. Army Beta* was not nearly as extensively used as *Alpha,* either during the war or subsequently.

Although hundreds of group intelligence tests have been developed since 1917, those which have been successful do not differ in fundamental respects from *Army Alpha.* This is not a criticism of newer tests, but rather a recognition of the basic soundness of this first venture, which, of course, was essentially a adaptation of Binet's ideas to group testing. The importance of Binet's contribution to the development of mental tests is obvious. Undoubtedly a genius, he established the basic principles and devised the appropriate techniques which have been followed, without material change, to this day.

Basic Concepts and Principles of Intelligence Measurement

Before discussing current procedures in measuring intelligence we should consider some of the fundamental ideas and associated problems of this field. Most of these problems are theoretical and do not affect to any great extent the actual use of the tests. Nevertheless, it is important for the user to understand this theory so that he can be more realistic in his approach and more aware of the strengths and limitations of the instruments he uses. In instances where the topics discussed are controversial issues, we have tried to present some of the facts on both sides.

Theories of Intelligence

Binet, like many in his field, revised his thinking as he gained more experience and witnessed the results of his tests. It will be recalled that at the time of the publication of his first scale in 1905 he believed "sound judgment" to be the central factor. This was in sharp contrast to the views held by most of his predecessors and contemporaries, who believed that intelligence consists of a large number of specifics. The tests of reaction time, acuity of vision, hearing, and so on, were consistent with this latter view, but they did not prove very useful in distinguishing between feeble-minded and normal children, or in identifying those who were considered brighter by their teachers, or those who did relatively poorly well in school or college.

Binet's definition of intelligence included the three factors or capacities: ability in thinking (1) to maintain a definite direction or to "stay on the track", (2) to choose appropriate means to ends, or to adapt procedures to goals sought, and (3) to evaluate objectively one's own actions (autocriticism). In general, Binet held that the mind is unitary and possesses one overriding function: effective adjustment to environment.

More precisely defined theories of intelligence have been advanced by various people contemporary with and following Binet. The first of these is the *two-factor theory* developed by Charles Spearman, an English statistician. On the basis of correlation studies, he proposed a theory that intelligence consists of two factors–a general factor *g,* and many specific factors, s_1, s_2, etc. The *g* enters into all intellectual activities, while each particular activity is also subject to one or more specific factors.

In contrast with the two-factor theory is one which has been referred to as the *multi-factor theory*, the beginnings of which are generally associated with the name of E.L. Thorndike. His theory holds that intelligence consists of a very large number of specific factors or functions ($s_1 + s_2 + s_2 + \ldots\ldots s_n$), and casts doubt on the existence of any *g*, or general factor. This is consistent with Thorndike's theory of learning called *connectionism,* which holds that learning consists of forming connections or bonds between specific stimuli and responses and that a person's learning increases with the number of connections formed. Consequently, his degree of intelligence would be determined by the ease with which bonds are formed and by their strength and number.

A third theory, somewhere between these two, is called the *group-factor theory,* usually associated with the name of L.L. Thurstone, an American psychologist and statistician. According to this theory, intelligence consists neither of *g* and *s,* nor of many *s's,* but of six to ten primary or group factors. The six named by Thurstone are number, verbal, space, word fluency, reasoning, and rote memory. While none of these factors is completely distinct from the others, statistical evidence has been presented to justify the assumption that they are not the same. The Thurstone theory is, in a sense, a compromise or middle ground between the other two.

In developing the theory of group factors, or Primary Mental Abilities, as Thurstone called them, he used the technique as factor analysis. By this statistical procedure, based on intercorrelations between tests, the factor analyst arrives at a limited number of factors which appear to be fairly distinct entities. Taken together they comprise what, in this instance, is called general intelligence or general mental ability.

Although all three of the theories discussed are based on statistical foundations, they illustrate the inevitable fact that different individuals will occasionally interpret the same or similar data differently. Present-day thinking leans toward the group-factor theory as being probably most consistent with the facts, but it recognises the probability of the existence of a general factor also.

The Intelligence Quotient

Apparently Binet did not come to the concept of the I.Q. himself, but he clearly saw and expressed the mental-age concept at the time of the publication of his first scale, and the idea emerged clearly with the 1908 revision. A German psychologist, Wilhelm Stern, seems to have been the first to formulate the concept of the intelligence quotient, in 1912, a year after Binet's death. The intelligence quotient, or I.Q., as it is generally known, was quickly adopted by Terman and others, and today is the generally accepted means of expressing intelligence, at least of persons below adulthood.

The ratio I.Q., as has been shown already, is the ratio of mental age or level to chronological or life age. Thus, it is reasoned that a child developing normally should have a mental age equivalent to his chronological age and therefore an I.Q. of 1, or, as it is commonly expressed, 100. The mental age or level for any given chronological age up to maturity is determined by testing a representative sample of children of that age. The mental age of nine, for example, is determined by giving that test to a representative sample of nine-year-old children. The average score in a group test made by these nine-year-olds is the mental-age norm for that life age. Subsequently, any child who makes that score is said to have a mental age of nine. On the other hand, this same score (and mental age) may be earned by children of varying life or chronological ages. Thus, John who is twelve may earn a score typical of nine-year-olds; therefore, his I.Q. is $\frac{9}{12} \times 100 = 75$. Again, Jean may be ten and if her mental age is nine, her I.Q. is 90; still another child with an M.A. of nine may be only seven, in which case his I.Q. is about 130. Thus, the I.Q. represents the ratio of mental age to chronological age or the rate of mental development compared to age. In the first instance above, there is, on the average, three-quarters of a year of mental growth per year of life; in the second, nine-tenths of a year; and in the third, 1.3 years mental gain for every year lived. The same facts may be shown in a different way by comparing children of the same age who have different mental ages.

The ratio I.Q. concept has been under fire from various quarters for a number of reasons. For example, it does not have the unqualified approval of educational statisticians because it does not have the same meaning at all levels or points on the scale. An I.Q. of 120 represents the ratio of $\frac{6}{5}$ in a five-year-old and the ratio of $\frac{12}{10}$ in a ten-year-old. Obviously, in the first case the difference between M.A. and C.A. is one year; in the second, two years. However, this disadvantage inherent in any ratio and applies to the I.Q. to no greater extent than it does to any other.

Another criticism of the ratio I.Q. is that such I.Q.'s are not comparable from one test to another. This was early pointed out by W. S. Miller, who gave ten different intelligence tests to a group of fifty-seven ninth-grade pupils and found that there was a range of more than three years in the mean M.A.'s on the ten tests. Thus, a child might have an I.Q. of 116 on one of the tests and 130 on another. Miller showed that this was largely due to differences in the tests themselves and differences in the standardisation population. He suggested a method of equating such differences by converting the I.Q.'s to standard scores.

Another shortcoming of the ratio I.Q. resides in the assumption of constant rate of mental development for a given individual. This assumption, although true, relatively speaking, for many, is not true for all. Research has shown that rate of mental development, as measured by existing tests, is not constant but fluctuates rather markedly in some instances.

One other aspect of the ratio I.Q. concept, also in the nature of a limitation, should be mentioned here. Experience has shown that the functions or capacities measured by existing intelligence tests reach their maximum about the same time as physical maturity is reached, which seems to be somewhere between the ages of fifteen and twenty, as reported in various studies. In some respects this would appear to be quite consistent, since we do not expect an individual to grow taller or to acquire more teeth or stronger eyesight once he is mature. On the other hand, most individuals like to think of themselves as gaining in wisdom and knowledge as long as they live, or at least until they grow quite old. Thus, as far as the I.Q. goes, if we continue to use $\frac{\text{M.A.}}{\text{C.A.}}$ and the individual's M.A. ceases to increase after a certain age, the I.Q. value declines. To illustrate, if $\frac{\text{M.A.}}{\text{C.A.}}$ were $\frac{16}{16}$ the I.Q. would be 100. If the M.A. was still 16 when the C.A. was 20, the ratio then would be .80, or, I.Q. = 80. This, of course, is an obviously erroneous conclusion, and certainly a demoralising one. Consequently, it is customary with subjects past the age of sixteen not to calculate I.Q.'s at all, but to express the individual's position relative to others in his group, either by percentile ranks or by standard scores. This is the procedure followed almost entirely with adult groups such as college and university students, men and women in military service, and so on. In effect, this procedure results in an equivalent of the I.Q., since we can assume that these persons have reached maturity. Therefore, the denominator of the $\frac{\text{M.A.}}{\text{C.A.}}$ ratio is a constant factor and the score or percentile rank is really a measure comparable to the ratio I.Q. rather than simply a measure of rank or relative position. Many studies show that for adolescents the correlation between scores on a mental ability test and I.Q.'s based on the scores is .98 or higher.

To overcome the major weaknesses of the ratio I.Q. the so-called deviation I.Q. has come increasingly into use in recent years. This is a standard core with an arbitrarily chosen mean and standard deviation. Although any values, such as a mean of 50 and standard deviation of 10 as used for the sigma scores could be employed, it has become quite general practice to use a mean of 100 and a standard deviation of 16. The reason for using these values is that they are the mean and standard deviation, respectively, of *Stanford-Binet* I.Q.'s. I.Q.'s based on these constants are therefore numerically comparable to *Binet* I.Q.'s. Thus, a ratio I.Q. one standard deviation above the mean of a particular group test becomes a deviation I.Q. of 116; one which is two standard deviations above the mean on this test becomes a deviation I.Q. of 132; a ratio I.Q. one standard deviation below the mean of the test becomes a deviation I.Q. of 84, and so on.

Constancy of the I.Q.

One of the continuing points of issue about the I.Q. concept is the question of constancy. Usually this means constancy from time to time in the development of the individual, though it may also mean constancy at different levels or points on the scale. The latter has been touched upon in the preceding section as a function of the ratio I.Q. and is a technical matter beyond the scope of this book. The question of constancy in an individual, however, is one of direct concern to every user of intelligence tests. In essence, this question is, "If I test a child today and he has an I.Q. of 90, what is the result likely to be if I test him again a year or more from now?" This is probably what most persons have in mind when they discuss the constancy of the I.Q.

Numerous longitudinal studies have been reported in which children have been tested annually or semi-annually over a period of years. In one study sixty-one children were tested at the preschool ages of one month to five years by the *California Pre-School Schedule,* from six to twelve years and at fourteen and seventeen years by the *Stanford-Binet.* At ages thirteen and fifteen they were tested by a group test, the *Terman-McNemar,* and at ages sixteen and eighteen by the *Wechsler-Bellevue.* The study began with sixty-one infants. At the last testing at age eighteen, thirty-seven cases were tested. The results showed that: (1) correlations between tests of children below age six ranged from –.13 to .73 (*California* with *Binet*), and (2) correlations between tests given between age six and eleven ranged from .73 to .93 (*Binet* at all levels).

In another study, 252 children were tested annually from age twenty-one months to eighteen years by the *California Pre-School Schedule,* the *Stanford-Binet,* or the *Wechsler-Bellevue* (an individual scale for adults). The results were similar to those reported by Bayley. In general they indicated that: (1) the results of tests made after age six are much more stable than those of tests made before age six; (2) individual children showed marked fluctuation in I.Q. over the sixteen-year period (the tested I.Q.'s of 58 per cent of the children changed 15 points or more); (3) the longer the interval between tests, the greater the possibility of change; and (4) the maximum shift in average I.Q. for the group as a whole, between twenty-one months and eighteen years, was from 118 to 123 or 5 points.

Another study is of interest since it examines the question of whether or not deviation I.Q.'s are more stable than ratio I.Q.'s, as has been suggested by some authorities. Fifty boys and girls were tested by the 1937 *Binet* every six months from age two-and-a-half to five and annually from six through twelve years of age. The results showed that : (1) average I.Q.'s in the 140–169 range increased over the years by about 30 points; (2) averages below this range tended to be much more stable; (3) variability of I.Q.'s of the entire group decreased between ages three and five, increased between five and ten and declined again between ten and twelve; and (4) no difference was found in the relative variability of ratio and deviation I.Q.'s.

Taken altogether, the evidence on stability of measured I.Q.'s can be summed up as follows: (1) average I.Q.'s for groups remain remarkably stable over many years; (2) I.Q.'s of many individual children fluctuate by substantial amounts; (3) tested I.Q.'s of children below age six are much less stable than those of the same children after age six; and (4) the results of intelligence tests of many children show remarkable consistency over long periods of time.

Finally, it must be emphasised that a single test, either individual or group, constitutes only a very limited sampling of a child's behaviour. Because of this fact, the results from a single testing should always be regarded as provisional and should be supplemented by additional testing whenever possible. It should be pointed out in this connection that many schools include in their testing programmes at least two and often three to five testings of intelligence between Grades 1 and 12.

Although it is currently fashionable to criticise all standardised tests, particularly intelligence tests, there should be no serious question of their overall value and usefulness. This point of view is epitomised in the words of a leading authority in the field, who says:

> The outstanding success of scientific measurement of individual differences has been that of the general mental test. Despite occasional overenthusiasm and misconceptions, and the fact that the established tests are rendered obsolescent by recent conceptual advances, the general mental test stands today as the most important technical contribution of psychology to the practical guidance of human affairs.

The great majority of counsellors and school psychologists know this, as do many teachers. To use these instruments wisely, with full recognition of their strengths and weaknesses, should be an objective of everyone involved in testing in the schools.

Distribution of Intelligence Quotients

Since there is no absolute standard of intelligence or of mental age, the basis for these must be relative. In other words, a mental age of twelve years is determined by what a sampling of children representative of the total population of twelve-year-olds can do on a given test. As has been pointed out, this varies from one test to another because of differences in the tests themselves and differences in the population sample. Nevertheless, distributions both of raw scores and I.Q.'s obtained from adequate population samples quite generally show results closely approximating the normal curve. One such distribution for the *Revised Stanford-Binet* is shown in Figure 4.1. This is based on a composite I.Q. on Forms L and M of the 1937 Revision for 2,904 subjects, ages two to eighteen, inclusive.

The close approximation to the normal curve in the form of the distribution of I.Q.'s is of considerable importance. If I.Q.'s obtained from intelligence tests did not yield this kind of distribution from adequate population samples, there might be a basis for doubting the validity of such tests, or at least the validity of the particular ones used. The basic assumption is that intelligence is normally distributed in the general population, and tests which do not yield results at least approximating the normal might be open to serious question. Also, this assumption provides a sound theoretical basis for interpreting the significance of any given I.Q. in comparison with the proportion of the general population having the same I.Q.

When the normal distribution of I.Q.'s is broken down according to the areas under the curve, and a mean of 100 and a

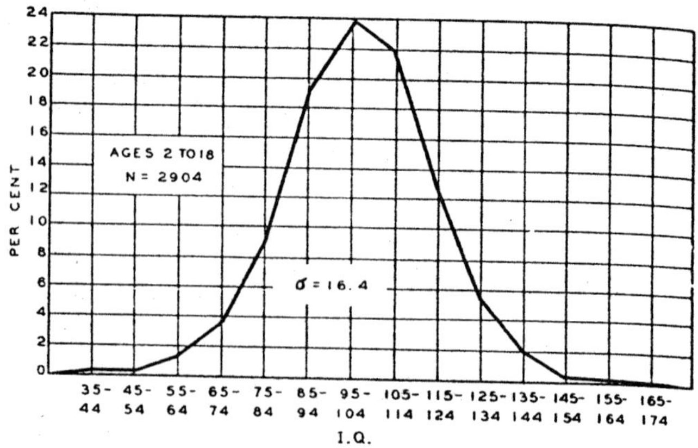

Fig. 4.1: Distributions of Composite L-M I.Q.'s of Standardisation Group.

(From Lewis M. Terman and Maud A. Merrill, *Measuring Intelligence*, Boston : Houghton Mifflin Company, 1937.)

standard deviation of 16 are used as the constant values (based on *Stanford-Binet* I.Q. distributions), the proportions of various levels of I.Q. are as shown in Table 4.1.

Table 4.1
Classification and Proportions of Various Levels of I.Q. in the General Population

Classification	*I.Q.*	*Percentage in General Population*
Very superior	140 and above	1.3
Superior	130–139	3.1
	120–129	8.2
High average	110–119	18.1
Normal average	100–109	23.5
	90–99	23.0
Low average	80–89	14.5
Borderline defective	70–79	5.6
Mentally defective	60–69	
	50–59	
	40–49	2.6
	30–39	

From Lewis M. Terman and Maude A. Merrill, *Stanford-Binet Intelligence Scale* (Boston: Houghton Mifflin Company, 1960), p. 18.

The classification of various I.Q. levels as shown in this table is generally accepted, though the limits are not to be regarded as exact. At the lower end of the distribution, the mentally defective have in the past been classed as morons, imbeciles, and idiots, in descending order; those whose I.Q.'s are below the lowest limit in the table are usually classed as idiots. However, today it is customary to use more functional designations such as "educable" or "trainable mentally retarded". Another recommended set of designations is "mildly retarded" (moron), "moderately retarded" (imbecile), and "severely retarded" (idiot).

Heredity versus Environment

Closely related to the question of the constancy of the I.Q. is the question of the relative influence of heredity and environment.

This controversy has raged for years with equally strong support on both sides of the argument. To a considerable degree the argument has been implemented and intensified by the development of intelligence tests. The widespread application of *Army Alpha* and its successors has supplied immense amounts of data, making possible comparisons among different racial, socio-economic and cultural groups or levels. Implicit in such comparisons, of course, is always the question of to what extent the differences among these groups are due to heredity or environment or both.

The debate on the relative influences of heredity and environment, while often apparently useless, is nevertheless concerned with a question of fundamental importance to educators and psychologists. Obviously, if a child's capacity for accomplishment were determined solely by inherited traits or abilities, education necessarily would have quite a different outlook and philosophy than it would in a less deterministic frame of reference.

Many investigations and experiments have been made on this question from the time of Galton to the present. One method of investigation involves studies of persons who are obviously brilliant, feeble-minded, or degenerate, to determine whether such traits tend to run in families. Results of such studies have generally been interpreted as showing the preponderant influence of heredity.

Another type of investigation involves the transplanting of children from a poor environment to a good one. The result of such studies are equivocal; some children show general and marked improvement in intelligence and other traits; others do not. One is almost forced to conclude that investigators tend to find the results they look for; much of the research showing marked changes has been severely criticised for poor control, careless procedures, or bad statistical treatment of data.

A third type of investigation uses twins as subjects. Identical twins are as nearly alike in heredity and environment as two humans can be. Starting with a large number of pairs of twins, the investigator studies may aspects of their resemblances—physical, mental and affective. Most of these studies show remarkable and, in some instances, almost incredible similarities among pairs of identical twins. In the few cases where studies have been made of identical twins reared in different environments, the resemblances have been less close in mental and social traits than in physical traits.

It can be said that the heredity-environment issue is still very much alive. During the first half of the twentieth century, there appeared to be a marked shift from a viewpoint strongly hereditarian to one strongly favourable to the environmentalist point of view. However, more recently the pendulum seems to be swinging again toward more emphasis on the role of heredity. At least there appears to be a tendency to question some of the assumptions and statements of those strongly convinced of the prepotency of the environment and to conduct further research on the matter implying that the question is far from being settled.

Most educators and psychologists, believing that what the individual becomes is the result of an interaction of heredity and environment, take a middle-of-the road view on this question. As one writer has put it, "The great mathematician, Sir Isaac Newton, if he had been brought up among African bushmen would probably have become a remarkable bushman but he would never have discovered the laws of motion." Similar statements might be made about a Mozart, an Einstein, or an Edison. In every instance, environmental opportunities were necessary to bring out a remarkable native endowment. On the other hand, it is improbable that any conceivable environment could make an Einstein, a Mozart, a Newton, or an Edison of a child having no special talents or unusual endowments.

Testing the Culturally Disadvantaged

It has been rather common in recent years to criticise all types of standardised tests whether achievement, personality, or intelligence. Some of these criticisms have been reviewed. One of the more persistent objections to the use of intelligence tests maintains that they are loaded or saturated with middle-class culture and are therefore unfair to children from lower socio-economic levels and especially to those who are considered to be culturally disadvantaged. It is maintained that existing groups tests penalise children who come from poor homes and whose cultural patterns, parental attitudes, and group standards are not the middle-class ones which are said to dominate the school and testing situations. Some critics have gone so far as to suggest that the use of current mental ability tests be discontinued. It has also been suggested that efforts be directed to the development of instruments on which the culturally disadvantaged will not be handicapped by previous experience or lack of it.

The question of the effects of cultural differences on performance on intelligence tests is not new. Numerous efforts have been made to develop "culture-free" or "culture-fair" tests of mental ability. The term "culture-free" has come to be regarded as meaningless if not positively misleading in this context. It is generally recognised that no test could be "culture-free" since the only way to respond to it is in terms of what has been learned, that is, in terms of one's culture. Attempts to develop "culture-fair" tests have concentrated on finding or devising tasks, responses to which are minimally or not at all affected by cultural differences. One method for doing this is to construct items of pictorial or performance nature, not requiring ability to read or even understand spoken directions, these being given in pantomime or "sign language". After tryout and item analysis, further refinement is made by eliminating items that show consistent differences in response by groups having different cultural backgrounds. An example of a test developed by this procedure will be described in detail later in this chapter. Suffice it to say at this point that none of the tests produced as "culture-fair" up to the present has been a success in any practical sense as evidenced by general usage or as a substitute for the more convential types of intelligence tests.

Recent concern with poverty, cultural deprivation, and related social problems in the United States has served to increase the tendency to question the use of intelligence tests in the schools and elsewhere, particularly with the so-called "disadvantaged". A recent publication outlines the common charges and attempts to answer the criticisms. Though it deals with testing in industry, the matters discussed and points made are generally relevant to testing in the schools. These will not be covered here but it is suggested that the student will find the bulletin thought-provoking and well worth careful reading.

The point we wish to make regarding this matter is that much of the discussion and criticism ignores the basic issue, namely, the purpose intelligence tests are intended to serve. Some critics seem to be saying that the tests are bad because they reveal individual differences and therefore result in some persons (e.g., the disadvantaged) being made to appear inferior to others. The fact is that the tests are *designed to reveal individual differences,* not to cover them up. A test that did not reveal differences in competence to perform or learn would be useless. Furthermore, the tests are designed to predict success in academic work, job performance, or ability to learn how to perform well. Their purpose is to differentiate between individuals, some of whom will do well, others less well, etc. The value of a test as predictor is measured by a criterion such as teachers' marks, performance on other tests, or on the job. A test that did not reveal differences between individuals would be quite useless for that purpose.

To date, no other measure or technique has been found or developed that equals the current best intelligence tests for the purposes for which they are intended. Some of the critics seem to be saying that we should kill the messenger who brings us bad news. Tests serve a useful purpose when they identify individuals' weaknesses and deficiencies as well as their strengths, whatever their cause or origin. The results of testing provide a basis for assisting the individual to remedy his shortcomings, to guide him into appropriate lines of activity, and to help him realise his potential to its fullest.

Current Procedures in Measuring Intelligence

Verbal and Non-verbal Material

The content of intelligence tests is generally classified as verbal or non-verbal. Verbal material requires the ability to read or, at the very least, to understand material spoken or read aloud by the examiner. Therefore, a strictly non-verbal examination is one that requires no use of language in its administration or in the pupils answers. Such a test was referred to earlier in the case of *Army Beta,* where it was stated that the directions for that examination could be given in pantomime. Tests are rarely non-verbal to this extreme; indeed we generally consider an intelligence test non-verbal as long as it does not require any reading ability. This type of test is useful and quite generally necessary in testing young children illiterates and the feeble-minded.

While non-verbal material may be pictorial, it may also be of the type known as "performance." Formboards, which are a kind of jigsaw puzzle, building blocks, and tracing mazes are typical of the performance type of exercises found in individual intelligence tests. Samples are shown in Figure 4.2.

In group tests the non-verbal material is generally pictorial, as will be illustrated later in this chapter.

Although the correlation between verbal and non-verbal types of tests of intelligence is far from perfect, it is generally high enough to justify the use of non-verbal material where verbal tests cannot be used. This is found most often in tests for young children. Non-verbal material of the performance type is also used extensively in tests of aptitude.

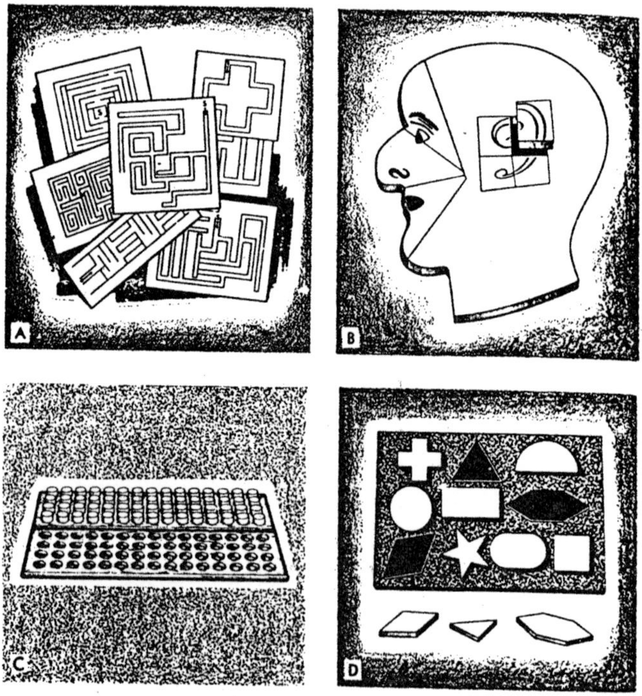

Fig. 4.2 : Examples of Typical Performance Tests. (A) Porteus Maze Test. (B) Knox-Kemp Feature Profile Test: Pintner-Patterson Modification. (C) Minnesota Rate of Manipulation Test. (D) Seguin-Goddard Formboard.

It should also be noted that many intelligence tests in current use include both verbal and non-verbal, that is, non-reading, material. This is true of both individual scales like the *Binet* and of numerous group tests. In some instances the materials are arranged so as to yield both a verbal and a non-verbal I.Q.

Individual Scales

A brief description has already been given of the nature and the procedure for administering a *Stanford-Binet* examination. The method is essentially the same in others of the *Binet* type, such as the *Kuhlmann*, except that the latter takes both accuracy and speed of response into account. It will be recalled that one of the criticisms of the *Stanford-Binet* (1916) was lack of adequate "ceiling" or "top" for testing adults. Although this was remedied to a large extent in the 1937 Revision, there was still some dissatisfaction on this point.

Another frequently voiced criticism of the *Binet* scale and its revisions was that the scales were designed for use with children, and the adult materials added later were really not essentially different. Consequently, it was said that the scales were not appropriate for adults and not intrinsically interesting to them. To meet these criticisms a scale for measuring adult intelligence was brought out by Wechsler in 1939. This was an individual intelligence scale known as the *Wechsler-Bellevue Intelligence Scale.* It departs in certain important respects from the *Binet*-type scale. The tests are not grouped at age levels and the scale yields standard score or deviation I.Q.'s. It was designed for and standardised largely on adults, but attained some popularity in use with children as well. In 1949, Wechsler published another scale, the *Wechsler Intelligence Scale for Children,* along the same general pattern as the adult scale. More recently he has published a revised and improved *Adult Intelligence Scale.*

The *WAIS* consists of eleven sub-tests divided into a Verbal Scale and a Performance Scale. The Verbal Scale includes tests called *Information, Comprehension, Arithmetic, Similarities, Digit Span* and *Vocabulary.* The Performance Scale includes tests called *Digit Symbol, Picture Completion, Block Design, Picture Arrangement* and *Object Assembly.* Each test is administered and scored separately; the scores of the Verbal Scale are combined to yield a Verbal I.Q.; the tests of the Performance Scale, to yield a Performance I.Q. All eleven tests combined yield a Full-Scale I.Q. Scores on each sub-test are expressed in standard score units with a mean of 10 and a standard deviation of 3. The I.Q.'s are expressed as deviation I.Q.'s with a mean of 10 and a standard deviation of 15. Five of the sub-tests are scored in terms of both speed and accuracy; the other six are scored on the basis of the number right.

The *WISC* is very similar to the *WAIS* in its composition. It consists of twelve sub-tests also grouped into Verbal and Performance Scales. Most of the sub-tests are of the same type as those in the *WAIS*, but they are easier. Procedures for scoring and calculating I.Q.'s on the two scales are almost identical.

Most recently, Wechsler has produced another scale for use with children from age 4–6½ years. This scale, abbreviated *WPPSI,* is primarily a downward extension of the *WISC*. It consists of eleven tests, eight of which are downward adaptations of tests in the *WISC;* three are new. Five tests constitute the Verbal scale and five, the Performance scale. One verbal test is an alternate. Procedures for administering and scoring are essentially the same as in other *Wechsler* scales.

These scales, together with the *Stanford-Binet,* are by far the most widely used individual intelligence tests and are regarded as standard in nearly all work where individual tests are used.

Typical Group Tests of Intelligence

There are many group intelligence tests available for use at all levels of human development from kindergarten to adult. Since it would be impossible to make a complete and up-to-date listing of such tests, to say nothing of describing them in detail, only a small number of illustrative ones will be discussed at length, as was done previously with achievement tests. Reference to catalogues of test publishers and to the various editions of *The Mental Measurements Yearbooks* will identify many other intelligence tests for those who are interested.

The first group test to be described is one which illustrates many excellent features of construction and standardisation. It has come increasingly into general use since its publication.

Lorge-Thorndike Intelligence Tests

1. *Name of tests and authors* : *Lorge-Thorndike Intelligence Tests*. Separate Level Edition, 1970. Irving Lorge, Robert L. Thorndike, and Elizabeth Hagen.

2. *Nature and purposes* : A series of tests of abstract intelligence defined as the ability to work with ideas and the relationships among ideas. The Primary Battery, Levels 1 and 2, is entirely non-verbal. Above these levels, both a Verbal and a Non-verbal Battery are provided.

3. *Grade levels* : Level 1, K-1; Level 2, 2-3; Level 3, 4–6; Level 4, 7–9; Level 5, 10–12.

4. *Number of forms* : Forms A and B.

5. *Publisher and date of publication* : Houghton Mifflin Company, 1954.

6. *Cost* : Levels 1 or 2, $ 3.90 per 35; Levels 3, 4, or 5, Verbal or Non-verbal, Consumable Edition, $ 3.45 per 35, Reusable Edition, $ 3.60 per 35. Answer sheets, scoring stencils, technical manuals, etc., extra.

7. *Content* : Sub-tests of the Primary Battery include *Oral Vocabulary, Pictorial Classification* (the one that doesn't belong) and *Pairing* (the two that go together). The items consist of pictures of familiar common objects or of simple geometrical figures.

The first three drawings are alike in that each has four sides and no lines inside it. The drawing at the right that goes with them is at D. It has four sides and no lines inside it. Make a heavy black pencil mark in the D answer space for question 0.

Now look at question 00. Find the drawing at the right that goes with the first three.

The Verbal Battery includes sub-tests of *Word Knowledge, Sentence Completion, Verbal Classification, Verbal Analogies* and *Arithmetic Reasoning.* The Non-verbal Battery includes sub-tests called *Figure Analogies, Figure Classification* and *Number Series.* No reading is involved.

IV A-H

One word has been left out of each sentence on this page. Choose the word that will make the best, the truest, and the most sensible complete sentence. Look at sample sentence 0.

0. Hot weather comes in the

(A) fall (B) night (C) summer (D) winter (E) snow

A B C D E

The best answer is summer. The letter before summer is C, so you should make a heavy black pencil mark in the C answer space for sentence 0.

Items for all the tests were chosen from a pool of 1,200 on the basis of tryout and statistical analysis of difficulty and item-test correlation.

8. *Time required* : The Primary Battery, Levels 1 and 2, has no time limits. Working time of 20 minutes and total time of 30 minutes is considered adequate. It is recommended, especially for Level 1, that the test at these levels be administered in two sessions.

For the Verbal Battery, Levels 3, 4 and 5, the working time is 34 minutes with total time not over 45 minutes.

For the Non-verbal Battery, Levels 3, 4 and 5, working time is 27 minutes, total time not over 40 minutes.

Time limits are based on preliminary tryouts and are considered ample for most pupils.

9. *Direction for, and Case of administering* : Directions are clear and complete. However, considering the amount to be read by the examiner, the sample items to be answered, and time required for distributing materials, answering questions, and for taking care of possible exigencies, together with the inexperience in test administration of the average examiner, it seems doubtful that the total times suggested will be adequate. The user should probably be prepared to allow from 5 to 15 minutes more than is suggested.

10. *Validity* : It is implied that the tests have content validity in that the items generally deal with familiar matters, and success in answering correctly depends primarily on the ability to deal with the relationships among the components.

Construct validity is believed by the authors to result from the facts that the tests deal with abstract and general concepts, require use and interpretation of symbols and relationships among them, require flexibility in organising concepts and symbols, and test power rather than speed.

Correlations with the *California Test of Mental Maturity*, the *Kuhlmann-Anderson*, and the *Otis* tests of mental ability given not more than three years earlier average respectively, .74, .66 and .73. Correlations with the *Pintner-Cunningham*, the *Stanford-Binet*, and the *WISC* range from .44 to .77, with a median of .54. Correlation with the *Stanford Achievement Test, Reading* was .87 and with *Arithmetic*, .76. In one study, the correlation between the *Lorge-Thorndike*, Level 4, given at the beginning of the year in the ninth grade, and average achievement at the end of the year was .672.

A factor analysis of the sub-tests of the *Lorge-Thorndike* showed a distinct communality for both verbal and non-verbal batteries in one general factor. All other factors together account for less than 15 per cent of the variance.

Taken altogether, the data on the validity of these tests is impressive.

11. *Reliability* : Alternate forms reliability coefficients for the different levels are as follows: Level 1, .810; Level 2, .761; Levels 3, 4 and 5, Non-verbal, average about .80; Levels 3, 4 and 5. Verbal, average about .87. Odd-even reliabilities are, with one exception, above .90. The standard error of measurement for the Primary Battery is approximately 7 points of I.Q.; for the Non-verbal Battery, about 6.5 I.Q. points; for the Verbal Battery, about 4.7 I.Q. points. They range at different score levels and in the three batteries, from 3.0 to 8.3. As would be expected, the lower the score and the lower the level, the larger the standard error.

Correlations between Verbal and Non-verbal batteries average about .65.

12. *Manual* : *Examiners' Manuals* contain instructions for administering and scoring, information on standardisation of the tests, a summary of the nature of the tests, and tables of I.Q. norms, grade percentiles, and grade and age equivalents.

A *Technical Manual* describes in detail how the tests were planned, constructed, and standardised.

Both manuals are clear and complete. They represent a high standard of excellence.

13. *Scoring* : All levels come in consumable editions which are hand scored by the use of strip or punched-out keys depending on level. Directions are printed on the keys. Levels 3, 4 and 5 are available also in a reusable edition with separate answer sheets. Answer sheets for reusable editions may be hand scored or scored by machine. Both Verbal and Non-verbal batteries yield deviation I.Q.'s with a mean of 100 and a standard deviation of 16.

14. *Norms* : More than 136,000 children in forty-four communities in twenty-two states were tested in establishing norms. Communities were selected on the basis of the per cent of adult illiteracy, the proportion of professional workers, home ownership, and home rental value. All pupils in the schools of each community, K-12, were tested.

Besides deviation I.Q.'s for both Verbal and Non-verbal batteries, norms are available in the form of grade percentiles, grade equivalents and age equivalents. Grade percentiles show the relative position of a pupil in abstract reasoning ability as compared with typical pupils in the same grade tested early in the school year. Grade equivalents are most useful for judging whether or not a pupil's measured achievement, e.g., on an achievement battery, corresponds to his mental ability. Age equivalents are the average raw scores made by pupils of given chronological ages near the beginning of the school year.

15. *Format* : In makeup, quality of materials, and printing these tests measure up to highest standards. The art work in the Non-verbal items and the arrangement on the page are excellent.

A new edition of the *Lorge-Thorndike* tests, called the *Multi-Level Edition,* was published in 1964. In the *Separate Level*

Edition, tests are provided in three levels for Grades 4–6, 7–9 and 10–12 respectively. In the *Multi-Level Edition* there are eight overlapping scales based on a graded series of items for use in Grades 3 through 13. For Grades K through 4 a *Cognitive Abilities Test* replaces the *Primary Battery* of the *Separate Level Edition.* In the description which follows, only significant changes are described.

1. ***Name of tests and authors* :** *Lorge-Thorndike Intelligence Tests, Multi-Level Edition* and *Cognitive Abilities Test.* Same authors.

2. ***Nature and purposes* :** Same.

3. ***Grade levels* :** Primary I, K-2; Primary II, Grades 2–4; Levels A-H, Grades 3–13.

4. ***Number of forms* :** 1 and 2.

5. ***Publisher and date of publication* :** Same, 1964, 1968.

6. ***Cost* :** *Cognitive Abilities Test.* Machine-scorable booklets, $ 9.00 per 35. Hand-scorable booklets, $ 5.25 per 35. Reusable test booklets, Grades 3-13, $.78 per copy. For Grade 3 (Level A) machine-scorable booklets, $15.00 per 35. Scoring stencils, answer sheets, technical manual, extra. Separate test booklets requiring answer sheets for Grade 13 (Level H), $ 6.00 per 35.

7. ***Content* :** As in *Separate Level Edition,* except that a sub-test on *Quantitative Concepts* has been included in the *Cognitive Abilities Test.* Item types otherwise are the same in both editions and about two-thirds of the items are identical. New items were added to replace weak ones or "to fill in gaps to provide more precisely graded scales".

Approximately 80 per cent of the items at each level overlap with those in the immediately preceding or the immediately following levels.

8. ***Time required* :** Primary I and Primary II of *Cognitive Abilities*–no time limits. Grades 3–13: Verbal Battery—35 minutes working time. Non-verbal Battery—27 minutes working time. Distributing materials, filling out answer sheets, giving directions, and attempting practice items will probably require about 15 minutes more for each battery.

9. ***Directions for and ease of administering* :** Directions are clear and complete with practice exercises for every sub-test.

The administration of the *Multi-Level Battery* may be complicated somewhat by the fact that pupils at each level begin and stop at different points in each sub-test. The examiner must see to it that pupils understand where they are to start and where to stop.

10. *Validity* : Most of the data on validity of the *Multi-Level Edition* are based on research with the original *Separate-Level Edition.* The authors justify this on the ground that types of items are the same in the two editions and because reliability coefficients of the *Multi-Level Edition* are as high as those of the older forms. For results of these studies see material under validity in the preceding description.

Correlations between the Verbal Battery of the *Multi-Level Edition* and composite scores on the *Iowa Tests of Basic Skills* range from .79 to .88 with a median value of about .85. For the Non-verbal Battery the coefficients range from .65 to .77. These correlations are based on results of joint administration of the two batteries. In the norming programme, *Tests of Academic Progress* were administered in Grades 9–12 concurrently with *Lorge-Thorndike.* Correlations for the Verbal Battery average about .77 with sub-tests and .88 with total score on the TAP. The corresponding Non-verbal figures are about .62 and .71.

Correlations between the *Multi-Level Verbal* and *College Board* and *American College Testing Programme* scores range from .63 to .85; between such scores and *Multi-Level Non-verbal,* they vary from .27 to .79. These are based on small numbers in Grade 12. Correlations between *Lorge-Thorndike Multi-Level* scores and scores on the sub-tests of the *Differential Aptitude Tests* are of approximately the same order.

11. *Reliability* : Alternate forms reliability coefficients for the Verbal Battery range from .851 at Grade 9 to .939 at Grade 5; for the Non-verbal Battery they vary from .845 at Grade 3 to .923 at Grade 12. These results are based on testing with the two forms at an interval of less than a week in one school system. Odd-even reliabilities for Form 1 average about .93 for the Verbal Battery and about .92 for the Non-verbal. For the *Cognitive Abilities Test, Kuder-Richardson* reliabilities average just under .90.

Standard errors of measurement are approximately 3.6 deviation I.Q. points for the Verbal Battery and about 4.5 for the Non-verbal.

12. *Manual* : *Examiners' manuals* contain instructions for administering and scoring, information on standardization of the tests, a summary of the nature of the tests, and tables of I.Q. norms, grade percentiles, and grade and age equivalents.

A Technical Manual describes in detail how the tests were planned, constructed and standardized.

Both manuals are clear and complete. They represent a high standard of excellence.

13. *Scoring* : *Cognitive Abilities Test* comes in both machine-scorable and hand-scorable booklets. The *Multi-Level Edition* comes in one booklet for each form, all levels, and requires the use of separate answer sheets. Level A (Grade 3) also comes in separate, machine-scorable booklets and Level H (Grade 13, college edition) in separate booklets requiring use of separate answer sheets.

14. *Norms* : Approximately 180,000 pupils in Grades 3–12 were tested in the fall of 1963 with the *Multi-Level Edition.* This population constituted a stratified sample chosen on the basis of size and location of community, and educational and socio-economic status of families so as to represent as closely as possible the national population. The sample included both public and parochial schools in seventy-two communities in forth states.

The *Cognitive Abilities Test* was normed by testing approximately 22,000 children in 1968 in Grades K-4 in 45 of these same communities. Pupils in Grades 3 and 4 took both the *CAT Primary II* and Level A of the *Multi-Level* in order to form a bridge between the two tests.

Norms for the *Multi-Level Edition* are provided in the forms of deviation I.Q.'s, percentile ranks, grade equivalents, and age equivalents for Form 1 with tables of raw score equivalents for Form 2. Separate norms are provided for both Verbal and Non-verbal Batteries. Norms for the *CAT* are presented as deviation I.Q.'s, percentile ranks, stanines and grade percentiles.

The next group test to be described represents a quite different approach from that used in the *Lorge-Thordike.* Although designed basically for the same purpose, it uses fewer types of items. In its development, standardisation, and subsequent evaluation it exemplifies the highest standards in care and thoroughness of procedures.

Cooperative School and College Ability Tests

1. *Name of tests and authors* : *Cooperative School and College Ability Tests, Series II.* Staff members of the Educational Testing Service with the advice and cooperation of many professional educators.

2. *Nature and purposes* : A measure of academic aptitude specifically designed to predict success in school or college. The *Series II* tests constitute a revision of the original *SCAT* series published in 1955-56. Efforts to equate scores on the two series were not entirely successful. For those who wish them, tests of the original series are still available.

3. *Grade level* : Grades 4 through 14; Level 1, 13-14; Level 2, 10–12; Level 3, 8–10; Level 4, 6–8; Level 5, 4–6; Level U, 15-16; (Restricted).

4. *Number of forms* : A and B; Level U, Form A only.

5. *Publisher and date of publication* : Educational Testing Service, 1966-67.

6. *Cost* : $ 7.00 per 20. Answer sheets $ 4.00 per 100. Scoring stencils, other accessories, etc.

7. *Content* : The content of all levels is of the same nature. There are two types of items.

(a) *Verbal Ability* consists of fifty verbal analogy items.

1. Tinkle: bells::

   A. whistle: tunes

   B. glide: snakes

   C. rustle: leaves

   D. wrinkle: fabrics

Answer

1. A B C D

(b) *Mathematical Ability* consists of fifty quantitative comparisons.

A. if the part in Column A is greater

B. if the part in Column B is greater

C. if the two parts are equal

D. if not enough information is given for you to decide.

Column A	Column B
Value of 1 nickel	Value of 1 dime

The items at the various levels differ only in difficulty. The tests yield three scores—Verbal, Quantitative and Total.

8. *Time required* : Twenty minutes working time for each part. Forty-five to 50 minutes altogether, including time for distribution materials, reading directions, etc.

9. *Directions for and ease of administering* : Directions are clear and complete. The tests are very simple to administer.

10. *Validity* : Evidence for validity is statistical in nature. Average correlations between *SCAT Series II* scores and teachers' grades in English and Mathematics and grade point average were determined in Grades 5, 8, 11 and 12 in some 150 schools. In Grade 5 these range from .54 to .69; in Grade 8 they range from .52 to .61; in Grade 11, from .50 to .65; and in Grade 12, from .41 to .59 with most in the .40's. Correlations of scores on *SCAT Series II,* Forms 1A and 1B (formerly the *Cooperative Academic Ability Test)* with rank in graduating class were .52 for Verbal, .51 for Mathematical, and .56 for Total scores, respectively. Correlations between scores on the same forms of *SCAT* and on the *Scholastic Aptitude Test of the College Entrance Examination Board* were found to be .83 and .86 for Verbal and Mathematics sections, respectively.

11. *Reliability* : All reliability data are based upon *Kuder-Richardson Formula 20* and are therefore measures of internal consistency. Reliability coefficients are based on Form A only. For Verbal scores they range between .87 and .91; for Mathematical scores they lie between .90 and .92; for Total scores the coefficients are .94 for each of the four levels. Standard errors of measurement for Verbal and for Mathematical scores are typically in the range of 2.75–3.00 points of raw score. For total scores they average slightly more than 4 raw score points.

12. *Manual* : There is a comprehensive manual called the *Handbook* which contains a description of the test, directions for administering and scoring it, and for interpreting scores. It also contains tables of norms, a brief discussion of the development of the test, and details of norming it. In addition, the *Handbook* contains an abundance of technical data on equating the forms, scaling, validity, reliability, and other matters. There is also a manual for interpreting scores containing norms tables and interpretive information. In addition, there are a separate, single sheet of directions for administering and a unique "student bulletin". The latter, a single page, tells prospective takers of the test what its purpose is and gives examples with answers of Verbal and Mathematical items similar to those in the test. This is obviously intended to allay anxiety and reduce tension.

13. *Scoring* : All forms and levels require the use of separate answer sheets. These may be IBM 805, IBM 1230, Digitek, or SCRIBE (the ETS special scoring service). IBM and Digitek answer sheets may be scored by hand or machine. SCRIBE can be scored only by ETS. Since only one side of an answer sheet is used for any level or form, scoring is rapid and easy. Three scores—Verbal, Quantitative and Total—are obtained for each student. Raw scores are changed to "converted scores", a type of standard score. These in turn are converted to percentile ranks. Comparisons of a student's score with that of other students at the same level or adjacent levels may be made by use of the converted score scale. Percentile ranks are interpreted in terms of percentile bands which represent confidence levels having a range of two standard errors, one on either side of a student's obtained score.

14. *Norms* : The normative population for these tests was chosen with great care. *SCAT Series II* was administered in October, 1966 to groups of approximately thirty students in a minimum of 100 schools in each grade from 4 through 12. These schools were chosen by a rather involved process to yield a sample that would be representative of the total school population of the country in these grades. However, no school system, public or private, enrolling fewer than 300 pupils was included. A total of 950 schools, representing every state, participated in the testing.

Three types of norms are provided for Verbal, Mathematical, and Total scores by grades, 4 through 12. These are converted score, percentile band and percentile rank.

15. *Format* : In quality of materials, printing, and attractiveness of format, the *SCAT* series is of the highest order. The use of colour on the covers of all booklets adds to their appeal.

The third intelligence test to be described is an example of an attempt to construct a test that is "culture fair" as described earlier in this chapter. The procedure discussed of trying out items and eliminating those that showed consistent differences in response (in this case, less successful choices by children with lower socioeconomic and cultural backgrounds) was used in producing the final forms. Although acceptance and use of the test in schools was insufficient to keep it on the market, it is described here as a prototype of the "culture fair" test and an interesting example of its kind.

Davis-Eells Test of General Intelligence or Problem Solving Ability

1. *Name of tests and authors* : *Davis-Eells Test of General Intelligence or Problem Solving Ability.* Allison Davis and Kenneth Eells.

2. *Nature and purposes* : To construct a test of intelligence, free of reading demands, based on common experiences shared by all urban American children. The test is said to consist of realistic problems in the experience of all children and is entirely pictorial except for directions read aloud by the administrator of the test.

3. *Grade level* : Primary, Grades 1 and 2; Elementary, Grades 3 through 6.

4. *Number of forms* : One form.

5. *Publisher and date of publication* : Harcourt Brace Jovanovich, Inc., 1953.

6. *Cost* : Primary, $ 4.00 per 35; Elementary, $ 4.45 per 35. (Now out of print).

7. *Content* : One part is called "Best Ways" problems. In each problem, three picture are presented. Each picture shows a person or group of persons starting to solve a problem in a different way. The task is to find the picture that shows the best ways of solving the problem.

Example:

Another type of problem is called "Analogies." This consist of pictorial situations like the example shown below:

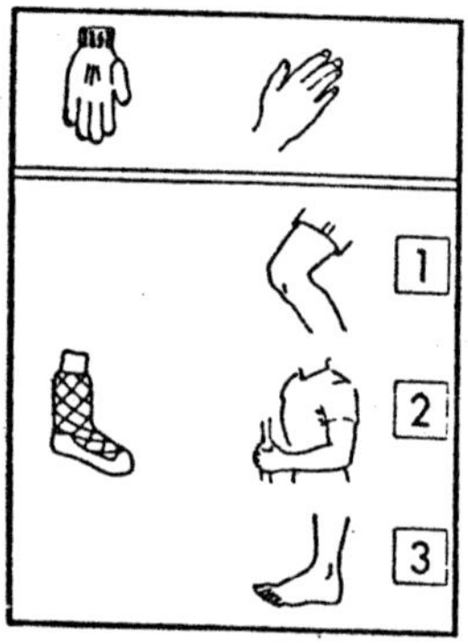

In each case the relationship between the first pair is made clear or suggested by the examiner before the child finds the answer.

A third type of problem is one called "Probabilities." In each case a picture shows a situation which is followed by three possible explanations. The task is to select the most likely explanation.

No. 1: The man *fell down* and hit his head.

No. 2: A ball *came through the window* and hit the man's head.

No. 3: The picture *does not show how* the man got the bump on his head. Nobody can tell because the picture doesn't show how the man got the bump.

Which number was true?

These three types of problems are found both in the *Primary* and the *Elementary* tests. In addition, the *Elementary* test contains some problems called "Money Problems." In these the pupil is required to indicate how a given amount of change could be made from certain available coins. For example, in the problem below the task is to select from the three pictures the one in which the coins on the right could be obtained from the group of coins on the left.

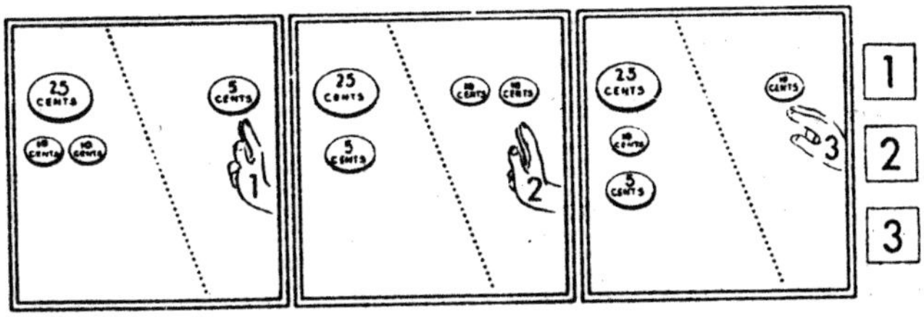

8. *Time required* : *Primary,* Grade 1: two 30-minute periods. Grade 2: three 30-minute periods. *Elementary:* two 60-minute periods.

9. *Directions for and ease of administering* : Directions for administering are very detailed and complete. Administration is comparatively complicated and time-consuming. Most of the time required to give the tests is consumed in reading directions and explanations.

10. *Validity* : The content of the tests is said to be independent of reading skill, in-school instruction, or speed of response. The test purports to be a measure of "over-all capacity to solve mental problems", and not a scholastic aptitude test. These problems are chosen as being of a kind which are encountered by most children. Correlations of the *Davis-Eells Test* with *Otis Quick-Scoring Mental Ability Tests* range from .39 to .66, with a median of .52. Correlations with scores on standardised achievement tests in reading, arithmetic, language and spelling are in the neighbourhood of .40.

11. *Reliability* : Split-half reliability coefficients corrected by use of the Spearman-Brown Formula average about .83 in Grades 2 through 6; for Grade 1 this coefficient is .68. The standard error of measurement of a score ranges from 2.5 to 3.5. Test-retest coefficients with an interval of two weeks were approximately .70 in Grade 2 and .90 in Grade 4.

12. *Manual* : The tests are accompanied by *Directions for Administering,* which include directions for scoring, tables for converting raw score to an *Index of Problem Solving Ability (IPSA),* and percentile equivalents. Information concerning development of the test, validity, reliability, and other statistical data is available in a separate manual.

13. *Scoring* : Scoring is quite simple. All items are of the three-response type, the pupil marking the number of the choice that seems best to him. Since there are only forty-seven items in the *Primary* form and sixty-two in the *Elementary,* and since these are widely spaced and in large print, it is easy to score the test. No separate answer sheets are provided, though they could be used, at least at the upper grade levels. The score is the number right. Printed scoring keys are provided. The raw score is converted to an *IPSA (Index of Problem Solving Ability)* by use of the tables previously referred to. Ages are used to the nearest half-year, which gives an approximate value for the *IPSA.* The *IPSA* is based on a normalised distribution with a mean of 100 and a standard deviation of 16. The authors state that this *Index of Problem Solving Ability* may also be called an I.Q.

14. *Norms* : Means, medians and standard deviations of raw scores are given for age groups by three-month intervals from 6–0 to 8–5 in Grade 1; from 7–0 to 9–5 in Grade 2; from 8–0 to 13–11 in Grades 3 to 6.

15. *Format* : The tests are well arranged and well printed. Figures are large and spacing is generous.

The *Davis-Eells Test* has been the subject of a substantial number of research studies correlating scores on it with scores on conventional intelligence tests and standardised achievement tests and with teachers' marks. Some studies have also compared correlations between scores of the *Davis-Eells* and various indices of socio-economic status with correlations between conventional intelligence tests and such indices. In general, it may be said that the results of research on the test have failed to justify or recommend its use in place of more conventional group tests of intelligence.

OTHER INTELLIGENCE TESTS

Individual

1. *Arthur Point Scale of Performance Tests.* 1947, Ages five to fifteen. *Knox Cube Test, Seguin Form Board (Arthur*

Revision), Arthur Slencil Design Test, Porleus Maze Test (Arthur Printing), *Healy Picture Completion Test II*. Revised Form II. Complete set, with manual and 100 score sheets, $ 79.00. 60–90 minutes. Psychological Corporation.

2. *Columbia Mental Maturity Scale.* Revised, 1959. Ages three to ten. One hundred cards each containing a series of drawings from which the examinee selects the one that does not belong. One form, $ 45.00 per set including manual. Record blanks, $ 2.20 per 35. 15–20 minutes. Harcourt Brace Jovanovich, Inc.

3. *Leiter International Performance Scale.* 1948–52. Ages two to eighteen. Fifty-four tests involving *matching of colours and of objects, picture completion, spatial relations, footprint recognition*, etc. One form, revised. $ 270.00, per set of test materials, 100 record blanks, carrying case and manual. 30-60 minutes. Stoelting Company.

4. *Minnesota Preschool Scale.* 1940. Ages one and a half to six, inclusive. Twenty-six tests: Verbal includes *pointing to and naming objects; comprehension, naming colours*, etc. Non-verbal includes *copying figures, Knox Cube Test, paper-folding*, etc. Forms A. $ 40.00 per set. 10–30 minutes. American Guidance Service.

5. *Revised Stanford-Binet Intelligence Scale.* 1960. Age two to superior adult. For description see text. One form. $ 39.00 per set. Record Booklets, $ 4.50 per 35. Manual, $ 4.80. Printed card material separately, $ 3.00. 1½ hours. Houghton Mifflin Company.

Group

1. *Academic Promise Tests.* 1959–62. Grades 6–9. *Verbal, numerical, abstract reasoning, language usage.* Forms A and B. $ 4.50 per 25. Accessories at additional cost. 90 minutes. Psychological Corporation.

2. *Army General Classification Test.* 1948. Grades 9–12 and adults. *Vocabulary, arithmetic, and block counting (spatial).* One form. $12.60 per 20 with manual. Answer pads, $ 3.15 per 20. Answer sheets for machine scoring, $ 6.30 per 100. 40 minutes. Science Research Associates, Inc.

3. *Boehm Test of Basic Concepts.* K-2. 1968. Fifty concepts basic to understanding oral communications. One form. $ 5.90 per 30. 30 minutes. Psychological Corporation.
4. *California Test of Mental Maturity.* Revised, 1963. K-adult. Short form—*opposites, similarities, analogies, numerical values, number problems, verbal comprehension, memory (delayed recall).* Long form—*rights and lefts, manipulation of areas, number series, inferences and immediate recall* added. One form. Short form, $ 5.25–5.50 per 35. Long form, $ 6.65–8.00 per 35. Accessories at additional cost. Short form, about 50 minutes. Long form, about 1-1½ hours. California Test Bureau.
5. *College Qualification Tests.* 1955–61. Grades 11–13. *Verbal, numerical, information, total.* Form A; Forms B and C, restricted to colleges and universities. $ 5.50 per 25. Accessories at additional cost. 80 minutes. Psychological Corporation.
6. *Henmon-Nelson Tests of Mental Ability,* Revised Edition. 1957-58. Grades 3–6; 6-9; 9–12; College. *Synonyms, analogies, number sequence, arithmetic,* etc. Forms A and B. $ 4.20 per 35. Accessories at additional cost. 30 minutes. Houghton Mifflin Company.
7. *Kuhlmann-Anderson Measure of Academic Potential.* 7th ed. 1963. Tests for K, Grades 1, 2, 3-4, 4-5, 5–7, 7–9 and 9–12. *Verbal and quantitative.* One form. K-4, $ 4.65 per 25; 4–12, $ 4.90 per 25. Accessories at additional cost. 50–60 minutes. Personnel Press.
8. *Kuhlmann-Finch Scholastic Aptitude Tests.* 1956-57. Grades 1, 2, 3, 4, 5, 6, 7–9, 10–12. *Verbal and non-verbal materials.* One form. $ 2.95 per 25. Accessories at additional cost. 45 minutes. American Guidance Service.
9. *Ohio State University Psychological Test.* 1958. Grades 9–13. *Vocabulary, word relationships, reading comprehension.* Forms 21 and 23. $12.60 per 20. Two hours. Science Research Associates, Inc.
10. *Otis-Lennon Mental Ability Test.* Grades K-12. 1967. *Pictorial items, verbal material.* Primary I, K; Primary II, Grade 1; Elementary I, Grades 1–3; Elementary II, Grades 4–6; Intermediate, Grades 7–9; Advanced, Grades 10–12. Forms J

and K. $ 6.00–6.30 per 35. 30–40 minutes. Harcourt Brace Jovanovich, Inc.

11. *Otis Quick-Scoring Mental Ability Tests.* Revised, 1954. *Alpha*, Grades 1–4; *Beta*, Grades 4–9; *Gamma*, High School and College. *Alpha* consists of *pictorial items, Beta* and *Gamma* of *verbal material.* Forms A, B of *Alpha*; EM and FM of *Beta;* EM and FM of *Gamma. Alpha*, $ 5.30 per 35; *Beta* and *Gamma*, $ 4.70 per 35. *Alpha*, 40 minutes; *Beta*, *Gamma*, 30 minutes. Accessories at additional cost. Harcourt Brace Jovanovich, Inc.
12. *Primary Mental Abilities Test.* Revised 1963. Grades K-1, 2–4, 4–6, 6–9, 9–12. *Verbal meaning, spatial ability, perception, number facility, reasoning.* One form. First two levels, $ 4.00 per 20. Three upper levels, $11.00 per 20. 55–60 minutes. Science Research Associates, Inc.
13. *S.R.A. Tests of Educational Ability.* 1957-58. Grades 4–6, 6–9, 9–12. *Language, reasoning, quantitative.* One form. $7.80 per 20. 26–42 minutes. Science Research Associates, Inc.
14. *Terman-McNemar Test of Mental Ability.* 1941. Grades 7–13. *Information, synonyms, logical selection, classification, analogies, opposites, best answer.* Forms C and D. $ 4.40 per 35. 40 minutes. Harcourt Brace Jovanovich, Inc.

5

The Measurement of Capacity : Special Aptitudes

In the preceding chapter we considered tests of general intelligence, which have shown their greatest usefulness as predictors of success in school and college, particularly in academic courses. There is another type of test, also used primarily for prediction, referred to as *aptitude tests*. These differ from general intelligence tests in that their usual purpose is to predict success in a more restricted field or area such as mechanical, clerical or artistic pursuits. Aptitude tests differ from achievement tests also in that they are designed to measure potential or promise. They do not presuppose training in a particular field but purport to measure an individual's capacity to profit by instruction in that field.

Specific aptitude tests are often designed to measure specific skills or knowledge essential to successful performance. Thus, a mechanical aptitude test may include such tasks as assembling a dismantled object like an electric bell, and a test of clerical aptitude may measure skill in locating numbers or alphabetising. Tasks or skills of this nature are often referred to as "work samples". Such skills may be based on job analyses which identify the specifics of successful performance in a given occupation or field. If a test is to screen applicants for a certain type of work, let us say that of an electrician, a detailed analysis of the job of an electrician may be made. On the basis of this analysis are determined the specific skills required of a successful electrician. Then a test is constructed to measure one or more of these abilities objectively and accurately. Job analysis is one widely used approach to the planning and developing of aptitude tests in special fields.

Another method used in constructing aptitude tests is based upon a theoretical, possibly more or less "armchair", attack. In this case an attempt is made to spell out basic qualities or abilities which are considered to underlie all successful, effective performance in a particular field. This approach is illustrated by aptitude tests in such fields as art or music. As we shall see when we examine prototypes of these tests, they purport to measure abilities of a fundamental nature, as for example in tests of art aptitude, they attempt to measure a feeling for line, colour, balance, and the like in a work of art or in producing the basis for a drawing, painting or sculpture. Similarly, in tests of musical aptitude we commonly find measures of pitch discrimination, tonality, rhythm, etc. As mentioned earlier, such tests do not presuppose previous training in the field, though it is generally agreed that scores on them are influenced by training.

One other approach is to test knowledge in a particular field. This is based upon the assumption that interest in and aptitude for a particular type of work will cause the possessor of these qualities to read widely in the field of such work, to experiment and work with the "tools of the trade," and thus to accumulate a fund of information which can readily be tested. The amount, depth, and accuracy of knowledge possessed is believed to reflect interest and aptitude. Many illustrations can be cited. The girl who likes to cook or sew, the boy who enjoys tinkering with an old "jalopy", or an old radio, will naturally accumulate information about these matters which indirectly reveals an interest and possibly an aptitude for cooking, sewing, auto mechanics, or radio, as the case may be. This point of view suggests the use of tests of knowledge in a particular field as elements of aptitude tests. And we often do find tests of knowledge included in aptitude tests as we shall see shortly.

Finally, there are the aptitude test batteries or multi-aptitude tests, a number of which are now available. These tests are designed in some instances primarily to predict success in specific school subjects; others are for the purpose of predicting success in a number of different occupations. An example of the former type will be described in detail later in this chapter. The *General*

Aptitude Test Battery of the United States Employment Service is widely used to assist in fitting applicants for employment into type of training or work that they seem to have some aptitude for. This is, of course, a very large and difficult task, since there are so many different occupations to be considered.

The aptitude test batteries are based for the most part on factor analysis, the purpose being to construct a battery of a manageable number of sub-tests which will, in various combinations, be optimally predictive of success in many different occupations. This constitutes a continuing and never-ending task as new occupations are studied and as additional data accumulate from the use of the tests in the battery.

All the approaches to testing aptitude that have been briefly discussed will be found illustrated in one or another of the tests to be described. There are many aptitude tests in many different fields, but we shall confine our descriptions to a few areas in which the most work has been done and which, in general, are of greatest interest and value to teachers and counsellors.

Mechanical Aptitude

One of the first specialised fields for which aptitude tests were developed is that of mechanical abilities. The reasons are not hard to find. There are many occupations requiring mechanical ability, and they engage large numbers of persons. Men and boys especially seem to have inclinations toward working with machines, mechanical toys, electrical equipment, and tools, although it has been found that women are more adept at operations involving small, delicate work such as assembly of intricate parts of machinery. It is not surprising, therefore, to find some of the earliest work in the measurement of special aptitudes in this area. Some of the first tests developed, like the *Stenquist Mechanical Aptitude Test,* published in 1921, and the *MacQuarrie Test for Mechanical Ability,* published in 1925, are no longer available. However, work in this field has continued, although no new tests have appeared recently.

Many of the older tests of mechanical aptitude included tasks of disassembling and assembling small pieces of equipment, such as an electric bell, as well as paper-and-pencil problems. The mechanical operations had the disadvantage of requiring individual testing. More recent tests have tended to concentrate largely on paper-and-pencil devices. The one to be described here, the *Minnesota Paper Form Board,* is a paper-and-pencil test measuring spatial perception as indicated by the ability to visualise assembly of two-dimensional shapes into a whole design. For example :

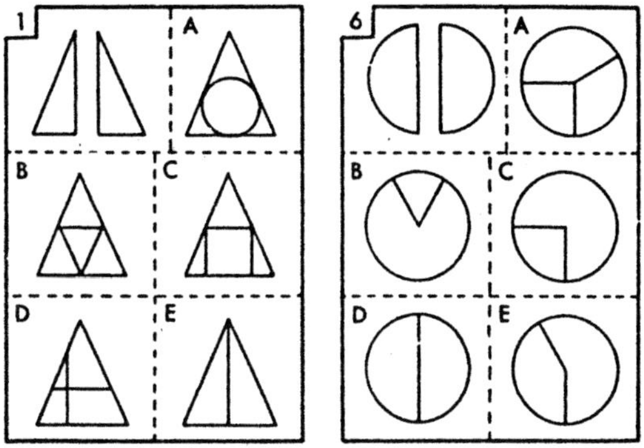

This test is part of a battery of mechanical ability tests developed at the University of Minnesota in the late 1920's. There has probably been more study and research of the *Paper Form Board* than any test ever developed in this field. Consisting of sixty-four items of the type illustrated, it is simple to administer and takes only twenty minutes of actual working time. Reliability of a single form is reported to be .85 and of both forms together, .92.

The test has been validated by correlating scores on it with ratings of performance in shop courses, mechanical drawing, descriptive geometry and machine drafting. Scores of engineering students have been compared with those of non-engineers. The test has also been given to students in dentistry and to workers in other mechanical pursuits.

Although the correlations between scores on the *Minnesota Paper Form Board* and ratings, grades in courses, production records of workers, and scores of criterion groups are not uniformly high or discriminatory, the mass of evidence accumulated about the test is generally quite favourable. It appears to be one of the best tests of a paper-and-pencil type yet devised for predicting success in a wide variety of fields of work that require more or less mechanical ability. It is, of course,, particularly useful for counsellors and guidance workers in helping boys and young men to achieve a better appraisal of their fitness for certain occupations.

Other Tests of Mechanical Aptitude

1. *Bennett Hand-Tool Dexterity Test.* Adolescents and adults. *Proficiency in use of wrenches and screwdrivers.* One form. $ 44.00 per set. 4–12 minutes. Psychological Corporation.
2. *Bennett Mechanical Comprehension Test.* 1965. Older adolescents and adults. *Mechanical relationships and physical laws in practical situations.* Forms S and T. $ 6.50 per 25. Spanish forms—$ 7.20 per 25. Answer sheets and tape recorded instructions at additional cost. 30 minutes. Psychological Corporation.
3. *Crawford Small Parts Dexterity Test.* 1946–56. Adolescents and adults. *Dexterity in use of tweezers and screwdrivers.* One form. $ 49.00 per set. 9–25 minutes. Psychological Corporation.
4. *Detroit Mechanical Aptitudes Examination.* 1939. Grades 7–12. *Tool recognition, motor speed, size discrimination, arithmetic fundamentals, disarranged pictures, tool information, direction and speed of pulley and belt movements*, and *digit-letter substitution.* One form. $ 4.95 per 35. 30 minutes. The Bobbs-Merrill Company, Inc.
5. *MacQuarrie Test for Mechanical Ability.* 1953. Grades 7-adult. *Tracing, tapping, dotting, copying, location, blocks* and *pursuit.* One form. $ 4.55 per 35. 20 minutes. California Test Bureau.
6. *Mellenbruch Mechanical Motivation Test.* 1956-57. Grades 6-adult. *Matching pairs of objects in picture.* Forms A and B. $1.95 per 20. 40 minutes. Psychometric Affiliates.
7. *Purdue Mechanical Performance Test.* 1957. Ages 17-adult. *Transfer boards, spatial relations, hub assemblies.* One form., $175 per set. 20 minutes. Lafayette Instrument Company.

8. *S.R.A. Mechanical Aptitudes.* 1947. High school and adults. *Tool identification, space visualisation* and *shop arithmetic.* One form. $17.50 per 20. Answer pads, $ 3.50 per 20. 40 minutes. Science Research Associates, Inc.
9. *Stromberg Dexterity Test.* Adolescents and adults. *Precision in placement of disks.* One form. $ 56.00 per set. 5-10 minutes. Psychological Corporation.
10. *Survey of Mechanical Insight.* 1955. Grade 9-adult. *Problems in the operation, maintenance, repair and designs of machinery.* One form. $ 4.20 per 35. 30 minutes. California Test Bureau.

Clerical Aptitude

The designation here refers to tests in the commercial and business field. There are aptitude tests for general office work, typewriting, bookkeeping and shorthand. Although extensive work has been done in the testing of these aptitudes, the tests so far developed have not been outstandingly successful as predictive measures, and they have not been widely used by teachers, employees or counsellors.

Detroit Clerical Aptitudes Examination

The *Detroit Clerical Aptitudes Examination* consists of eight parts. Part 1 is a test of rate and quality of handwriting, and involves the copying of a short selection. Part 2 consists of a comparison between two sets of numbers to determine whether they are the same or different, e.g., 2 7 3—2 7 5. Part 3 contains arithmetic problems. Part 4 is a test of manual dexterity and requires the student to perform such tasks as drawing crosses in circles as rapidly as possible without touching the circles. Part 5 tests miscellaneous knowledge related to office and business. Part 6 is a series of pictures, each presented in several sections or parts of the whole; the task is to indicate their proper order or sequence. Part 7 is a substitution test in which letters are numbered according to a key which is constantly changing. Part 8 is a test of alphabetisation.

Each part of the *Detroit Clerical Aptitudes Examination* is timed separately. The test is designed for use with pupils at the intermediate and junior high school grade levels to identify those who will probably succeed in commercial courses in high school.

The reliability, test-retest, is .85. The correlation between scores on the test and scholarship in bookkeeping is .563; between test scores and scholarship in shorthand, .366; between test scores and scholarship in typewriting, .317. The *Detroit Clerical Aptitudes Examination* is available in one form only at $ 4.15 for 35 copies. The handwriting scale used in Test 1 must be ordered separately at $.50 per copy.

Other Tests of Commercial and Business Aptitude

1. *Bennett Stenographic Aptitude Test.* 1939. High school and college. *Substitution of numbers for symbols and symbols for numbers* and *spelling*. One form. $ 2.70 per 25. 25 minutes. Psychological Corporation.
2. *E.R.C. Stenographic Aptitude Test.* 1944. Grades 9-10. *Word discrimination, phonetic spelling, vocabulary, sentence dictation,* and *speed of writing.* One form. $ 4.20 per 20.33 minutes. Science Research Associates, Inc.
3. *General Clerical Test.* 1950. High school and above. *Clerical speed and accuracy, numerical ability, verbal facility.* One form. $ 7.00 per 25. 43 minutes. Psychological Corporation.
4. *Minnesota Clerical Test.* 1933–46. Grades 8–12 and adults. *Speed and accuracy in checking numbers and names.* One form. $ 3.00 per 25. 15 minutes. Psychological Corporation.
5. *Personnel Research Institute Clerical Battery.* 1945–47. Adults. (*1*) *classification*, (*2*) *number comparison*, (*3*) *name comparison*, (*4*) *tabulation*, (*5*) *filing*, (*6*) *alphabetising*, (*7*) *arithmetic reasoning*, (*8*) *spelling*. Form A of 1–3; Forms A and B of 4–8. $ 2.00 per 25 copies of any test. Total time, including time for directions, 100 minutes. Personnel Research Institute.
6. *Purdue Clerical Adaptability Test.* 1949–56. Applicants for clerical positions. *Spelling, computation, checking, word meaning, copying, reasoning.* One form. $ 5.00 per 25. 60 minutes. Purdue University Bookstore.
7. *Short Employment Tests.* 1951. Adults. *Vocabulary, arithmetic computation, clerical skill.* Forms 1, 2, 3, 4 (1 is restricted). $ 3.00 per 25 for each test. 15 minutes. Psychological Corporation.

8. *Short Tests of Clerical Ability.* 1959-60. Applicants for office positions. *Coding, checking, filing, directions—oral and written, arithmetic, business vocabulary, language.* One form. $ 3.20 per 20. 35–70 minutes. Science Research Associates, Inc.
9. *Turse Clerical aptitudes Test.* 1953–55. Grades 8–12, adults. *Verbal skills, number skills, written directions, checking speed, classifying-sorting, alphabetising.* One form. $ 5.90 per 35. 40 minutes. Harcourt Brace Jovanovich, Inc.
10. *Turse Shorthand Aptitude Test.* 1940. Grades 8 and above. *Stroking, spelling, phonetic association, symbol transcription, word discrimination, dictation* and *word sense.* One form. $ 5.90 per 35. 40 minutes. Harcourt Brace Jovanovich, Inc.

Musical Aptitude

Seashore Measures of Musical Talents

Various tests of musical aptitude have been devised, though the total number of such tests is not large. Probably the best known is the *Seashore,* which consists of tests of *pitch, loudness, rhythm, time, timbre* and *tonal memory*, all on phonograph record or tape. The tests are as follows: *pitch* (the higher of two tones); *loudness* (the louder of two tones); *rhythm* (comparison of two rhythmic patterns); *time* (the longer of two sounds); *timbre* (comparison of tonal quality to decide whether two tones are the same or different); *tonal memory* (comparison of two short musical figures differing in one note, to indicate by number which note is different). The tests are said to be applicable from the fourth grade up, but they seem to work best with older subjects. Reliabilities range from .62 to .88 with an average of about .80. The tests require about one hour to administer, and may be given to individuals or groups. They show little relationship to differences in amount of musical training at advanced levels, but when administered in combination with an intelligence test, the *Seashore* shows a definite relationship to success in advanced musical study.

Many musical aptitude tests are largely paper-and-pencil tests which measure knowledge and understanding of musical terms and symbols, though a few include tests of some of the types of performance that are measured by the *Seashore.*

Other Tests of Musical Aptitude

1. *Aliferis Music Achievement Test.* 1954. Grades 13–15. *Matching melodies, harmonies, or rhythms with musical notations.* One form. $ 3.00 per 20. (Piano or tape recording necessary.) 45 minutes. University of Minnesota Press.
2. *Drake Musical Aptitude Tests.* 1954. Grades 3 through college. *Musical memory and musical rhythm.* One $33\frac{1}{3}$ LP record. One form. $ 6.25 per record and manual; answer pads, $ 6.30 per 100. 30–80 minutes. Science Research Associates, Inc.
3. *Musical Aptitude Profile.* 1965. Grades 4–12. *Tonal imagery, rhythm imagery, musical sensitivity.* One form. Set of three tapes, $ 24.00; single tapes, $ 9.00 each. Test T, 29 minutes; Test R, 36 minutes; Test S, 45 minutes. Houghton Mifflin Company.

Art Aptitude

Another area of aptitude testing in which considerable work has been done is the field of visual or graphic arts. A number of tests have been developed which purport to get at potential along these lines. As in other specialised areas, the distinction between achievement and aptitude in art is not easy to make or maintain. In some instances, as has already been pointed out, so-called aptitude tests have measured information or learned abilities on the theory that such outcomes are indicative of interest and possibly aptitude as well. This is perhaps less relevant in the measurement of art aptitude than in some other areas since the most successful of the tests so far developed deal with abstractions. Some, however, are in the nature of work samples testing the ability of the subject to draw or to create.

The test of art aptitude to be described is the *Meier Art Judgment Test,* one of the best and most widely used tests of its type. It consists of one hundred pairs of pictures in which the task is to select the better in each pair. One of the pair is a picture of a work of established merit. The other is the same except that the picture has been altered in some way to impair a fundamental and universal principle of art contained in the original (see Fig. 5.1).

The material used was chosen from the works of old masters and contemporary artists. Three hundred pairs of pictures were

Fig. 5.1 : Sample Pair of Figures from the *Meier Art Judgment Test.* Reproduced by permission of the author, Norman C. Meier.

tried out and eventually reduced to one hundred. The pairs were submitted to twenty-five art experts and were responded to by 1,081 persons ranging in age from eleven years to past middle life. Final selection of item pairs was based upon favourable critical reaction by the experts and a 60 to 90 per cent preference by the 1,081 subjects. Scores on the final one-hundred-item test differentiated consistently between various groups in expected directions. Correlations between scores on *Meier Art Judgment* and intelligence are generally low, averaging close to zero. Reliabilities, split-half, and Spearman-Brown range from .70 to .84. Norms are based upon students in junior and senior high schools, primarily those interested in art.

More recently (1963) Meier has produced a test of *Aesthetic Perception* designed to measure individual differences in perception of aesthetic merit of different ways of constructing an art object. The subject observes four versions of the same work of art and ranks them in order of aesthetic merit. There are fifty plates of such test items. The score on the test show a wide range with means for different groups varying in keeping with expected directions according to artistic propensities and talent.

The usefulness of these tests as measures of art aptitude is based upon the principle or theory that aesthetic judgment is an important factor in the complex of factors that make up this aptitude. This factor, said to be the product of heredity and experience, is the unfailing response to a work of art embodying good principles of line, proportion, balance and the like.

Other Tests of Art Aptitude

1. *Graves Design Judgment Test.* 1948. Grades 7–16 and adults. Ninety sets of two- and three-dimensional designs calling for *discrimination on the basis of eight principles of art.* One form. $ 1.70 per booklet. 20–30 minutes. Psychological Corporation.
2. *Horn Art Aptitude Inventory.* 1951. Grades 12–16 and adults. *Outline drawings of simple objects* and *creative composition.* One form. $ 5.50 per set. 50 minutes. Stoelting Company.
3. *Tests in Fundamental Abilities of Visual Art.* 1957. Grades 3-adult. *Proportion, line drawing, light and shade, vocabulary, visual memory of proportion, cylindrical, parallel and angular perspective, colour.* One form. $7.25 per set of 9 tests. One hour and 25 minutes. California Test Bureau.

Foreign Language Aptitude

In recent years interest in foreign languages has increased materially for reasons that are fairly obvious. The growing importance of international relations, improved means of travel, and the great increase in foreign travel have all affected foreign language instruction. The support of such instruction by the Federal government through the National Defence Education Act has encouraged such developments. Instruction in foreign languages has been added to the curriculums of many elementary schools, and colleges and universities have greatly expanded their offerings in this field.

As a result there is an awakened interest in the measurement of aptitude for learning a foreign language. A few tests of this nature have been developed over the years but these have not been widely used. Some new tests have been developed, one of which will be described. It is called the *Modern Language Aptitude Test.* Although its title suggests that it is designed primarily as a measure of an individual's probable degree of success in learning a modern foreign language, it is claimed to be useful also in measuring potential success in Latin and Greek.

The test has five parts. "Number Learning" is intended to measure aural memory. "Phonetic Script" measure the ability to learn correspondences between speech sounds and orthographic symbols. "Spelling Clues" presents words spelled in disguised form as "luv" for "love". The task is to select from a group of five words the one which means the same or nearly the same as the disguised word, e.g., affection. "Word In Sentences" tests the ability to identify a word in a test sentence which has the same function as a designated word in another "key" sentence. For example:

LONDON is the capital of England.

He liked to go *fishing* in *Maine*.

A B C D E

Here, the word "he" has the same function in the second sentence as LONDON has in the first.

The last part is called "Paired Associates". It measures the ability to learn and recognise a short set of equivalents of English words in a foreign language.

All directions for the tests are given by tape recording. A short form consisting of Parts III, IV and V may be given either by use of the tape or with oral instructions in about thirty minutes. The test may be scored either by hand or machine.

Validity of the *Modern Language Aptitude Test* was determined on the basis of correlations between scores on it and course grades in Latin, Spanish, French, German, Russian, Chinese and Indo-European. These correlations range from .13 to .83, with the majority in the range of about .35 to .65. Included were classes in foreign language in Grades 9–11, college classes, and intensive courses for adults. The coefficients with scores on the total test and the short forms are generally almost identical, differing in most instances by less than .05.

Odd-even reliabilities for the total test are above .90; for the short form, slightly less, ranging from .83 to .93. Norms are based upon approximately nineteen hundred students beginning the study of a foreign language in Grades 9–12 in fourteen high schools and approximately thirteen hundred students in ten colleges and universities. No students of current enrolment who had studied a language previously were included.

This test represents a praiseworthy attempt to develop a valid and reliable predictive instrument in the field of foreign language study. It has many features that make it outstanding among those of its type.

Other Tests of Foreign Language Aptitude

1. *Pimsleur Language Aptitude Battery.* 1966. Grades 6–10. *Grade point average, interest in studying a foreign language, verbal ability and auditory ability.* One form. Test tape, $ 9.50. Test booklets, $ 6.50 per 35. 50–60 minutes. Harcourt Brace Jovanovich, Inc.
2. *Symonds Foreign Language Prognosis Test.* 1930. Grades 8-9. Forms 1, 2. $7.35 per 100. 65 minutes. Bureau of Publications, Teachers College, Columbia University.

Aptitude Batteries

A comparatively recent development in measuring aptitudes is the aptitude battery, or what is sometimes called the *differential* or *factored* aptitude battery. Such batteries have grown out of the development of factor analysis mentioned earlier in this chapter. The attempt to isolate and identify specific factors in general intelligence has carried over into the measurement of particular aptitudes. It was reasoned that test batteries could be devised which would measure a number of important abilities or traits that enter into many types of work or activities. Then if the scores on the parts of the battery could be related to specific occupations or groups of occupations, these part scores could be differentially weighted according to their importance in such occupations.

In addition to the impact of factor analysis, the growing number of persons engaged in educational and vocational guidance or counselling has increased the interest in and the demand for such batteries. Obviously, no counsellor could test his client with all aptitude tests to determine how to advise him. Therefore, a single battery or group of tests would be very useful.

Broadly speaking, one might include in the category of aptitude batteries the *Primary Mental Abilities Test* and any others which yield part scores that can be demonstrated to have *low intercorrelations.* Obviously, if the parts of a battery have high correlations with each other, they are measuring the same thing to a substantial degree and thus have little "differential" value. Not many test batteries meet this criterion very well. We are concerned here with batteries developed to meet the criteria as outlined above and those which are designed primarily for general counselling purposes. Several such batteries are now available and a typical one will be described below.

Differential Aptitude Tests

The *Differential Aptitude Tests* were some of the first of this type. They consist of tests of *Verbal Reasoning* (analogies), *Numerical Ability* (arithmetic computation), *Abstract Reasoning, Space Relations, Mechanical Reasoning, Clerical Speed and Accuracy* and *Language Usage* (spelling, grammar, punctuation).

Abstract Reasoning consists of items like the following:

Problem Figures ***Answer Figures***

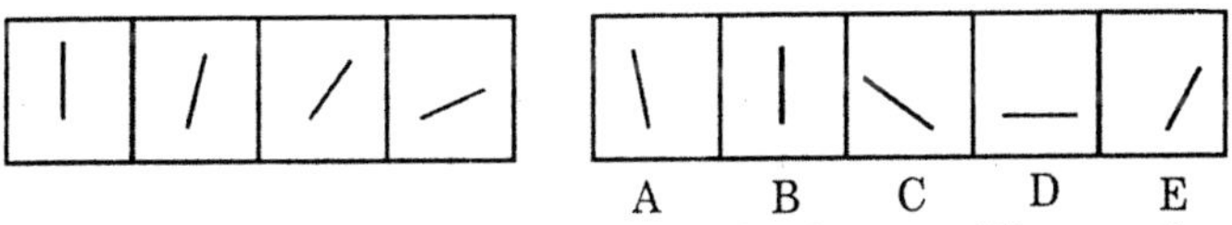

The task is to select from among the Answer Figures the one that should come next in the series of Problem Figures.

Space Relations consists of items in which a pattern that can be folded into a figure is followed by five figures, one or more of which can be formed from the pattern. The task is to identify the figure that can be formed from the pattern at the left.

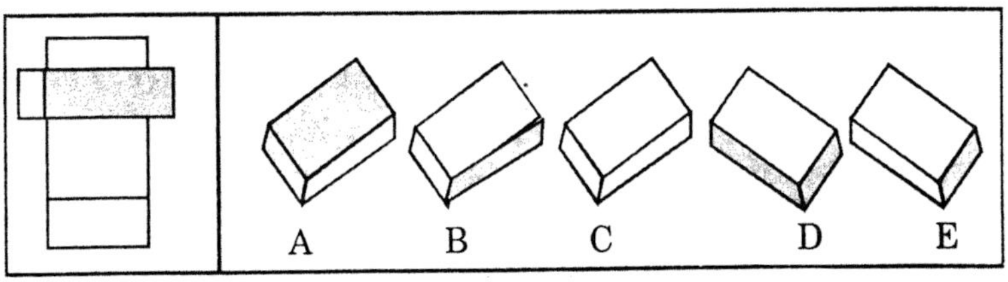

Mechanical Reasoning consists of a series of problems like the following:

X
Which man has the heavier load?
(If equal, mark C.)

Clerical Speed and *Accuracy* consists of sets of letter and number combinations in pairs. In the first set one combination is underlined. The task is to find the same combination in the second set.

Test Items

V	AB	AC	AD	AE	AF
W	aA	aB	BA	Ba	Bb
X	A7	7A	B7	7B	AB
Y	Aa	Ba	bA	BA	bB
Z	3A	3B	33	B3	BB

Sample of Answer Sheet

V	AC	AE	AF	AB	AD
W	BA	Ba	Bb	aA	aB
X	7B	B7	AB	7A	A7
Y	Aa	bA	bB	Ba	BA
Z	BB	3B	B3	3A	33

Originally, the eight tests in the battery were printed in separate booklets as Forms A and B, and each was separately administered. Later these were issued in three booklets containing (1) *Verbal Reasoning* and *Numerical Ability,* (2) *Mechanical Reasoning, Language Usage* and *Space Relations,* and (3) *Clerical Speed and Accuracy* and *Abstract Reasoning.* In 1963 a new edition with new norms was issued in a two-booklet format. Booklet 1 contains the *Verbal, Numerical, Abstract, Reasoning* and *Clerical* tests. Booklet 2 contains the *Mechanical, Space* and *Language Usage,* 1 and 2, tests. There are two forms, L and M, with which either IBM or MRC answer sheets may be used. There is also a booklet containing the *Verbal Reasoning* and *Numerical Ability* tests only.

The tests are designed for use in junior and senior high schools, but may also be used with young adults in employment counselling. Reliability coefficients (split-half except for *Clerical*

Speed and Accuracy) for the sub-tests are generally in the .80's and low .90's with the exception of scores on *Mechanical Reasoning* for girls where co-efficients are typically in the .70's. Alternate form (L vs. M) reliability coefficients for *Clerical Speed and Accuracy* range from .76 to .88.

Ideally, in a battery such as this the correlations between the sub-tests should be low. They range from .06 to .67 and the authors believe that these correlations indicate that what the separate tests measure is sufficiently different to warrant the inclusion of every test in the battery. By statistical analysis it is shown that the separate tests meet a rather high standard of differentiating power.

A continuing programme of validation of the test battery for predictive purposes is conducted by the authors and publishers. The studies reported are concerned principally with correlations between the sub-tests of the battery and grades in a wide variety of courses, tests of intelligence, other aptitude batteries, and objective achievement tests and occupational data. In general, these results show that the tests do exhibit a differential relationship to achievement in various subject-matters and to mental ability levels as well as to occupational classifications and ratings by supervisors in a limited number of fields.

Other Aptitude Batteries

1. *Aptitude Tests for Occupations.* 1951. Grades 9–13. *Personal-social, mechanical, general sales, clerical routine, computational* and *scientific aptitudes*. One form. Five booklts, $ 3.00; $ 3.75 per 35. 107 minutes. California Test Bureau.

2. *Flanagan Aptitude Classification Tests.* 1953. High school and adults. *Inspection, coding, memory, precision, assembly, scales, coordination, judgment and comprehension, arithmetic, patterns, components, tables, mechanics, expression.* One form. Each of the 14 tests, $ 3.70 per 20. Tests 1–13 in one booklet, $17.85 per 20. Tests 14–19 in one booklet, $.30 each. Three half-day sessions, each with ten-minute break. Total time, including time for directions, 2 hours, 46 minutes and 2 hours, 42 minutes. Science Research Associates, Inc.

3. *General Aptitude Test Battery.* 1947–1963. Ages 16 and up. *Intelligence, verbal, numerical, spatial, form perception, clerical*

perception, eye-hand coordination, motor speed, finger dexterity, manual dexterity. One form. $ 54.65 per complete set. 135 minutes. United States Employment Service, United States Department of Labour.

4. *Multiple Aptitude Tests*. 1959. Grades 7–13. *Word meaning, paragraph meaning, language usage, routine clerical facility, arithmetic reasoning, arithmetic computation, applied science and mechanics, spatial relations—two dimensions, and spatial relations—three dimensions*. One form. Three booklets, $ .4.90 per 35. Fourth booklet, $ 9.80 per 35. 177 minutes. California Test Bureau.

Creative Thinking

During the past decade there has been much interest and activity in the field of "creative thinking." Perhaps it would be more appropriate to say "renewed" or "increased" interest, since such famous personalities as Galton and Terman have long been identified with studies of genius which have obvious bearing on "creativity". More recently, work in this area has been directed chiefly along two lines, namely the development of measures of creative thinking and their validation. New impetus was given to such endeavours by the work of Guilford, who theorised two different processes or types of thinking, which he called *convergent* and *divergent*. In the former the major emphasis is said to depend on use of known information in arriving at new information or principles. In the latter, new information is held to be determined or derived with a minimum use of, or reference to, known information.

Guilford has also raised the question of the relation of creativity to intelligence as measured by conventional tests. His work has led to a great deal of activity in the development of tests purporting to be measures of creativity and in investigation of the relation of scores on such tests to performance on intelligence tests. Research on this question has produced conflicting results, although the preponderance of evidence seems to show that intelligence and creativity as measured by available instruments are not identical and that correlations between them tend to be low, i.e., in the range of .20 to .40.

On the prior consideration—the development of valid and reliable tests of creativity—most work is still in the experimental stage. The tests that have been produced generally exemplify attempts to measure divergent thinking. Guilford himself has investigated a number of approaches to such measurement, including ideational fluency (quantity of ideas produced), associational fluency (synonyms for words), expressional fluency (making sentences using words beginning with a certain letter), alternate uses (uses of a common object like a brick), and consequences (possible results in a new situation).

The central problem in the development of tests of creative thinking is that of validity. From the standpoint of construct validity the question becomes one of the relationship of divergent thinking to creativity. Assuming that it is possible to develop measures of unusual, unconventional, divergent thinking, is this characteristic of, and even a necessary element in, creativity? No one really knows as yet, though some studies appear to suggest that it may be. Second, from the standpoint of criterion-related validity, the problem becomes one of the validating tests purporting to measure creativity by comparing scores on them made by individuals of recognised creative ability with scores on the same tests made by persons who have displayed little or no creative talents. Data of this nature are difficult to come by though some attempts in this direction have been made.

To close the discussion of this interesting subject we present a brief description of one of the very few standardised tests of creative thinking. These tests appear in verbal and figural versions with Forms A and B of each. The verbal form tests are entitled *Thinking Creatively with Words,* the figural, *Thinking Creatively with Pictures*. In the former, a line drawing is the core element to which subjects respond by (1) asking all the questions they can think of about the picture, (2) listing as many possible causes as they can of the action shown in the picture, and (3) listing as many possible consequences of the action in the picture as they can. The next part of the test presents a picture of a stuffed toy animal to which the subject responds by listing as many ways as he can think of to change the toy to make it more fun to play with. The next activity is to list (1) as many unusual uses of cardboard boxes as possible, and (2) as many questions about such boxes as possible, with emphasis on unusual aspects. The last activity asks the subject to list the most number of consequences of an improbable happening that he can—in this case, if clouds had strings attached to them which hang down to earth.

Thinking Creatively with Pictures consists of the following tasks: (1) constructing a picture around a curved shape and giving it a title; (2) adding lines to incomplete figures to produce interesting objects or pictures; (3) making objects or pictures from a number of pairs of parallel lines or circles.

The actual working time on the verbal test is 45 minutes and on the figural test it is 30 minutes. In each case about 15 minutes additional must be allowed fcr preliminary instructions, distributing papers, etc. The separate parts of each test are timed exactly with no deviations permitted.

Scoring is rather complicated and subjective, although detailed instructions are given. It should not be attempted without careful study of instructions. Some supervised practice would also seem desirable. Four types of scores are determined. These are (1) Fluency (total number of relevant responses); (2) Flexibility (number of different categories used in responses); (3) Originality (number of more infrequent responses, i.e., those given by less than 2 per cent of the subjects); and (4) Elaboration (number of details over and above what is necessary to communicate the basic idea).

A large amount of data on reliability and validity of the *Torrance Tests of Creative Thinking* is provided in the *Norms—Technical Manual.* Norms for grades one through twelve obtained in several school systems are also provided.

Interscorer reliabilities for Verbal Forms are quite high for Fluency, Flexibility, and Elaboration, being generally in the high .80's and .90's. The coefficients for Originality range from .66 to .94. For Figural Forms the reliability coefficients range from .86 to .99. *Interform* reliability coefficients range from .50 to .93, with a median in one situation for the seven sub-tests of .84; in another situation the median was .71 and in a third group, .73.

A large number of studies of the *Torrance Tests of Creative Thinking* that bear in one way or another on their validity have been reported in the literature. Many of these are reviewed in the *Norms-Technical Manual.* Under a category labelled Content Validity the author maintains that his tests sample a rather wide range of the abilities in a universe of creative thinking abilities.

Under Construct Validity many studies are cited purporting to show that scores on the *Tests of Creative Thinking* support hypotheses regarding their relationship to such constructs as rigidity, originality, playfulness, non-conformity, sense of humour, etc. The validity of most of the criterion measures appears not to have been determined. At least it is not commonly reported in this review. Under Concurrent Validity, scores on the tests are related to peer nominations and teacher nominations on creativity. Generally, these show significant differences between the mean scores of the high and low groups in the predicted direction. A number of studies of the relationship of scores on the tests to educational achievement as measured by standardised test batteries and tests of tool subjects in the grades are reviewed. The results are equivocal. Correlations reported range from near zero to as high as .77. No correlations between I.Q. and scores on creative thinking are reported, although one investigator reported a correlation of .54 with scores in kindergarten on the *Metropolitan Reading Readiness* test, the tests of Creative Thinking being taken in the sixth grade. The author attempts to explain these widely varying findings on the basis of differences in instructional methods and classroom climate; some teachers encourage creativity, others, by their methods and attitudes, engender conformity.

The amount of work done with the *Torrance* tests is impressive. However, the basic questions of what they measure and their relationship to educational achievement, intelligence, and criteria of creative accomplishment need further and more definitive investigation.

Recognising that knowledge and understanding about creative thinking are yet in a relatively underdeveloped state, the *Torrance Tests of Creative Thinking* are designated by author and publisher as a Research Edition. The tests constitute a pioneering effort to develop and standardise tests in this field. Further studies are under way and both author and publisher are conducting and supporting ongoing research.

Other Aptitude Tests

In addition to the aptitude tests described or listed in this chapter, a number of such tests have been developed in other fields. A perusal of Buros' *Sixth Mental Measurements Yearbook* shows listings of one or more tests or batteries in each of the following areas: medicine, nursing, dentistry, law, engineering, selling, accounting, dental hygiene, firefighting, driving and traffic safety, business management, law enforcement, carpentry, coach operation and truck driving. This is not a complete list but it indicates the variety of purposes for which such tests have been devised.

The use of aptitude or prognostic tests was given considerable impetus during World War II. Large numbers of men and women were inducted into service with little or no training or experience that could be used in the armed forces. These people had to be screened and assigned either to training or to jobs, and this had to be done quickly. The need for reasonably accurate, objective, and rapid methods for appraising an individual and assigning him was obvious. Consequently a great deal of effort was expended on the development of aptitude tests, some of which have continued to be used in civilian life.

The development of aptitude tests or batteries is a challenging task. Research and development in this field are likely to continue, particularly in business and industry. Perhaps the most promising development is that of the factored aptitude batteries, but these require great expenditures of talent and money as exemplified by the *General Aptitude Test Battery* of the United States Employment Service. They also demand continuing research and appraisal to meet changing requirements in occupations. However, valid and reliable aptitude tests are well worth what they cost if they save time, money and energy and if they help avoid frustration and disappointment for millions of young people faced with the necessity of making decisions about their life's work. Aptitude tests for specific occupations or types of work should also prove useful in guiding the so-called "hard-core unemployed" into types of training for productive work commensurate with their abilities.

6

The Measurement of Personality and Adjustment: Self-report Techniques

Personality is often considered synonymous with popularity. The individual who knows a large number of people, who is present at all functions and who is persuasive in his dealings with others is said to have a "wonderful personality". While there is undoubtedly some slight basis for this point of view, it is quite inadequate as an acceptable definition of personality. In a deeper sense, personality is the most inclusive frame of reference in which an individual can be judged. It includes the sum of all his characteristics and his behaviour—his intelligence, knowledge, attitudes, interests, and his responses to and interaction with his environment. Personality thus broadly conceived is the total of all of these qualities together with the effects of the combination of them on what he thinks, feels, says and does.

If we can accept such a broad definition of personality, we may go a step further and suggest that personality has two aspects: inner and outer. The inner phase refers to the adjustment of the individual within himself. That is, does he have a realistic and satisfying self-concept? Is he confident, sure of his personal worth? Has he set suitable and challenging goals for himself, keeping in mind his own limitations as well as his strengths? Is he satisfied with his occupation? Of course, there are many more factors which importantly affect one's inner personality, but these are among the chief elements.

The outer or interpersonal phase of personality concerns the individual's relationships with other people. Is he a useful member of family and community groups? Does he have the respect and affection of his associates? Is he capable of enjoying group activities? Such questions point up the social or interpersonal aspect of personality as it is conceived here.

We cannot emphasise too strongly the importance of adjustment in the definition of personality. Indeed, the individual who is well adjusted is most likely to be happy and to have a personality which makes a favourable impression on others. Conversely, the poorly adjusted person, almost by definition, is unhappy, and consequently his relationships with others will tend to be strained and difficult. Thus, one's personality is not some superficial characteristic that may be briefly adopted; rather, it is a reflection of a person's innermost self, and it influences and becomes a part of everything he or she does.

There are two fundamental approaches to the measurement of personality or adjustment. In the simplest terms, the first approach involves asking the individual himself what he thinks, feels, says and does; the second involves finding out about the individual from others who have known him. The first may be called the *self-report* approach; the other, the *observational* approach. The examiner who uses the self-report technique asks questions or presents stimuli to which the individual being measured responds. From the replies obtained, the examiner can formulate some idea of the subject's personality or certain aspects of it. The examiner using the observational technique asks someone who knows the subject well to express opinions about him. Both of these methods are widely used. Self-report techniques may be distinguished from observational by the fact that the former are more often tests or other devices which yield scores. Thus, personality inventories, tests of attitudes, and tests of interests are typical self-report instruments, whereas rating scales, anecdotal records, and sociograms are examples of the observational type of report.

The nature advantages, and disadvantages of self-report techniques will be discussed in this chapter, and those of the observational techniques will be treated in Chapter 7.

Personality Inventories

The typical personality inventory of earlier years was an instrument planned in terms of some rationale conceived either in term of areas of activity such as school, home, and job, or a set of psychological constructs conceived by the author. In the latter case an author's constructs might include such traits as sociability or confidence. As a matter of fact, most inventories, past and present, represent one or the other of these two basic patterns of organisation.

More recently, two developments in measurement theory have been applied to the construction of self-report inventories, one of which is *factor analysis*. Considerable research has been done in the application of this technique to the development of these instruments. The results have been promising in that the technique has helped to isolate a limited number of fairly distinct factors or traits of personality.

The other development is the so-called *"forced choice"* technique. One of the nagging concerns of those who use any type of self-report device is the possibility of the subject's faking or slanting responses. Presumably, the individual, by judicious selection of his responses, can create an impression that is false but favourable to himself. The forced choice technique purports to eliminate or at least reduce the possibility of such faking. Typically, it presents a choice between pairs of equally complimentary or equally uncomplimentary alternatives. One of each pair, however, is a more significant response than the other with respect to some criterion such as emotional stability. The subject is required to choose one response which he considers to be most like him and one least like him. Since both of one pair sound equally complimentary and both of the other pair sound equally uncomplimentary, his chances of faking are believed to be greatly reduced. The forced choice technique was developed during World War II and has found considerable application in fields in which measurement depends on self-report. An example of forced choice items is presented below in connection with the discussion of a personality inventory prototype.

Gordon Personal Profile–Personal Inventory

The *Gordon Personal Profile* and *Gordon Personal Inventory* are companion pieces designed to measure eight factors of personality. Those included in the *Profile* are *ascendancy, responsibility, emotional stability* and *sociability.* The *Inventory* covers *cautiousness, original thinking, personal relations* and *vigor.* These eight traits or personality aspects are reported to have been arrived at and identified through several successive factor analyses.

Data presented in the manuals for the two tests tend to support, at least in part, the claim that the tests measure significantly different aspects of personality. Intercorrelations among the four scales of the *Profile* range from —.18 (sociability with emotional stability) to .71 (ascendancy with sociability). The correlation between emotional stability and responsibility is about .50. Other intercorrelations for the *Profile* are low positive or low negative.

Intercorrelations among the four scales of the *Inventory* range from .42 (cautiousness with personal relations) to —.45 (cautiousness with vigor).

Intercorrelations among scales of the *Profile* and scales of the *Inventory* range between .47 (emotional stability with personal relations) and —.21 (sociability with cautiousness). Most of the coefficients are between zero and .40.

The forced choice type of item is used in both instruments. A sample item follows:

1. Likes to work primarily with ideas.
2. Does things at a rather slow pace.
3. Very careful when making a decision.
4. Finds a number of people hard to get along with.

Here the first and third items are judged to be equally complimentary, the second and fourth, the opposite. The person taking the test is to mark one that is *most* like him and one that is *least* like him in each tetrad or group of four. Each set of four consists of one item related to each of the four scales or traits. Thus, one item of a tetrad in the *Profile* pertains to cautiousness, one to original thinking, etc., and similarly with the *Inventory.*

Extensive studies of the validity of both tests have been reported. They consist mainly of reports of scores of groups expected to differ as, for example, males, females, clerks and stenographers, foremen, executives, and many other occupational groups. Comparisons between students in various curriculums in high schools are also reported. Correlations between scores and personality ratings by peers, counsellors, teachers, supervisors and with scores on other personality measures are reported in a substantial number of investigations. The data on validity are more extensive than usual with instruments of this type and, on the whole, are quite encouraging, especially in the case of the *Profile*. Those for the *Inventory* are less extensive.

Reliability of the two tests is reported in terms of split-half coefficients. They are typically in the high .70's and .80's. In one study involving several hundred high school students the separate reliabilities of the four parts of the *Profile* were found to be about .60.

Percentile norms are provided for college students, high school students, and adult groups in various occupations. Norms are provided in each case by sex. On the whole, the *Gordon Profile* and *Inventory* are promising devices. They were developed by use of the best available techniques and have been extensively evaluated by independent researchers. Either of the pair may be used alone or they may be used together, seemingly without substantial overlap or duplication.

The Mooney Problem Check Lists

The Mooney Problem Check Lists, yield data on problems or difficulties in such categories as *Health and Physical Development, Home and Family, Morals and Religion, Sex, Economic Security, School or Occupation* and *Social and Recreational*. Obviously, this represents a different approach or analysis from that of the Gordon tests. A number of other personality inventories yield scores that are indicative of adjustment is similar areas.

The Mooney Problem Check Lists are available in different forms for the junior high school, high school, college and adult levels. The areas covered are essentially, the same in each form, although there are differences in the items at the various maturity levels. The person responding is asked to read the list of several hundred items, underline those problems which are troublesome to him, and indicate the two or three which are of real concern. The items are so arranged that a count can easily be made of the check marks in each of the different areas. In the junior high form the areas are *Health and Physical Development; School; Home and Family; Money, Work and the Future; Boy and Girl Relations; Relations with People in General;* and *Self-Centered Concerns*. In the high school and college forms these same areas are included, with additional ones such as *Morals and Religion*, and *Curriculum and Teaching Procedure*. The check lists can be completed by most persons in about thirty minutes. The following samples from the junior high school form show the nature of the arrangement:

	1.	Often have headaches
Health	2.	Don't get enough sleep
and	3.	Have trouble with my teeth
Physical Education	4.	Not as healthy as I should be
	5.	. . . .
	6.	Getting low grades in school
	7.	Afraid of tests
School	8.	Being a grade behind in school
	9.	. . . .
	10.	. . . .
	11.	Being an only child
Home	12.	Not living with my parents
and	13.	Worried about someone in the family
Family	14.	. . . .
	15.	. . . .

In the junior high school form there are 210 items in seven areas; in the high school, college, and adult forms there are 330 items in eleven areas. In every area there are thirty items.

The Mooney Problem Check Lists are not tests in the usual sense, and do not yield scores. However, they do provide a useful tool for teachers and especially for counsellors in locating problem areas which may then be investigated by the use of more refined techniques. The *Mooney Lists* can also be used as a basis for guidance and orientation programmes, and as a foundation for increasing teacher understanding in the classroom.

Several questions are perennially raised concerning the self-report type of personality inventory. One of these has to do with its validity and reliability. A second, already mentioned, relates to the problem of the subject's faking or simulating responses. A third question concerns the usability of such inventories in schools. How much use should be made of them? By whom should they be used? Full discussions of these questions are beyond the scope of this book, but a few statements will be made to provide some information on each point.

First, concerning validity, a little reflection will make it clear that the usual methods of establishing validity cannot apply to personality inventories. It is not possible to establish validity of personality inventories by correlating the scores with age, grade, or I.Q., except possibly in a negative way by showing a lack of relationship between such measures. One criterion often used is a comparison of scores with teachers' ratings of adjustment; another is a comparison of scores with case histories to see if those who make poor scores on the inventory show a history of maladjustment, problem behaviour, and personality disorders. On the whole, such studies show the self-report inventory to have fairly satisfactory validity as a screening device. Although these instruments generally do not reveal minute adjustment differences, they serve to identify most of the serious cases of maladjustment.

As to reliability, data vary widely. Some inventories report reliability coefficients as high as .90. Some, as in the case of the *Mooney,* do not yield scores and thus do not lend themselves to statistical analysis. In general, the reliability of personality inventories is lower than that of good standardised tests of intelligence or achievement. The reliability coefficients range from the .60's to the .80's, with the average falling somewhere between .70 and .80. In this connection, it must be kept in mind that it is not the subject's response to one or even a few items that is meaningful, but rather, the *trend* of his responses to a large number of items. For example, in the *Gordon* there are seventy-two items; in each of the two tets; in the *Mooney* there are more than two hundred.

On the problem of faked or simulated responses there is considerable evidence from research. The information obtained from a number of these studies may be summed up briefly as follows:

1. It is possible to fake or slant answers on a self-report inventory.
2. It is not as easy to do this as might be supposed, especially to take and maintain consistently a pose. Ability to slant answers is affected, among other things (a) The sophistication of the subjects, (b) the subtlety of the statements on the inventory, (c) the number of items.
3. Some individuals cannot consistently fake answers in a desired direction even when told to do so.

It is obvious that a personality inventory differs from a test of achievement in this respect. In the latter case there is little chance for faking or bluffing if it is a good test, while in the former, the value of the responses depends on the subject's willingness to be truthful and his ability to give accurate representations of his behaviour and feelings. Unless he is cooperative, the responses are of no value.

As to the question of whether personality inventories should be used in schools, it may be said, first of all, that they should be used very conservatively. Whereas the average classroom teacher can handle standardised tests of achievement and intelligence with some help and guidance from the counsellor or school psychologist, this is seldom the case with personality tests. The use and interpretation of these tests require more training and experience than most teachers posses. As a rule, the personality test should be given on an individual rather than a school-wide basis. When a child asks his teacher or counsellor for help or shows symptoms of maladjustment, the use of a personality inventory certainly may be indicated. It is important that the results be held in strictest confidence and used only with caution by a person qualified to interpret them. Even a tool like the *Mooney Check Lists* should probably be used selectively rather than on a school-wide basis, and the results should be made available only to guidance workers or school psychologists. When these principles are not adhered to, the results will often prove detrimental to pupil morale as well as to the parents' confidence in the method used.

The words in the preceding paragraph were written, the principles expressed seem as sound today as they were fifteen years ago. In fact, developments in the use of personality inventories during the past decade have intensified the need for care in their use. The issue of "invasion of privacy" has been lively and at times, hot, in a number of areas, especially in government and education. In 1965 and 1966 three Congressional investigations were held, two in the House and one in the Senate, on the use of psychological, especially personality, tests with applicants for government employment. In education the clamour has been somewhat less resounding but still of great concern to many persons, especially parents whose children are asked to respond to inventories containing questions concerning such matters as home conditions, family relationships, sexual attitudes and practices and religious beliefs. The concern revolves about several questions. Probably foremost in the minds of critics is the "invasion of privacy" issue. Is the gathering of such types of information a violation of an individual's privacy and, indeed, of his constitutional rights? Perhaps equally serious is the question of the confidentiality of such information. What guarantee is there that, since every individual has a social security number by which he can always be identified, information which he is led to believe will be held in strictest confidence cannot and may not be collated by computer or used by others than those to whom it was originally confided? A supplementary question, also raised by many critics, has to do with the validity of scores on psychological and, especially, personality tests as predictors of performance.

There is a wide range of viewpoints on these questions. Some more violent critics would go so far as "to prohibit the giving of psychological tests by any Federal agency, under any circumstances, at any place, and to make it a Federal crime for any Federal official to do it." At the other extreme would be those who would place little if any restrictions on the use of psychological tests. A more reasonable middle ground would hold that such tests could be employed, provided that their use could be justified on the basis that they make a contribution to useful knowledge and are administered and interpreted by qualified professionals.

One of the most reasonable and helpful discussions of this issue is to be found in the report of a symposium entitled "Invasion of Privacy in Research and Testing." The members of the symposium included a test publisher, officials of the federal government and of an educational foundation, a director of educational research, and university professors of psychology and education.

The consensus of this group and of other students of the issue at this time could be summarised somewhat as follows:

1. There is a real issue here that will continue to exist and that users of psychological tests for whatever purpose and in all circumstances must recognise.
2. The right of privacy of the individual and his right to refuse to divulge information which he considers his own personal business must be respected. For research purposes it may often be unnecessary to identify the respondent.
3. Those who employ psychological tests must be prepared to justify their use as contributing to some useful purpose or need. Furthermore, they must be able to show that such tests are more effective and efficient than other means.

On the other hand:

4. Critics have the obligation to demonstrate that the tests are in fact harmful or demeaning.
5. They also have the obligation to base their objections on real and substantial, rather than on fanciful and trivial, faults.
6. Critics must recognise that the greater good that may accrue to the community, to government, to education, or to society in general from use of psychological tests should not be lost because of some trivial or fancied offense to a comparatively few individuals.

The issue boils down to a conflict between methods and values. On the one hand, we have the behavioural scientist seeking new knowledge and developing instruments and methods to obtain such knowledge. On the other hand, we have the public—the people—who are jealous of their rights as individuals. Between these two sets of forces some accommodations must be found or there can be no progress. The social scientist must find a very fine, sometimes seemingly invisible line, which permits him to proceed with his work with the willing support and cooperation of the people who in the last analysis will be served.

Other Personality Inventories

1. *Adjustment Inventory.* 1934–38; student form revised, 1962. Grades 7–16 and adults. *Home, health, submissiveness, emotionality, hostility, masculinity-femininity.* Student form and adult form. $ 3.25 per 25. 35 minutes. Consulting Psychologists Press.

2. *A-S Reaction Study.* A scale for measuring ascendance-submission in personality. 1928. College students and adults. Measures the *tendency to dominate or be dominated in face-to-face relationships*. Form for men and form for women, $ 3.90 per 35. 20 minutes. Houghton Mifflin Company.

3. *California Test of Personality.* 1953. Primary, K-3; Elementary, 4–8; Intermediate, 7–10; Secondary, 9-College; Adults. *Personal adjustment and social adjustment.* Forms AA and BB. $ 3.85 per 35. 50 minutes. California Test Bureau.

4. *Detroit Adjustment Inventory.* 1942–53. Ages 5–8, Grades 3–6 and 7–12. Adjustment in four areas: *self, home, school and community*. Forms Delta, Gamma, Alpha. $ 4.50 per 35. 30 minutes. The Bobbs-Merrill Company Inc.

5. *Edwards Personal Preference Schedule.* 1953–57. College and adults. *Achievement, deference, order, exhibition, autonomy, affiliation, intraception, succorance, dominance, abasement, nurturance, change, endurance, heterosexuality, aggression.* One form. $ 4.00 per 25. 45 minutes. Psychological Corporation.

6. *Guilford-Zimmerman Temperament Survey.* 1949–55. Grades 9–16 and adults. *General activity, restraint, ascendance, sociability, emotional stability, objectivity, friendliness, thoughtfulness, personal relations, masculinity.* One form. $ 4.00 per 25. 45 minutes. Sheridan Supply Company.

7. *IPAT Anxiety Scale.* 1957. Ages 14 and up. *Self-sentiment development, ego strength, paranoid trend, guilt proneness, ergic tension.* One form. $ 3.00 per 25. 10 minutes. Institute for Personality and Ability Testing.

8. *Minnesota Counselling Inventory.* 1953–57. Grades 9–12. *Family relationships, social relationships, emotional stability,*

conformity, adjustment to reality, mood, leadership. One form. $ 4.00 per 25. 50 minutes. Psychological Corporation.

9. *Minnesota Multiphasic Personality Inventory*. 1951–67. Age 16 and up. *Hypochondriasis, depression, hysteria, psychopathic deviate, masculinity and femininity paranoia, psychasthenia, schizophrenia, hypomania* and *social introversion*. Individual form and group form. Individual, $ 25.00 per set, plus $ 1.50 per manual; scoring keys and manual, $ 9.00. Group, $ 6.50 per 25, plus $1.50 per manual. New Form R, $ 2.00 per copy. Scoring keys and manual, extra. 60–90 minutes. Psychological Corporation.

10. *Study of Values*. Revised, 1951. College and adult. Aims to measure the relative prominence of six basic interests or motives in personality: *the theoretical, economic, aesthetic, social, political* and *religious*. One form $ 4.20 per 35. About 20 minutes. Houghton Mifflin Company.

11. *Survey of Interpersonal Values*. High School and College. *Support, conformity, recognition, independence, benevolence, leadership*. One form. $ 3.35 per 20. 15 minutes. Science Research Associates, Inc.

12. *Survey of Personal Values*. High School and College. *Practical mindedness, achievement, variety, decisiveness, orderliness, goal orientation*. One form. $ 3.35 per 20. 15 minutes. Science Research Associates, Inc.

Projective Techniques

Another type of self-report is the projective test, which is a clinical instrument to be used only by psychiatrists or clinical psychologists. It derives its name from the fact that in his responses the subject "projects" his feelings, emotions, conflicts and problems. The projective tests are less structured than the personality inventories in that the questions, items, or stimuli are less definite and specific, and the subject is far more free to make responses in his own words.

The Rorschach Ink-Blot Test is a well-known example of a projective test. It consists of a series of what purport to be ink-blots, some black, some in colour. These are shown to the subject one at a time, and he is asked to tell what they suggest or remind him of. From the subject's responses the psychiatrist can determine something of the presence and nature of deep-seated emotional conflicts and maladjustments which the subject himself may not understand or even be conscious of. Obviously, such a test requires much training and experience to administer and interpret.

A simpler form of projective technique, and one probably antedating such instruments as the *Rorschach,* is the *word-association test*. The procedure in this type of test is to present a list of words one at a time to the subject, asking him to give the first word that comes to mind in each case. Some of the words are "loaded", that is, they may carry emotional aspects for some individuals under certain circumstances. To be more specific, suppose a teacher or psychologist presented the words in the following list to a group of fifth-grade children, and asked each pupil to tell or write the first word that came to mind in each instance. Let us assume that the list of words has been used in this way with many children, and that certain conventional or non-emotional responses have been identified. The results might reveal that two pupils responded as follows:

Stimulus Word	*Pupil A*	*Pupil B*
House	big	white
Apple	eat	sour
Paper	write	burn
Teacher	lady	ugly
Sky	blue	high

On the basis of the previous trials of these same words the responses of Pupil A might be regarded as quite conventional and normal. In the case of Pupil B, however, certain responses are found to be different in character. To apple, he responds "sour"; to paper, "burn"; and to teacher, "ugly". The psychiatrist might interpret these responses as reflecting some factors in Pupil B's emotional makeup that would warrant further investigation. Not only the response itself, but other considerations as well, have significance. For example, long hesitation before responding to a given word may be a sign of emotional blocking. Such a word list is a simple projective device in that the subject often "projects" his complexes or problems in the responses he makes.

Some projective tests consist of pictures of people, and still others use objects such as toys or simple mechanical devices. There are many projective tests and devices and they are especially popular with European psychologists and psychiatrists.

Before closing this brief discussion, it may be appropriate to mention one rather well-known application of the association technique, i.e., the polygraph or "lie detector." By this method, the person suspected of a crime is asked if he will submit to such a test. Usually he agrees to do so. If he is innocent he has nothing to fear or lose by taking it; if guilty, he is afraid that refusal will reflect on him adversely, so he generally agrees to take it with the hope of "beating it." The test depends upon the known effect of strong emotion on blood pressure, pulse rate and amount of palmar sweating, all of which are increased by heightened emotion. Normal rates of each are established for the subject under simple and innocuous questioning, then loaded questions are introduced. If the pulse, blood pressure and palmar sweating increase, it is judged that the subject is not telling the truth. This, of course, is not accepted as proof of guilt, but the results, when shown to a guilty suspect, often bring about a confession. In general, specialists in crime detection are of the opinion that the results of lie detector tests are quite reliable, and that few persons are successful in beating the test. The harder the individual tries and the more determined he is to beat it, the more pronounced are the telltale signs when a loaded question or some significant piece of evidence is suddenly introduced.

Interest Inventories

Though interest inventories are not measures of personality and adjustment in a technical sense, it seems appropriate to consider such inventories at this point, since a person's interests reflect his personality and are a part of it; moreover, his interests in relation to his abilities, opportunities, and background may have a definite bearing on his adjustment. Interest inventories are useful tools for counsellors and school psychologists in helping the individual make appropriate educational and occupational choices; inappropriate or unsuitable choices often lead to maladjustment and serious loss of time and energy.

The interest inventory is based on the theory that a dependable picture of a person's interest pattern can be obtained by asking him to express likes and dislikes of a large number of diverse activities and things. It is assumed, furthermore, that persons successful in the same occupation or field of work will have patterns of interests that are similar. Thus, a successful motion picture actor will usually have patterns of interests that are similar to the patterns of other successful actors. Finally, it is assumed that the patterns of interests of persons successfully engaged in one occupation—teaching, for example—will differ from those of persons in another field, such as engineering or chemistry. These three assumptions are at the root of the development of interest inventories. Two typical inventories of this type will be briefly described. The total number of such inventories is not large, as compared with the number of tests in other types of personality measurement.

Strong Vocational Interest Blanks

One of the earliest and best-known interest inventories was developed by Strong. It consists of items listed under such topics as "Occupations," "School Subjects," "Amusements," "Activities," and "Peculiarities of People." In each group of items the individual is asked to express a preference, either in terms of "Like," "Indifferent," or "Dislike," or an order of preference for the items. For example, in "Part I—Occupations":

1. Actor -- L I D
2. Advertising Man ---------------------------------- L I D
3. Architect --- L I D
4. Military Officer ---------------------------------- L I D
5. Artist -- L I D

the subject encircles "L" if he would like or be interested in that occupation, "D" if he would dislike it, and "I" if he is indifferent toward it.

Again, in "Part VI—Order of Preference of Activities":

Indicate by checking in Column 1 the three activities you would enjoy most; in Column 3 the three you would enjoy least; and the remaining four in Column 2.

	1	2	3	
311.	( )	( )	( )	President of a Society or Club
312.	( )	( )	( )	Secretary of a Society or Club
313.	( )	( )	( )	Treasurer of a Society or Club
314.	( )	( )	( )	Member of a Society or Club
315.	( )	( )	( )	Chairman, Arrangements Committee
316.	( )	( )	( )	Chairman Educational Committee
317.	( )	( )	( )	Chairman, Entertainment Committee
318.	( )	( )	( )	Chairman, Membership Committee
319.	( )	( )	( )	Chairman, Programme Committee
320.	( )	( )	( )	Chairman, Publicity Committee

The men's blank of the 1966 edition of the *SVIB* contains 399 items, the women's, 398. The categories in the two blanks are the same, but the activities, occupations, etc. are different. On the basis of responses, a profile is constructed which permits comparison of the individual's pattern of interests with that of a sample of men (or women) in general and with that of persons successfully engaged in a particular occupation. The individual profile may also be interpreted against twenty-two basic interest scales for men and nineteen for women. These include such areas as office practices, social service and music. Items on these scales are related in turn to high and low score on various occupational scales. The men's blank can be scored for fifty-four different occupations; the women's for fifty-eight. Other scales have also been developed over the years for the *Strong*. For both men and women there are scales for Diversity of Interests, Masculinity-Femininity, and Academic Achievement, plus several others for men.

Although earlier forms could be machine-scored or hand-scored the latter is laborious and time-consuming. It is still possible to score the men's blank manually for the occupational scales and a few of the non-occupational scales. All other scoring must now be done by machine.

The *Strong* scales are the result of a great deal of careful work from their beginning in 1938 to the present. In the latest edition, obsolete items were eliminated, some were re-worded and over 100 new items were added. Scoring was simplified, new scales were added and additional data on reliability and validity were collected. Use of the scales is restricted to mature high school students, college students and adults. This limitation constitutes a deficiency in the opinion of some users of the scales; however, in view of the evidence on changeability of interests, especially at younger ages, this may be a desirable feature.

Reliabilities determined by test-retest over varying intervals range from .91 for periods up to thirty days to the .50's and .60's for periods up to thirty years. Reliability coefficients of the separate occupational scales are nearly all above .80 and many are in the .90's.

Validity of the earlier scales was determined by the fact that men or women entering a particular occupation make higher scores on the scale for that occupation than on any other; that men or women continuing in a suggested occupation make higher scores than those who change from that occupation to another one; and that a person changing from some other occupation to occupation X ten years later made higher scores as a college senior on the scale for occupation X or one other occupation than he did on the scales for eighteen other occupations. While such data do not show that scores on the blank predict success in an occupation, they do indicate that scores are related to occupational preference as judged by entrance into and persistence in an occupation

More recent pronouncements on validity follow the form now widely accepted—Content, Concurrent, Predictive. With respect to the first, it is said that the item content of the *SVIB* is heavily oriented toward vocational activities; feelings toward such content constitute useful information for vocational planning. Concurrent validity rests on the discriminatory power of the scales to distinguish the individual's profile from that of men or women in general. The median per cents of overlap are generally in the .30's, a separation of roughly two standard deviations. Predictive validity based upon earlier studies has already been discussed. Additionally, for college seniors and high school seniors with definite patterns it has been found that the odds are about 3 to 1 over a 10–20 year period that the individual will be found in an occupation consonant with his earlier profile. For the general population of college-bound high school seniors the odds are about 2 to 1. Those found to be in an "inappropriate" occupation according to an earlier interest profile will report dissatisfaction about four times as often as those in "appropriate" occupations.

Kuder Preference Records—Vocational and Personal

Another well-known and widely used set of interest inventories are the *Kuder Preference Records—Vocational C, Vocational B, Personal A, Occupational D*, and most recently *General Interest Survey E. Vocational C* measures ten broad areas of interest: *outdoor, mechanical, computational, scientific, persuasive, artistic, literary, musical, social service* and *clerical. Vocational B* measures all these except *outdoor interest*. The *Personal A* measures five different kinds of personal preferences referred to as *sociable, practical, theoretical, agreeable* and *dominant. Occupational D* relates preferences to specific jobs, and the publishers state that scoring keys for fifty-two occupations may be obtained. *General Interest Survey E* was developed to provide a measure of interests primarily to meet the need for such an instrument at the junior high school level. All the other scales in the series are designed for use in grades 9–12 and with adults. Vocabulary is sixth-grade level and concepts used are those believed to be fairly stable. It can be scored for the same ten areas as *Vocational C. Occupational Interests Survey DD,* also a newer form, contains 100 items with six possible response patterns per item. It permits comparisons of an individual's preferences with those of a large number of occupational groups and those of persons pursuing various college majors. It is designed for use in grades 11-12, college, and with adults.

These inventories call for choices among a wide range of activities as does the *Strong,* but the choices are not grouped into categories such as occupations, subjects, etc. The alternatives are presented in groups of three; in each group the subject selects the one alternative which he would most prefer and the one which he would least like. For example:

P. Visit an art gallery

Q. Browse in a library

R. Visit a museum

S. Collect autographs

T. Collect coins

U. Collect butterflies

The activities in each group are not necessarily in the same category, though in most groups they are. The blanks are scored for preferences in terms of the areas or fields as listed above and for specific occupations.

The scoring of the *Kuder Preference Records* is very simple. By means of a special type of answer booklet the scores of each individual on the group or area scales can be readily determined and the scores transmuted into a profile. Machine-scorable answer sheets may also be used.

A large amount of research bearing on the validity of the *Kuder Records,* particularly *Vocational C,* has been published. The general trend of such studies has been to show marked differences in scores on the separate scales for different occupational groups and for different college majors and curricula, and definite relationships to job satisfaction. The reliabilities of the various scales, determined by the *Kuder-Richardson Formula,* are mostly between .85 and .90.

It may be appropriate to note at this point that the two major approaches to measurement of vocational interests or perhaps more precisely the scoring rationales of two methods have been coming together. In the earlier forms, the *Strong* was scored only for specific occupations, whereas the *Kuder* was scored only for broad, general areas—outdoor, mechanical, artistic, etc. Today the *Strong* scales can still be scored for many specific occupations but they can also be scored for basic interest areas such as merchandising, adventure, religious activities, homemaking, etc. Likewise, the newer *Kuder* scales, especially *Forms D* and *DD,* permit scoring for many specific occupations.

Although interest inventories are very useful in certain situations, especially in guidance and counselling, the results obtained by their use can be overgeneralised if certain facts are not kept clearly in mind. In the first place, the inventories are not aptitude tests. Although a similarity-of-interest pattern such as that of persons generally engaged in a given occupation is undoubtedly a desirable attribute for one considering that occupation as his life's work, such resemblance is not a guarantee of success in the occupation. An inventory might reveal a pattern of interests which resembles very closely resembles that of successful engineers, for example, but much more than an interest pattern is needed to achieve success in such work; the same is true of any other profession or occupation. Teacher and counsellors should guard against becoming uncritical, over-enthusiastic users of these instruments; students should not be advised to choose a given occupation solely on the basis of scores on an interest inventory.

In the second place, it should always be kept in mind that interests change, particularly for persons below the age of twenty-five years. When an interest inventory is given in the junior high school, for example, the results should be considered as very tentative and likely to change markedly, perhaps more than once, before the individual "settles down." It is common knowledge that many persons change their goals even after leaving college. The results of an interest inventory should always be regarded as provisional, at least until the individual has attained full maturity.

Finally, it should be recognised that few persons have the breadth of knowledge and experience to make valid choices among such a wide range of activities as these inventories present, and that many such choices must, at best, be based upon questionable or very limited information. Moreover, when the inventories are used with children in junior high schools it seems likely that many of the words in them may pose vocabulary problems. If a pupil does not know the meanings of the words or terms, he certainly cannot make intelligent choices.

In the light of these considerations, the use of interest inventories with subjects below the senior high school level seems questionable. When they are used, it should always be with full cognizance of the limitations and safeguards that have been pointed out. Interest inventories are valuable tools and their use can be recommended particularly for counsellors and guidance workers provided the results are interpreted and used with appropriate caution.

Other Interest Inventories

1. *Brainard Occupational Preference Inventory*. 1945. Grades 8–12 and adults. *Commercial, personal service, agricultural,*

mechanical, professional, aesthetic and *scientific*. One form, $ 3.50 per 25. 30 minutes. Psychological Corporation.

2. *Guilford-Shneidman-Zimmerman Interest Survey.* 1948. Grades 9–16 and adults. *Artistic, linguistic, scientific, mechanical, outdoor, business, social personal office.* One form. $ 4.00 per 25. 50 minutes. Sheridan Supply Company.

3. *Minnesota Vocational Interest Inventory.* 1965. Age 15 to adult. *Twenty-one scales in semi-skilled and skilled occupations.* One form. $ 4.50 or $ 5.50 per 25. 45 minutes. Psychological Corporation.

4. *Occupational Interest Inventory.* 1956. Intermediate, Grade 7 to average adult; Advanced, Grades 9 to adult. *Personal-social, natural, mechanical, business, arts, sciences, verbal, manipulative, computational.* One form, $ 5.25 per 35. 40 minutes. California Test Bureau.

5. *Ohio Vocational Interest Survey.* 1969. Grades 8–12. *Occupational plans, school subject preferences, curriculum plans, post-high school plans and vocational course interests;; 24 scales to measure interests in a broad spectrum of occupations.* One form. $ 20.00 per 35. 60–90 minutes. Harcourt Brace Jovanovich, Inc.

6. *School Interest Inventory.* Grades 7–12. *150 item scale designed to differentiate between stay-ins and drop-outs.* One form. $12.00 per 100. 20 minutes. Houghton Mifflin Company.

7. *Thurstone Interest Schedule.* 1947. High school and college. *Physical science, biological science, computational, business, executive, persuasive, linguistic, humanitarian, artistic, musical.* One form, $ 3.00 per 25. 15 minutes. Psychological Corporation.

The Measurement of Attitudes

Attitudes may be considered one phase of personality. They are closely associated with feelings and emotions, and are a large factor in determining our reactions and behaviour. An attitude may be thought of as a response pattern, or a tendency to think or act in a particular way under a given set of circumstances. Thus, a person has established attitudes towards certain activities, facts, geographical regions, political parties, and towards particular individuals such as the principal of his school, his biology teacher, his classmates, etc. When situations arise in which one or another of these is involved, he tends to react in each case in a certain way. His attitude toward Communists may be strongly antagonistic; toward his principal, neutral; and toward the football coach, strongly favourable. In the first instance, the attitude may be generalised to include all Communists; in the second and third, the attitude is specific with respect to a single individual. In every case, there is likely to be some emotional reaction, however slight.

It has already been pointed out that attitudes condition behaviour. An unfavourable attitude will usually cause a reaction either of avoidance or of aggression; a neutral attitude, indifference; and a favourable attitude, a seeking behaviour. Of course, not all attitudes can be neatly classified as favourable, neutral, or favourable. Attitudes range by degrees from one extreme to the other, and the use of the three terms is merely for convenience.

The Method of Equal-appearing Intervals

The measurement of attitudes is carried out by self-report methods. One method is to present to the subject a list of statements expressing attitudes varying widely from very favourable to neutral to very unfavourable; the subject is asked to check those with which he agrees. This method, known as the method of *equal-appearing intervals,* was devised some years ago by Thurstone and Chave. A large number of statements of attitudes toward something, e.g., the Republican Party, are collected. These statements must vary by fine degrees in the attitudes they express, from extremely favourable to extremely unfavourable. A number of competent judges sort the statements into eleven piles or groups according to the shade or degree of opinion expressed. All statements in one pile are those judged to be expressive of the same attitude. Each pile differs from the adjoining ones above and below by apparently equal intervals or equal differences in attitude. Each judge sorts the statements independently.

Next, the judges together select from each group the two or three statements which they regard as most typical of that group and which express most nearly the same degree of attitude. When these are assembled there are generally twenty-five to thirty statements varying in expressed attitude from very favourable through neutral to extremely unfavourable. Each statement has a scale value according to its position or grouping. Thus, those at the most unfavourable end of the scale may each have a scale value of 11, the neutral ones, 6, and the more favourable ones 5, 4, 3, 2 and 1, in that order. The statements are reproduced in random order and the person whose attitude toward the Republican Party is to be measured is asked to check those statements with which he agrees. His score or attitude is based on the average scale values of those he checks.

To illustrate this type of scale, a few statements from a scale constructed to measure attitudes toward vocational education in secondary schools are given below.

I think that for his own good, every high school student should be required to take one shop course. (2.9)

I think that one course is as good as another. It all depends on what you can do and are interested in. (5.4)

Students in a regular high school should have an opportunity to take vocational courses if they want to. (4.2)

Vocational subjects are taken by many students because they require very little homework and outside study. (8.0)

I think that academic courses should all be elective and that only vocational courses should be required. (1.0)

I see no value to anyone in vocational subjects; they are an absolute waste of time. (10.5)

I think that vocational subjects are usually spoiled by the practice of "dumping" failures from other subjects into them. (7.7)

These statements represent a sampling from some thirty that constituted a scale of attitudes toward vocational subjects in high school. The scale value of each statement is given in the parentheses following it. These values are generally not shown on the scale that is checked by the person taking the test. This scale, one of four devised for use with high school students, was developed by following very closely the procedure of Thurstone.

The Linkert Method

The Likert method of measuring attitudes is somewhat less time-consuming than that just described. It, too, begins with a considerable number of statements of attitude toward something. However, in this case they are either decidedly favourable or decidedly unfavourable. Each statement usually has five possible responses: "SA" ("Strongly Agree"); "A" ("Agree"); "U" ("Undecided"); "D" ("Disagree"); and "SD" ("Strongly Disagree").. The person taking the test reacts to *every* statement by making one of the five possible responses. The responses have weights of 5, 4, 3, 2 and 1 for favourable statements, and 1, 2, 3, 4 and 5 for unfavourable ones. The subject's score is the sum of the weights of the responses he checks. A high score indicates a highly favourable attitude, a low score, the opposite.

The Likert method eliminates the sorting by judges and therefore it requires less time to prepare a scale than the method of equal-appearing intervals. It also uses more statements, as a rule, and the subject is required to check all of them, both of which factors tend to increase not only the reliability of scores but also the time required.

A sample set of statements set up by the Likert method might read as follows:

SA A U D SD All parents today are too strict with their children.

SA A U D SD The old saying, "Children should be seen and not heard," is more applicable today than ever before.

Other methods used for measuring attitudes require the subject to react to pictures, and still another method requires a series of choices from paired alternatives such as "salesman and mechanic," "banker and professor," "owner and operator," etc. However, the two methods that have been described above are probably as good as any developed to the present time. Both give fairly high reliabilities for the type of measurement. Correlations between scores on comparable scales of the two types are reported to be quite high.

One of the chief problems in connection with attitude scales is their validity. As with all self-report instruments, the value of the score is dependent upon the cooperation of the person taking the test. It is very easy for him to simulate an extreme attitude if he wishes to do so, simply by checking all the strong statements one way or the other, or by strongly agreeing or strongly disagreeing with all the statements of one type or another. Generally this is much easier to do in an attitudes scale than in a personality inventory. In the latter the implications of specific statements are not always obvious. Unless the subject is honestly trying to cooperate when he checks the attitudes scale, the results are of little or no value.

In the second place, what a person agrees or disagrees with on paper is not necessarily a reflection of how he really feels or acts. There is no way of determining whether or not the subject is honestly expressing what he believes. Furthermore, what he endorses on the test is one thing, but his actual behaviour in the same or a similar situation may not be consistent with his verbal responses. Some research has been done on this with widely varying findings. Some studies report substantial correlations between scores on an attitude scale and observed behaviour; others report negligible correlations. Corey, for example, found practically no correlation in a college class between scores on a scale of attitude toward cheating and actual behaviour in an examination.

Much of the research suggests that there is a positive correlation in the neighbourhood of .50–60 between scores on attitude scales and actual performance or behaviour. This is not a close relationship, but is does indicate a substantial tendency. The ultimate validity of attitude scores depends on how well they correlate with action. It may be interesting and in some instances useful to know what an individual's verbalised attitudes are, but unless they can be used to predict how he will act, such data are of limited value for practical purposes. In this respect there is still much to be accomplished in the area of attitude measurement.

7

The Measurement of Personality and Adjustment: Observational Techniques

In Chapter 6 various self-report approaches to the measurement of personality and adjustment were presented. In this chapter we shall continue and conclude the discussion of the measurement of personality and adjustment with a consideration of observational techniques. Observational techniques employ information from sources other than the individual being studied. The techniques which will be discussed here are rating scales, systematic observation, anecdotal records and sociometric methods. Each will be described and illustrated. There will also be a brief discussion of the effective use and the particular advantages and disadvantages of each technique.

Rating Scales

The basic purpose of rating devices is to obtain systematically and objectively a sampling of opinion on certain characteristics of a given individual. Such judgments should be obtained from people who are well acquainted with the person being rated and who can express accurate and dependable opinions. In order to obtain satisfactory results it is essential to follow certain well-established and tested procedures. Among other things, it is necessary to define the traits or characteristics on which the ratings will be based, to provide some kind of scale or range by which the rater can indicate his judgment of the amount or degree of the trait, and to give the rater some specific and carefully worked out instructions regarding the purposes and use of the instrument. In addition, it is highly desirable to meet with the persons who are going to do the rating in order to discuss the use of the device with them, and, if possible, to give them some practice in using it. Instruction and information in addition to that which is printed on the scale *must* be given to persons untrained in the use of rating scales if the results are to be valid and reliable.

In constructing a rating scale the first step is to divide the broad area to be analysed into specific traits or characteristics. To ask for ratings in such wide areas as "personality" or "adjustment" would give results that are practically meaningless. Therefore, the concept of "personality" should be broken down into more specific and definable terms such as "persistence," "cheerfulness", "aggressive tendencies", "generosity", or "resourcefulness".

When such an analysis has been made, the next step is to define each of these traits in terms which will be meaningful to the rater and will convey similar meanings to the various persons using the scale. This is a difficult task and, of course, it is never possible to be sure that one has succeeded. However, if the traits are clearly defined in terms of *behaviour,* rather than vague abstractions, it helps materially to insure that those using the scale will have common understandings of the traits being rated.

Finally, the specific traits should be defined in such a way that the definitions provide descriptions of the varying degrees of each trait and lead the rater to make quantitative judgments rather than vague, meaningless generalisations.

The most widely used form of rating device is generally referred to as the *graphic rating scale.* In this form each trait is represented not only by descriptions of varying degrees of the trait but also a line divided into the same number of equal segments as there are trait descriptions. The rater expresses his judgment by placing a check mark on the line to indicate his estimate of the person being rated.

BEC Personality Rating Schedule

An excerpt from a graphic rating scale of personality is shown in Figure 7.1. It clearly illustrates the principles of construction and organisation that have just been discussed.

Fig. 7.1 : Excerpt from *BEC Personality Rating Schedule*

V. Judgment	5	4	3	2	1
1. Sense of Values	Is unfailingly keen of insight in distinguishing the important from the unimportant in classwork	Generally distinguishes the important from the unimportant in classwork even when confusion might be easy	Distinguishes satisfactorily between the important and the unimportant in classwork	Occasionally confuses the important with the unimportant in classwork	Commonly neglects crucial issues in classwork through attention to the unimportant
2. Deliberativeness	Always considers carefull, all aspects of problem situation before proposing solution	Usually considers all important aspects of problem situation before proposing solution	Seldom proposes solution to important problem situation without some preliminary analysis	Sometime proposes solutions to problem situations without any preliminary analysis	Is constantly jumping at conclusions
3. Tact	Extremely gifted in discerning the best thing to do or say when dealing with others; never gives any offense	Usually says or does the suitable thing when dealing with others	Only rarely gives any offense through ill-considered speech or action	Sometimes says or does the wrong thing when dealing with others	Frequently gives offense through lack of discernment in speech or actin
4. Worth of Opinions	His opinion invariably sought by colleagues in deliberative assemblies	His opinion usually valued by colleagues in deliberative assemblies	His views generally accorded a courteous reception	His opinion not generally sought by colleagues	His opinions accorded little esteem in deliberative meetings

This rating scale, or rating schedule, as it is called, provides opportunity for ratings on twenty-nine traits grouped in eight categories: *Mental Alertness, Initiative, Dependability, Cooperativeness, Judgment, Personal Impression, Courtesy* and *Health*. A score may be obtained on each trait and these scores may be averaged within each category or for all twenty-nine traits, if desired.

A check mark placed as shown indicates the rater's appraisal of the person being rated, in this case, between average and somewhat above average. This rating could be given a numerical value of 3.5 if desired.

Michigan Department of Mental Health Rating Scale for Pupil Adjustment

Another rating scale, set up somewhat differently, is the *Michigan Department of Mental Health Rating Scale for Pupil Adjustment*. This provides for letter ratings on eleven characteristics or traits: *Over-all Emotional Adjustment, Social Maturity, Tendency Toward Depression, Tendency Toward Aggressive Behaviour, Extroversion-Introversion, Emotional Security, Motor Control and Stability, Impulsiveness, Emotional Irritability, School Achievement* and *School Conduct*. In addition, there is an opportunity to check physical conditions of the child such as height, weight and physical handicaps and defects. The sample below shows how this scale is set up.

IX. Emotional Irritability

(Definition: Tendency to become angry, irritated, or upset.)

A. Usually good-natured.

B. Good-natured—rarely irritable.

C. Fairly good-natured—occasionally irritable.

D. Moderately irritable—frequently shows *moderate* irritation.

E. Extremely irritable—frequently shows *marked* irritation.

A B C D E

Obviously, this is not a graphic rating scale in the usual sense of the term. There is no line or continuum upon which a check mark can be placed anywhere according to the rater's best judgment. Instead, there are five levels for each trait, and the rater simply checks the one of these which is most appropriate. He cannot signify an in-between rating. In the opinion of some persons this is a disadvantage in that it does not permit as much differentiation as the graphic scale.

A score is obtained on each trait by multiplying *A* ratings by 5, *B*'s by 4, *C*'s by 3, *D*'s by 2 and *E*'s by 1. These products are added to get a total score. The authors state that the best index of *Total Emotional Adjustment* is a score based on a combination of four traits, namely, *Over-all Emotional Adjustment, Social Maturity, Emotional Security* and *Impulsiveness*. It is recommended that this score be used as the adjustment criterion until results of further research on validity are available. Ratings on various combinations of traits may be used to obtain scores in other areas such as *Aggressive Behaviour* or *Inhibitory Control*.

This rating scale is suggested by its authors for use as a screening device. After pupils have been rated by their teachers and the scores have been calculated, a distribution of scores is made. Pupils scoring in the lower third or lower fourth of the distribution may be referred to the proper clinical services for further study and therapy. The proportion suggested for referral will depend on a number of factors such as the quality and availability of clinical services, and the character of the school population with respect to such factors as culture, socio-economic status and geographical area.

Rating scales and devices may be used for purposes other than rating personality and adjustment. For example, they may be used to rate performance on a job, the quality of a product such as a cake or a lampstand made by a pupil, or the quality of handwriting. The use of rating scales for such purposes has already been discussed in a previous chapter.

In closing the discussion of rating scales it may be helpful to present a few suggestions regarding their effective use. We mentioned earlier that it is not safe to assume that anyone can use a rating scale properly and effectively without instruction; indeed, it is generally recognised that some instruction is necessary if the results are to be of value.

Some of the common errors in using rating scales may serve as a starting point in developing suggestions for effective use. A frequent cause of error is the *halo effect,* the tendency of the rater to let his general, over-all impression of the person being rated influence his ratings on every trait. If he likes the subject, he will tend to rate favourably on everything. Contrariwise, a rater's dislike of a subject will tend to colour all his ratings.

Another common error is the tendency to avoid the ends of the scale, that is, to avoid rating persons very high or very low. This is sometimes referred to as the *error of central tendency* and is likely to occur where raters are not well acquainted with the persons being rated. A similar type of tendency is known as the *generosity error,* which refers to the practice of rating everyone average or above. When this happens no one gets a rating below the middle of the scale, a fact which is manifestly unrealistic in most situations since there are usually as many below the average in a given group as there are above.

Another common error is called the *stereotype error,* which means that some raters will have preconceived ideas regarding members of certain groups—racial, religious, economic, or occupational—and will tend to rate them accordingly.

There are other types of errors in using rating scales, but the foregoing are among the most common and serious. The suggestions listed below should help to counteract, if not entirely overcome, such tendencies toward error.

Suggestions for Users of Rating Scales

1. Rate each member of a group in comparison with all the others in his group. If only one person is being rated compare him mentally with others of his same level, class, occupation, etc. Do not rate him on the basis of some ideal that exists only in your imagination, or on the basis of some unrealistic and unattainable standards.

2. Rate each person on one trait before going to the next. For example, if there are thirty-five pupils to be rated on ten traits, rate all thirty-five on Trait 1, then all thirty-five on Trait 2, and so on. This is believed to make ratings more accurate and dependable in that the rater concentrates on one trait at a time and compares each member of the group with all the others on the same trait before considering another trait.

3. Wherever possible use multiple ratings. That is, have several teachers or observers rate the same pupils without consulting each other. Ratings which are made independently by several raters and then considered collectively are much better than single ratings by one individual.

4. In making ratings try to think of the individual's behaviour in as many different situations as possible. Isolated incidents, although they may be very striking, are not always typical of his usual behaviour.

5. Do not rate individuals on traits or categories for which you cannot cite specific evidence or behaviour to support your rating. If you have no basis for making a judgment, *do not rate.* Rather, leave that item unmarked and use "NOTO" (No Opportunity To Observe). A false or inaccurate rating is worse than none at all.

6. If you are responsible for obtaining ratings, give those who are to make them some instruction and assistance. A staff meeting or two could well be devoted to the development and discussion of such points as the five preceding.

Other Rating Scales

1. *KD Proneness Scale.* 1950. Grades 7–12. *Delinquency proneness (truancy record, home background, attitude toward school, club membership, family mobility,* etc.). One form, $ 6.50 per 25. 15 minutes. Western Psychological Services.

2. *Vineland Social Maturity Scale.* 1946. Birthday to maturity. *Self-help, self-direction, occupation, locomotion, communication and socialisation.* One form, $ 2.00 per 25. 30 minutes. American Guidance Service, Inc.

Observation

Although each of the methods described in this chapter involves observation, there is an *observation technique* which has several features that merit individual consideration. The observation technique has been developed primarily in connection with child study. Nursery schools and kindergartens, particularly where these are part of a laboratory or demonstration school, are commonly equipped with one-way-vision screens so that children may be observed without their seeing the observers or knowing that they are being observed. Some efficient and dependable procedures for making and recording such observations have been developed through experience and research, and these procedures will be considered briefly as a means of evaluating behaviour, personality and adjustment.

As in the case of rating scales, one basic principle in observation is to define the behaviour to be observed. It has not been found very useful or satisfactory just to "observe" children. It is much more productive first to define what is going to be observed, and then to concentrate on observation in terms of the definition established. For example, suppose one were interested in making a study of personality traits in a group of four- and five-year-olds. The first step would be to identify and define the traits to be observed—such traits, for example, as cooperative behaviour. What constitutes cooperative behaviour at this age? Probably a dozen or more kinds of behaviour (sharing toys, helping the teacher, picking up, etc.) could be thought of that would be evidence of cooperation among five-year-olds.

When the particular characteristic in question has been analysed and divided into specific acts or behaviour patterns, these elements are listed on a schedule or check list which the observer uses as a means of recording observations. Each time a particular behaviour is observed it is recorded on the check list. In addition cooperative behaviours not listed can be added as they occur.

A second principle is that there should be frequent and distributed observations. This means that it is better to divide the total observation time per child into smaller amounts for frequent observation than to use it all in one or two observations. Assuming, for example, that the observer has two hours of observation time per child, what is the best way to use it? It can be used in one two-hour block, two one-hour periods, and so on, down to 120 one-minute observations. Although no arbitrary, hard-and-fast rule can be given, it is generally agreed that a total of two hours divided into twenty-four five-minute periods would be preferable to longer and less frequent observations. Some investigators would use shorter and more frequent periods than this. In general, expert opinion seems to favour frequent, short observations distributed over a period of several weeks and falling at different times of the day. The chief advantage of such a plan is that it is likely to yield a more adequate sample of a child's behaviour and thus reduce the chances of getting erroneous impressions from a long observation on what might be a very non-typical day. Rotating the time of observation so that the same child is not observed at the same time of day each observation period reduces the probabilities of getting consistently biased samples of behaviour at a particular time of day, such as just before lunch.

It must be recognised, of course, that longer observation periods may be preferable under certain conditions or for certain purposes. This is particularly true where sequence of behaviour is to be studied and where the development from beginning to end of certain behaviour situations is to be observed.

Instead of defining and concentrating the observation on a specific behaviour, one may keep a continuing or running account of the total behaviour of a given child over a period of several days. This procedure, often used by clinicians, has the advantage of giving a more complete picture of the child, though it usually lacks the objectivity of the other method and it does not yield data which can readily be expressed in quantitative terms, such as a count of the number of times the defined behaviour occurred.

Much depends on the training and the skill of the observer. He must be able to observe and record objectively, keep personal bias out of his observations, and distinguish clearly between observation and interpretation. He should record only what happens and do so as promptly as he can so that he does not have to rely too long on memory for important data. It is generally best to concentrate on obtaining a complete and accurate record at the time of observation and to make interpretations of the record later when there is more time for careful study.

An illustration or two of the observation method should serve to make it more definite and meaningful. One of the earliest applications of the *time-sampling* method of observing behaviour in young children was a study reported by Olson in 1929. He observed nervous habits in elementary school children by using five-minute observation periods for each child and recording the incidence of nervous habits (such as nose-picking, twitching, etc.). Although later investigators have improved upon and refined his procedure, Olson's was one of the first to yield quantitative data based on systematic time samples of children's observable behaviour.

Another illustration of the observation technique will show how it can be used for evaluative purposes in the classroom. An experiment was conducted in seventy elementary schools in New York City to compare the effects of "activity programme" with a more conventional type of programme. The methods used to evaluate the results of the experiment included a wide variety of tests, anecdotal records and observations. The observers, after a period of orientation and training, carried out a series of half-hour observations on each class in the experimental and control schools. The observer recorded by use of a code each occurrence of pupil activity which the experiment was designed to encourage. The number of observations varied from six to fourteen per class. When observations were checked by having two observers present at the same time, a substantial amount of agreement (averaging above 85 per cent) was found. The results of the observations showed a distinct superiority for the activity-programme schools in the number and variety of pupil activities. The control classes showed a reliable superiority in recitational behaviour. Here, in contrast with the Olson study, the technique was used for group comparisons.

It should be mentioned before closing this discussion of the observational method that the importance of training and skill in observation can scarcely be overemphasised. People vary greatly in their ability to observe and report accurately what they have seen. It is well known, for example, that witnesses to an accident may give diametrically opposite accounts of what took place. Even under less strained conditions observers in a laboratory or in a theatre may differ in the accuracy of their observations, even though they have witnessed the same circumstances or events.

In research the observers are usually carefully selected on the basis of tests, and they are thoroughly trained. Furthermore, their reports are checked against those of other observers for agreement and consistency. Data gathered under such conditions are likely to be acceptable in validity and reliability. However, there are many situations in which such precautions and safeguards are impractical, even though systematic observations are desirable. Observations must often be made by classroom teachers who are relatively untrained for this work. Not only where educational experiments are being conducted in the schools, but in the daily activities in the classroom, much of our information about pupils and activities is based on observation by teachers. Observation by classroom teachers is generally informal and unsystematic and is carried on without benefit of check lists or planned procedure. Anything that can be done to make teachers more reliable and accurate observers should add to our understanding of children, which in turn should contribute to better adjustment and more wholesome personalities. To become better observers teachers must first of all have a genuine interest in improvement; they must be willing to accept instruction and assistance, and they must be willing to have their observations checked for accuracy and dependability. Perhaps above all, teachers must be able to put aside their personal preferences and dislikes of individual children if their observations are to have any value.

Anecdotal Records

The method discussed in the preceding section is a systematic procedure for gathering observational data and is used more often in research than in everyday classroom situations. A method used more frequently and informally is the *anecdotal record*, which is the teacher's written record of an occurrence or incident involving a child. For example, the following might be typical:

Grade 5—Miss Jones

9/15/70 A new boy, Jimmy Long, came to school this morning. He is large and strong for his age. I heard him telling some of the other boys during recess about his dad, who is a professional baseball player. (He didn't seem to be boasting—just proud of his dad.)

9/18/70 Jimmy, the new boy, got into an argument with Bob about a percentage problem dealing with baseball batting averages. Later, Jimmy hit John with a ruler and John cried. I made Jimmy say he was sorry. (Jimmy may be inclined to bully. Time will tell.)

These are samples of what Miss Jones might record as significant anecdotes concerning a new pupil. They illustrate some of the generally accepted principles of making anecdotal records.

First, it should be noted that the record is in two parts—the incident itself and, in parentheses, Miss Jones's interpretation. This inclusion, but separation, of fact and interpretation is desirable and important if the records are to be maximally useful. When fact and interpretation are mingled it makes the records less objective and more difficult to interpret. Also, different persons may interpret an anecdote differently.

Second, the examples suggest that Miss Jones will keep a continuing record on Jimmy over a period of time and in a variety of situations. By this means she will secure a more complete and accurate picture of Jimmy's personality and will certainly be in a good position to give him help if he needs it.

Third, the samples indicate what Miss Jones considers to be significant aspects of Jimmy's behaviour. There are undoubtedly other occurrences which she might have recorded, but these seemed to her to give the most insight into his personality during the first few days of school.

It is not easy to know what is significant and worth recording. Teachers inevitably have preferences and dislikes among their pupils, often without being fully aware of them, and these biases tend to influence the choice of children about whom anecdotes are recorded, as well as the nature of the anecdotes. It is quite natural, also, to overlook the shy, quiet child and to record anecdotes only on the more aggressive children. The observation that "Ruth sat in her seat and looked out the window while the other children came up to the desk to see the turtle," may be just as significant as the fact that "David brought a live turtle to school today which attracted is great deal of attention to him as well as to the turtle."

A recurring question on the matter of anecdotal records concerns the number of children on whom to keep such records and the number of anecdotes to record. Some authorities advocate that anecdotes should be regularly recorded for all children. Ideally this is certainly desirable, but in most situations it would be impractical for busy teachers. A goal of only one anecdote per week per pupil would mean something like thirty-five or forty per year per pupil. Thus, a teacher with thirty-five pupils in her room would have 35 × 35, or 1,275 anecdotes per year to record, which would be no small task in itself, to say nothing of the time required for the interpretation and use of the anecdotes. In this connection it should be noted that keeping anecdotal records presents quite different problems for elementary and high school teachers. The former usually has about twenty-five to thirty pupils in her room all day every day, which provides ample opportunity to observe significant happenings. The high school teacher, on the other hand, may see 150 pupils every day for only one period each. Observing and recording significant anecdotes in this case is obviously even more difficult.

In most situations it is probably best to begin by keeping records on a few pupils. As the teacher gains some experience and confidence he can undertake the recording of anecdotes on additional pupils. Even with a modest beginning, however, the teacher should take care to avoid the common mistake of keeping records on "problem cases" only. As we have already suggested, the shy, reticent child may be just as much in need of study and help as the one who is always causing trouble. In the beginning, when records are kept on only a few children, it would be well to select the children with a view to including some of the less obvious cases as well as some who demand attention.

Records of anecdotes should be made as soon as possible after the incident has been observed, but never so that pupils are aware that this is being done. Many teachers find it best to make a few notes at the first opportunity and then to make a complete record during free time at noon or after school. Anecdotes should always be recorded on the same day if their occurrence if at all possible, for the longer the time lapse between the occurrence and the recording of it, the less distinct and accurate one's memory of the incident becomes. Anecdotes are probably best recorded on cards. Each anecdote may be recorded on a single small card, or, as is sometimes preferred, several anecdotes may be recorded on one large card. The latter system makes the interpretation of trends or developments a little easier for some teachers. In any case, cards are the most convenient means of record-keeping since they are easy to file, sort, handle and arrange.

To be most useful, anecdotal records on a pupil should be kept over an extended period of time. To obtain a reliable sample of a child's behaviour and to make any useful assessment of changes that may occur, it is essential that an adequate number of anecdotes or observations be made. These principles apply here no less than in the case of systematic observations discussed in the preceding section. It is of little value to record an anecdote or two about an individual and then neglect him for a month. By observing him long enough to see how he functions in a variety of situations from day-to-day it is possible to gain much better insight into his personality and whatever difficulties he may have. The only exception to this principle might be in a school system where anecdotal records are a part of the regular cumulative records kept on all pupils. In such a system it would probably be impossible to record anecdotes frequently and regularly on every child; occasional anecdotes would have to suffice. Nevertheless, the principle still holds that, other factors being equal, the more frequent and regular the anecdotes recorded for a given individual, the more dependable the results will be.

If anecdotal records are to be valuable they must be used, and if they are to be used they must first be interpreted. To interpret the records it is, of course, necessary to study and summarise them. Several anecdotes on a single pupil must be studied and compared. They tell a story, reveal characteristic behaviour, show the individual in his interaction with others in a natural setting. In these respects anecdotal records have certain advantages over other methods such as ratings or systematic observation. However, the task of summarising and interpreting is not an easy one, and it invariably takes much thought and time. Ordinarily, summarising should be done often enough to keep abreast of typical behaviour and developments of the individual, and yet not so frequently that the process will become too much of a chore. Perhaps two or three times per year is often enough under ordinary circumstances. However, in individual cases it may be desirable to summarise and interpret more frequently.

Summarising and interpreting are usually best done by the teacher who has written the anecdotal record, though this may also be done by a committee of two or three teachers, especially in difficult cases. The guidance teacher, counsellor, or the school psychologist may be brought into the picture if needed.

The anecdotal record and summaries should be passed on to successive teachers as the pupil progresses so that each teacher will have the benefit of previous observations and can add to them. By this means a quite complete and valuable "behaviour journal" of a pupil may be built up over a period of years.

It probably goes without saying that anecdotal records should always be related to all the other available information concerning a given child. Information on home conditions, health, ability, success in schoolwork, participation in extra class activities, etc., should be considered along with the anecdotal records, and the whole taken into account in any interpretations that are made.

One factor which often causes difficulty in maintaining a system of anecdotal records is the clerical work involved. Reference was made earlier to the time involved in recording even one anecdote per pupil per week. Where a schoolwide programme involving hundreds of children is maintained, the total amount of time and labour can grow to large proportions. Nevertheless, some programmes of this nature have been tried and found feasible. In one school system six teachers in Grades 4 to 7 recorded anecdotes for three months on every pupil. During this time an extensive testing programme was carried out with the same pupils. At the end of the three months the anecdotal records were compared with test results to determine how well the two types of data agreed. Although the findings are two extensive to cite in detail here, it was found that teachers could keep such records without too much difficulty and that they were able to judge the social relations of their pupils accurately by comparing anecdotal records with test results. Among the most significant conclusions were: (1) The success of anecdotal records depends in large measure on the outlook of the teachers. Those having a formal, academic viewpoint will probably find little use for anecdotal records, and those they write will be of little value. (2) Unless the child has opportunity for many varied experiences it is probable that little useful information about that child will be found in anecdotal records. (3) Classes enrolling from seventeen to twenty-eight pupils show no appreciable difference in the number of anecdotes recorded.

The results of this study are encouraging. They suggest that keeping anecdotal records, at least in the elementary grades, is not an inhuman task, that teachers who are interested in studying problems of pupil adjustment can do it, and that the results seem to bear significant relationships to other measures of personality and adjustment.

Sociometric Methods

The last of the observational methods to be discussed are those known as *sociometric,* sometimes referred to as *interpersonal,* methods. The instrument usually associated with these is called a *sociogram.* It is a pictorial or graphic representation of relationships of a specified nature among members of a group, and is based on information gathered from members of the group. Thus it differs from other observational methods discussed in this chapter in that the data are collected about individuals from their peers, rather than from teachers or other observers.

The use of sociometric techniques probably dates from the work of Jacob L. Moreno, first published in 1934. Much study has been made of the sociogram during the last forty years, and it has been widely used in schools. The sociogram has proved valuable when properly used, but it has definite limitations and some dangers in the hands of those not adequately prepared.

A sociogram is generally based upon the written answers to a question put to members of a group. For example, a fifth-grade group might be told that they were about to begin work on a certain project and that they were to be grouped for this into committees of three. They might then be asked to list the names of two pupils with whom they would like to work as a committee. Or, they might be asked to indicate a first choice and a second choice.

It may sometimes be desirable to ask for more than two choices, a third and perhaps even a fourth, depending on the purposes of inquiry. If only a tabulation of the responses is to be made, recording more than two choices presents no great problem. However, the construction of a sociogram involving three or four choices becomes quite complicated and its interpretation correspondingly difficult. Moreover, as the size of the group increases the complexities also increase. It is suggested, therefore, that unless the situation actually demands more than two choices, and especially with persons inexperienced in sociometric techniques, most purposes can be adequately achieved with two.

Members of a group may also be asked to name "rejects", that is, one or more with whom they would rather not work, play, sit, etc. There is some disagreement with respect to the desirability of this procedure and there are arguments on both sides of the question. We tend not to favour the inclusion. For one thing, it seems to emphasise negative feelings, which would appear to have some undesirable aspects. Furthermore, rejection is surely implied in the case of individuals who are not chosen at all or chosen by hardly anyone. The possibility of such interpretations seems sufficient in almost all situations, excepting possibly those in which it is necessary to identify an object of genuine hostility.

Once the data have been collected, the next step is to tabulate them in a form that is useful. There are two methods commonly employed, the table and the sociogram. Either or both may be used with a given set of data. An illustration will help to make this clear. Suppose a fifth-grade teacher has asked seventeen pupils to nominate their first and second choices of members of the class to work with on a certain project. The responses of the pupils may be tabulated as shown below:

Table 7.1

Chooser	*First Choice*	*Second Choice*
Ken	Guy	Fran
Jack	Kevin	Len
Helen	Fran	Kathy
Ted	Mike	Kevin
Fred	Ken	Karl
Fran	Jane	Milly
Jean	Kathy	Kevin
Sally	Milly	Jane
Jessie	Helen	Fran
Karl	Fran	Ken
Mike	Jean	Kevin
Len	Fran	Ken
Guy	Karl	Ken
Milly	Fran	Jane
Kathy	Helen	Jean
Jane	Sally	Fran
Kevin	Ted	Jean

These choices may be organised into a chart somewhat like the one shown in Figure 7.2. Here each pupil's first choice is indicated by a *1* under the name of the pupil chosen, and the second choice by a *2*.

	Ken	Jack	Helen	Ted	Fred	Fran	Jean	Sally	Jessie	Karl	Mike	Len	Guy	Milly	Kathy	Jane	Kevin
Ken						2							1*				
Jack												2					1
Helen						1									2*		
Ted											1						2*
Fred	1									2							
Fran														2*		1*	
Jean															1*		2*
Sally														1		2*	
Jessie			1			2											
Karl	2					1											
Mike							1										2
Len	2					1											
Guy	2*									1							
Milly						1*										2	
Kathy			1*				2*										
Jane						2*		1*									
Kevin				1*			2*										
First choice	1		2	1		4	1	1		1	1		1	1	1	1	1
Second choice	3					3	2			1		1		1	1	2	3

Fig. 7.2 : Pupils' Choices of Class Member to Work on Project.

The number of times each pupil is chosen as a first choice and as a second choice is shown at the bottom. Those not chosen at all have no numbers in the columns under their names. Mutual choices are indicated by an asterisk. For example, Guy is Ken's first choice, and Ken is Guy's second choice.

A better way of showing the relationships in this group is by the sociogram shown in Figure 7.3.

There are several methods of constructing such a chart, but to discuss these in detail is beyond the scope of this book. One of the easiest and most practical methods is described in a publication dealing explicitly with this matter, and any teacher or counsellor can learn the method with a little study and practice.

A conventional terminology has come to be used in interpreting a sociogram, which may be illustrated by reference to Figure.7.3.

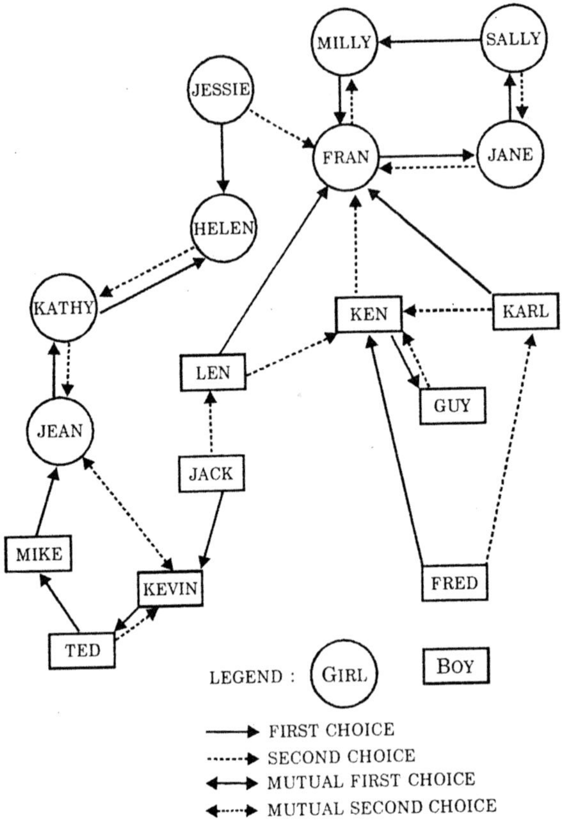

Fig. 7.3 : Sociogram Showing First and Second Choices of Seventeen Fifth-grade Pupils.

A "star" is an individual who is chosen by many. Fran is an example; so are Kevin and Ken. A "chain" is a sequence of choices in a line, none of whom is chosen by many; an example here is the Jessie-Helen-Kathy-Jean-Mike-Ted alignment. They are marginal and not actually members of a group. An "isolate" is one not chosen; examples are Jack, Jessie and Fred. The term "island" refers to a small, more or less self-contained, group or clique; an example is Milly, Sally, Fran and Jane; another is Ken, Karl, Guy and Fred. Such cliques are often the cause of concern to the teacher and may have an undesirable effect on the relations of the group as a whole.

In studying Figure 7.3 some other facts about the relationships become apparent. For one, there seems to be a distinct tendency for boys to choose boys and girls to choose girls. No boy is a girl's first choice, and only two girls are named as first choices by three boys. Perhaps at fifth-grade level this would not be unusual. However, one might expect the trend to be in the opposite direction, namely, more girls choosing boys than boys choosing girls in view of the greater maturity of girls at this age. Again, the sociogram reveals what appears to be some tendency for the class to split into two parts. The link between the right-hand group and that on the left seems to be Fran, who apparently is extremely popular with most of the class; the only other link between the two is the choice of Ken (another star) by Len.

So far, we have dealt with methods of collecting sociometric data and ways of tabulating and summarising them. Perhaps a more important question concerns the purposes for which the results may be used. A further question concerns the advantages and disadvantages of a sociogram.

It may be said that a sociogram is probably the best instrument yet devised to reveal the social structure of a group. It shows interrelationships among individuals and relationships of each individual to the entire group. It provides a teacher or group leader with information that will help him to understand the behaviour of the group and function more effectively in working with that group. There are many relationships and sub-groups within any class or group which are not apparent on the surface.

It is important that appropriate action be taken soon after the sociogram has been completed and examined. If the teacher has asked pupils to tell with whom they would like to work, groupings should be formed on the basis of what the children have requested, as far as that is possible. The effect on pupils of carrying through is very wholesome. It goes without saying that not to do so has the opposite effect, and that pupils will lose interest in sociograms if they come to believe that nothing happens as a result of their expressions of preference.

The booklet mentioned earlier suggests the following uses of a sociogram:

1. To identify mutual choices, stars, isolates, chains, islands and triangles or circles.
2. Studying race or nationality in relation to group structure. In this case racial groups may be coded by use of different shaped figures (as was done for sex in Figure 7.3).
3. Studying age or maturity in relation to group structure.
4. Studying the relation of total group structure to out-of-school groupings, such as scouts, sororities, etc.
5. Studying the effect of certain experiences. In this case there should be a sociogram "before and after". Thus it may be used to study the effect of various methods of choosing committees on the structure of the group.

In the same publication some limitations of sociograms are mentioned. First, it is pointed out that sociograms are only as valid as the rapport between teacher and pupils will permit. Pupils must sign responses if the results are to be most useful, and if there is resistance to doing this or to answering the questions the responses are not likely to be worth much.

Second, it is pointed out that since group structure, especially among younger children, is quite fluid, the reliability of a single sociogram may not be very high.

Third, the way in which the data are gathered may force responses which are misleading. For example, the sociogram does not reveal differences between strong and weak feelings, or even hostility The point is made that to require three choices may force the nomination of someone for whom there is really no feeling of attraction and for whom there is perhaps even a feeling of dislike.

Fourth, it is important to remember that a sociogram merely reveals conditions; it does not give answers or solutions. A teacher may decide that acceptance of an isolate by other members of a group must be brought about by authority, if necessary. Measures taken to accomplish this, even though subtle, may result in stronger feelings of rejection instead of larger acceptance. The solution or amelioration of conditions revealed by a sociogram depends upon the use of other techniques such as anecdotal records, interviews with individual children and further careful study of the total situation. Perhaps the status of sociograms is best summed up by this quotation from the same bulletin.

Once a sociogram has been plotted, it is a beginning not an end. It raises questions rather than answers them. Perhaps its greatest value is that it directs the attention to certain aspects of group structure which will lead to further observation of individual and group behaviour. To data, we have few, if any, generalisations which can be applied in the interpretation of sociograms, although we are beginning to find certain tentative hypotheses. We are in great need of carefully reported anecdotes of group behaviour recorded by teachers who are sensitive to problems of group behaviour. If the making of sociograms encourages such observation and recording, they shall have fulfilled an important function.

8

The Measurement Programme

What is a Measurement Programme

Large-scale or national testing programmes are quite generally referred to as "external testing programmes" because they are directed and administered by agencies outside the local school authorities. Among the most prominent of such programmes are those of the College Entrance Examination Board, the National Merit Scholarship Qualifying Examinations, the American College Testing Programme and the Statewide Testing Programmes.

The type of measurement or testing programme with which we are concerned in this chapter is the locally initiated and directed, systematic use of tests to meet local needs, solve local problems, and contribute to the attainment of local educational goals. If such a programme serves wider purposes, so much the better, but its focus is basically on meeting the needs of a particular school or school system.

Without the support and cooperation of teachers and counsellors, the results of a measurement programme can scarcely be utilised to the fullest extent. When some action is to be taken as a result of the programme, whether it is grouping, counselling, remedial work, or some other, teachers and counsellors may defeat the very purposes for which the testing was done by not cooperating in the programme. If the programme has been "dictated" by authorities rather than carried out with their advice and cooperation, it is possible that those involved will not respond wholeheartedly. Unfortunately, administrators, though fully aware of this fact, do not always take the trouble and time to secure the support of their staffs. The result is that the programmes sometimes fall far short of attaining their maximum usefulness, or fail entirely.

On the other hand, it must be recognised that it is not always easy to stimulate the active cooperation and interest of teachers in the systematic use of measuring instruments. Some teachers resent the interruption it may cause in their usual routine, some do not appreciate the extra demands on their time and energy, and a few are prejudiced against "outside" tests of any kind. They do not like the idea of having their pupils examined by any means other than those which they themselves have devised. Where such attitudes exist, they must be changed before a measurement programme can be carried on with any reasonable assurance of cooperation and success. It may take some time to accomplish this, yet there are a number of ways of creating more favourable attitudes: selected teachers can be sent to summer school to take courses in measurement, professional libraries can be built up, and teachers can be urged to participate in workshops and institutes dealing with problems of measurement and evaluation. In-service training programmes may also focus attention on measurement as a means of facilitating curriculum revision and improving instruction.

A measurement programme of any consequence is always undertaken with the cooperation and responsibility of more than one person. The programme may involve only classroom teachers and their supervisors or principals, or the work may be planned and carried out with the cooperation of the entire staff of a school or school system. In the latter case it is customary to entrust most of the actual direction to one qualified person or to a representative committee. As we have said, it is almost axiomatic that unless a measurement programme has the active cooperation and support of all concerned it cannot achieve its maximum usefulness. When a measurement programme is carried out to meet needs or to solve problems which the teachers themselves regard as important, and when those teachers participate actively in planning and carrying out the programme, it will have a good chance of succeeding. It is also helpful to have parents understand the reasons for measurement so that they too will support the programme. If parents can see that the results of measurement help to bring about better learning and adjustment on the part of their children, their confidence in the usefulness of measurement and their faith in the school will be increased.

Planning a Measurement Programme

Purposes

A measurement programme will be successful to the extent that it accomplishes the purposes for which it is designed and carried out. Therefore, it must be planned in accordance with those purposes. This is a matter for cooperative endeavour by all concerned. Although many teachers are not well acquainted with standardised tests and techniques of measurement and appraisal, most will know what the educational problems are, and they will know of many situations in which measurement may be helpful. School psychologists, counsellors, directors of research, and other personnel with more specialised training can usually supply the leadership, the technical knowledge, and the skills needed for setting up a measurement programme.

Whereas in a smaller school or community the planning of a measurement programme may be undertaken by the entire staff, such a procedure will generally be too cumbersome or unwieldy in a larger system. In the latter case it is generally better to have a committee made up of representatives of various groups, grade levels, schools, or districts to assume responsibility for planning and carrying out the programme. This is not to say that the entire staff loses contact with the programme. On the contrary, general teachers' meetings from time to time may be devoted to overall planning, progress reports, discussions and implementation of results. Furthermore, occasional reports to the community may be used as a means of improving relations between the schools and the parents.

Listed below are some of the major purposes for which a measurement programme may be carried on. A more extensive discussion of each of these purposes, together with practical suggestions on using test results, will be found in the next chapter.

Purposes of Measurement Programmes

1. Placement and promotion
2. Homogeneous grouping
3. Diagnosis and remedial work

4. Counselling and guidance
5. Marking
6. Curriculum evaluation
7. Motivation
8. Identification and study of exceptional children
9. Interpreting schools to the community
10. Improvement of school staff
11. Educational research

The above list is based on various studies and reports of the use of measurement in schools, and, while not exhaustive, it probably includes most of the common purposes for which educational measurement is used.

Time of Year for Testing

When the purposes of the measurement programme have been decided, several other considerations immediately come to the fore. One of these is the time of year for giving the tests. Often this matter resolves itself into a choice between giving the tests at the beginning of the school year or near the end. The decision on timing will usually depend on the purposes for which the tests are intended. For example, diagnostic testing and testing for purposes of grouping or grade placement will most profitably come early in the school year, while testing for purposes of promotion, educational counselling, marking, and comparison of achievement with norms will usually occur near the end of the term or year. On the other hand, some of the purposes for which measurement programmes are carried on are unrelated to the time of year. (See above list.)

Frequency and Grade Levels of Testing

Questions which must be decided upon early are the frequency of the testing and the grade levels at which particular tests are to be given. In part, these matters are determined by the purposes for which the testing is intended. For example, if tests are to be given for counselling purposes there will generally be less emphasis on and less need for testing below the secondary level. On the other hand, diagnostic testing in arithmetic or reading will almost certainly be started in the earlier grades of the elementary school.

The frequency of testing also depends on the purposes, but it is further affected by such considerations as the kinds of measuring instruments being used and the amount of money and time available for the work required. Many a measurement programme, undertaken with enthusiasm and high hopes, has failed because those responsible greatly underestimated the expense, the time, and the effort necessary to carry it through. The initial cost of standardised tests is frequently the smallest item of expense; getting the tests properly administered, scored, and interpreted requires much time and effort. *It is far better to undertake a modest programme and complete the work required to put the results to effective use than to try to carry on a more extensive and ambitious programme, only to have it bog down.*

A Minimum School- or Community-wide Measurement Programme

No programme can be prescribed which will fit every situation. Nevertheless, some suggestions will be made to help the prospective teacher, counsellor, or administrator set up a kind of priority list for the planning of a testing programme.

If only one type of test is to be given, at least as a beginning, the first choice should almost certainly be a group intelligence test. If no standardised tests have been used before, it is desirable to give a group intelligence test to every pupil. Since the I.Q. based upon one group test is not completely reliable, any cases which raise questions or present discrepancies with other known facts about an individual should be tested as soon as possible with *another form of the same test.* This point is important because two forms of the same test will give results which are directly comparable, whereas I.Q.'s obtained through the use of two different tests must be equated by standard scores or similar derived scores before they can be directly compared.

The recommendation of a test of intelligence as the essential minimum is based on several considerations. In the first place, the I.Q. of a pupil cannot be accurately determined without such a test, whereas a teacher can determine a pupil's educational achievement with tests of his own devising. In the second place, for educational purposes this information about a pupil is probably the most useful and important that we can learn. The I.Q. gives more accurate insight into his work, achievement, and general mental ability than any other single fact about him can provide.

If testing is to be done at regular intervals after the first year in which a measurement programme is started, it would be advisable to give intelligence tests in the second grade and again in the fourth grade; they should be given again in the sixth grade if there is a junior high school, or in the eighth grade if the system is organised on the 8–4 plan; and again in the tenth grade. The results of these measurements should always be made a part of the cumulative record which accompanies the pupil as he progresses through the elementary and secondary grades.

If more than one type of test can be given, and the results put to use, a reading readiness test should be administered at the end of the kindergarten year or early in the first grade, an achievement battery in the third or fourth, and sixth or seventh grades, and an interest test or inventory in the ninth and twelfth grades. These tests will supplement the results of the intelligence tests at critical points in the pupil's school career in ways which are most useful and appropriate at those points.

The use of other types of tests, such as diagnostic, personality, aptitude, reading, and those in specific school subjects should be undertaken where necessary, with a view to the available resources of the school and to the other factors peculiar to each situation. In every case, the purposes of the measurement programme should be the dominating factor in determining its nature and extent.

A tabulation of a recommended minimum school- or community-wide annual testing programme is given here:

Grade Level	Type of Test
K or I	Readiness
2	Intelligence
3 or 4	Intelligence
3 or 4	Achievement Battery (including reading)
6 or 8	Intelligence
6 or 7	Achievement Battery (including reading)

9	Interests
10	Intelligence
12	Interests

This programme amounts to nine separate tests given annually at various levels throughout the usual grades of the elementary and high schools. An achievement battery may also be given in the eleventh grade if time and resources permit, although separate subject-matter tests may be preferred for various reasons. Where two tests are recommended for use in either of two grades, it probably would be best, other things being equal, to distribute the burden by giving one test in each grade instead of giving both tests at the same grade level. This is particularly desirable where the scoring is done by teachers, and it also requires less of the pupils' time for such testing in any given grade.

Such a programme should not be undertaken lightly. It will require much time and work, although the results should be worth the effort many times over. The cost may safely be reckoned on an average of thirty cents per pupil annually, provided that scoring the tests and tabulating and interpreting the results will not necessitate additional expenditures, and provided that most test blanks can be used over and over again with separate answer sheets.

Larger school systems often carry on testing programmes far more extensive than the one outlined. With a central staff organised for such work, and ample financial support, a great deal more can be done. However, the above plan will provide a good foundation, and it represents the type of programme that most schools with limited funds for measurement can carry.

It will take three or four years under this plan for every pupil to be reached unless a group intelligence test is given to every pupil the first year. If a school-wide test is given the first year of the programme, there will be information available on every pupil as soon as the tests can be given and scored, and this will be a real advantage to teachers. The regular programme may be launched the second year. Even if the school-wide intelligence test is not given the first year, there will still be test results available at four important levels of the child's progress through the school. This will be a useful beginning and will help to introduce the programme gradually so that those responsible will more easily be able to absorb the load.

Selecting and Obtaining the Tests

Selecting the Tests

In planning a measurement programme one should use the best available instruments for it. The criteria of *validity, reliability, objectivity, ease of administration, scoring* and *interpretation,* availability of *equivalent forms, adequate norms* and *economy* provide a sound basis for appraising any measuring instrument, although, as has been mentioned, all of these criteria do not necessarily apply to every type of instrument.

In addition to the criteria mentioned above, a number of less tangible considerations usually influence the selection of instruments. In the case of standardised tests, for example, the deciding factor may be simply a general impression of the whole test. If those responsible for the selection like an instrument, if it seems to measure objectives which are important, and if they think it is suitable for their situation, that test or instrument will often be chosen in preference to one that meets the technical criteria more adequately. Probably the best that can be hoped for is an objective choice based on careful consideration of *all available information* about the test and the situation in which it is to be used.

In a measurement programme the task of selecting tests may be delegated to a committee. Sometimes the tests are selected by a member of the supervisory or administrative staff and occasionally by the director of research or by the counselling staff. However, if the programme is to be of the type outlined above for all-around basic purposes, the tests should be selected by a committee on which teaching, counselling, research, supervisory and administrative personnel all have representation.

This committee should have full responsibility and authority to obtain, examine, select and purchase the tests in the quantities needed. It should also have the authority and the initiative to encourage local groups to develop measuring devices for local needs where commercially available instruments are not adequate. The committee should feel free to consult with experts and with any school personnel in making its choices, yet its decisions should be final and should be accepted as such by all concerned. That is, as long as all elements of the school staff have representation on the committee, and as long as the committee makes a thorough study of available instruments in relation to the purposes of the programme, its choices should not be subject to veto by administrative authorities or other groups except in the most extraordinary circumstances. If the committee responsible for the over-all programme is a large one, smaller sub-committees may be appointed to look after various phases of the programme. The selection of tests might well be done by such a sub-committee.

Obtaining the Tests

It is common practice for test publishers to put up tests in packages of twenty-five or thirty-five. Each package contains the specified number of copies of the test, a manual of directions, a scoring key, a class record sheet, and any other materials necessary for proper use of the tests, except answer sheets, which are sold separately. Test publishers, as a rule, will not break packages of tests; in ordering, therefore, it is advisable to request a number which can be shipped in unbroken packages. For example, if tests are needed for 170 pupils, one would ordinarily order 175 (seven packages of twenty-five each or five packages of thirty-five each). The same is true of answer sheets. Prices are usually quoted for quantities of twenty-five or more.

Of course, the above applies only to paper-and-pencil tests. If the programme involves the use of other types of materials such as sets of pictures, toys, nuts and bolts, phonograph records, etc., such equipment will usually have to be bought in single complete sets. Such material is not consumable, and the same instruments therefore may be used repeatedly.

Handling the Tests Prior to Administration

The committee or person responsible should take charge of all measurement materials when they are received and keep them in a safe place until they are to be used. The assumption in the use of a standardised test is that everyone who takes it has an equal chance and that no one has an unfair advantage. Although classroom teachers are usually most scrupulous in such matters, their enthusiasm and eagerness to see pupils do well will sometimes lead them to give assistance which they should not give.

The story is told about a high school principal and the teacher of mathematics who had agreed that a certain test should be given in the plane geometry classes. The tests were ordered, received, and turned over to the teacher for safe-keeping until the time set for the testing. A few days before the tests were to be given, the principal dropped into the room to speak to the mathematics teacher, and he was surprised to find several problems from the test copied on the board, and the teacher discussing these problems with his pupils. After the class had been dismissed, the principal asked the teacher to explain. The teacher replied, "I was so anxious to see what they would do with the problems that I couldn't wait. I just had to try them out on a few." While this teacher's enthusiasm and interest were highly commendable, it is clear that his understanding of the purposes and use of standardised tests left much to be desired.

Answer Sheets

The use of printed answer media has developed greatly in recent years, as have techniques and services for scoring them. Several different types of answer sheets and answer cards are commercially available, and the organisations that produce them usually also offer a scoring service. The most advanced of these, using electronic equipment, not only score the answer sheets but also provide distributions of scores and part scores, intercorrelations between scores, percentile and standard score equivalents, and almost any type of analysis desired. For larger systems or large-scale testing programmes such services are both efficient and economical.

Some type of separate answer sheet is now available with nearly all standardised tests for Grade 4 and higher. For testing in grades below this level it is still customary to have answers written or printed by the children in the test booklets. Research has shown that separate answer media may be used safely beginning at about the fourth- or fifth-grade level. Although marking answers in test booklets adds to the expense of testing since the booklets cannot be used again, this practice has certain advantages. First, of course, is the removal of the possibility of confusion on the part of the children taking the test if a separate answer sheet is used. Probably of equal importance is the value to the teacher, who scores the papers, of seeing which items each child answers correctly or misses. Teachers often feel that this type of information is the most valuable result achieved by testing.

A facsimile of one of the most widely-used types of answer sheets is shown in Figure 8.1. This form, known as IBM 805, though designed primarily for use with multiple-choice items, may also be used with true-false items by using only the first two spaces—1 for true and 2 for false. It may also be used for the 3×5 type of matching item. It may be scored by hand with a punched overlay stencil or by machine.

Ethics

A word on the ethics of using standardised tests may be appropriate at this point. In the first place, it must be recognised that published standardised tests are copyright material. No part of such tests may be copied, duplicated, or reproduced in *any form* without written permission from the holder of the copyright. To do so is to violate copyright law. Aside from the legal aspects, there is a moral obligation which is equally great. Authors and publishers of standardised tests must expend large amounts of time, professional competence, and money in producing these tests. A single test may have involved the work of several persons for three to five years, as well as the cooperation of dozens of other people and the expenditure of thousands of dollars. Except for the professional recognition accorded the authors and, to some extent, the publishers, the only recompense they receive is a small profit from the sale of tests and answer sheets. Therefore, to reproduce such tests or accompanying materials or parts thereof without express permission is not only unlawful, but also unethical since it deprives those who have produced the tests of their rightful compensation.

Another aspect of the ethics of using standardised tests has already been touched upon obliquely in the anecdote about the mathematics teacher and the principal, but it will bear amplification here. The continued use of standardised tests of intelligence and achievement requires that their nature and content be kept confidential until the tests are administered. Obviously, if persons who are to be tested have prior knowledge of the contents of a test, standardised or otherwise, the results are invalidated. Such prior knowledge is even more undesirable

Fig. 8.1 : Portion of the IBM 805 Answer Sheet

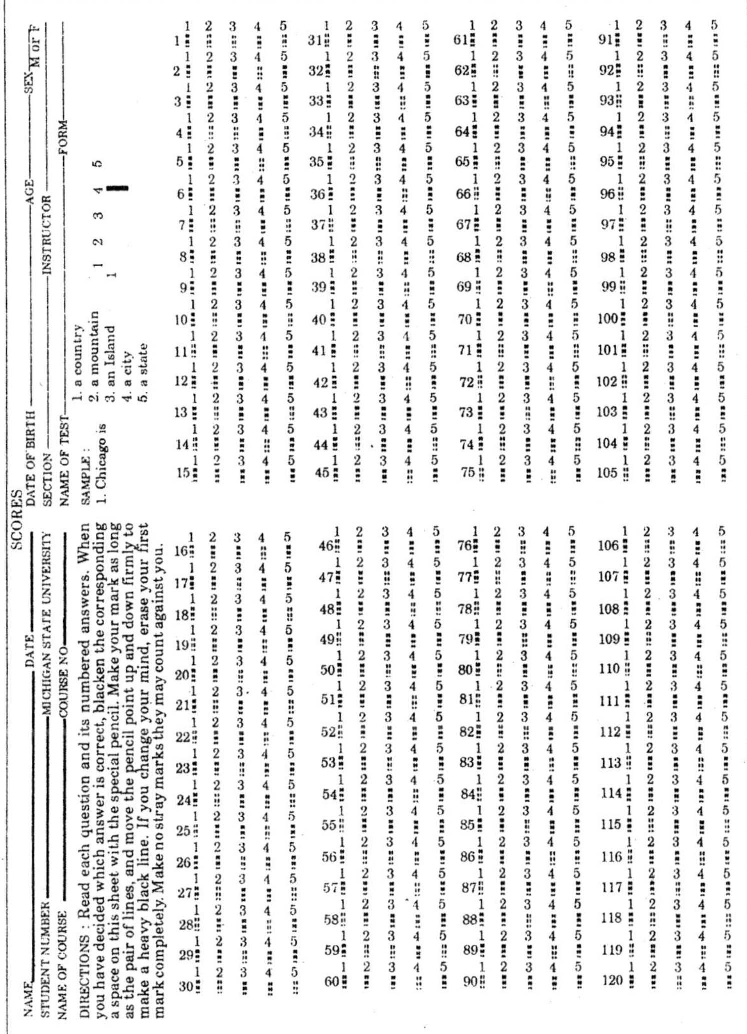

if some individuals have it but not all. In either case, the results are meaningless and no comparison with norms is possible. The continued use of standardised tests with meaningful, dependable results requires that the content must not be passed along from one person who has seen the test to another who has not. Consequently, it is axiomatic that tests should be safeguarded by their users as confidential material if their use *as tests* is to be continued.

The only possible exception to this principle is the standardised diagnostic test. With this type of instrument it may be permissible under certain circumstances to go over the test with the individual pupil so that he can see his errors, but even here it is usually possible to accomplish the same objective in other ways. The manual of directions for such tests contains specific instructions regarding how the results of a diagnostic test may be used most effectively in remedial work. If the user adheres to these directions and suggestions he will usually be successful *and* ethical.

If pupils are permitted to go over their diagnostic test papers for the purposes mentioned above, the teacher should always make sure beforehand that two or more equivalent forms of the test are available. Then, if retesting is to be done, a different form can be used, thus minimising the effect of familiarity with specific details of the form first used. What we have said about achievement tests applies with even greater force to tests of intelligence and personality, and to evaluative devices such as ratings, sociograms and anecdotal records. The results of these as well as the original instruments are to be held in strict confidence and should be accessible only to authorised school personnel. These principles of usage may seem strict, especially to the inexperienced student and user of standardised tests, but they are not unduly so. Psychologists and educators involved in the production and proper use of measuring instruments are genuinely concerned with this problem and have published a code of ethics which includes recommendations for the proper use of psychological tests.

Nothing said above should be interpreted to mean that teachers themselves should not analyse the results of standardised achievement tests to identify strengths and weaknesses of pupils. On the contrary, this is one of the most important uses to which test results can be put. A teacher may thus determine which objectives or outcomes of instruction have been achieved to a satisfactory degree and by which pupils. Also, he can identify weaknesses both of individual pupils and of the class as a whole, and proceed to remedy such weaknesses. More will be said about this matter in Chapter 9.

Scheduling the Tests

Day of Week and Time of Day for Testing

Considerations relating to the time of year for testing have already been mentioned. It is also necessary to decide when each test is to be given, particularly if a school-wide or community-wide programme is planned. This involves a decision on the day of the week and the time of day for testing. It is usually best to have the tests administered to all pupils at the same time, for such a plan causes less disruption of the school programme and has the added advantage that pupils' discussion of the tests will not work to the benefit of some and to the disadvantage of others. It also reduces or eliminates entirely the period of worry and dread which some children inevitably suffer if they known in advance that they are to take some tests.

With regard to the matter of pupil concern about forthcoming tests, it has been the writer's experience that it is best to give standardised tests without any previous announcement to pupils. This eliminates all fear in advance of the testing, it eliminates hasty "cramming", and pressures on the teacher for hints on the nature of the tests. Nothing may be gained by announcing such tests in advance, and much suffering and annoyance may result for both pupils and parents. On the other hand, it is quite possible that in some situations a careful discussion with pupils about the importance of tests and the value of results obtained to all concerned is preferable to "springing" the tests unannounced. In such instances it should be emphasised that "cramming" is largely useless and that the pupils have nothing to fear from taking the tests.

It is probably best to give the tests in the morning because pupils are likely to feel more alert then than later in the day. There is a psychological advantage, if not an actual, measurable difference in performance, in this. It is also desirable, generally speaking, to give tests near the middle of the week. Monday is often "blue Monday", and Fridays are likely to be crowded with activities of more compelling interest. While none of these factors may have a demonstrable effect on test performance, they may all have some effect on the state of mind of pupils, their attitudes toward the programme, and their concentration. A favourable attitude toward the testing is advantageous to the teacher and to the pupil. Ideally, the pupil should feel that he has been able to do his best on the test.

Since absentees create additional problems it is well to give the tests when absences are likely to be at a minimum. If the tests require more than one sitting, it may be necessary to spread the testing over a period of several days. Some achievement batteries require several hours of testing time, which will require several sittings, especially for younger pupils. If there are large numbers to be tested it is probably best to arrange a schedule of sessions to which every class or group will adhere. If a small number of pupils are involved—perhaps one or two classes—the schedule can be arranged to suit the convenience of those concerned.

Ordinarily, it is desirable to plan a schedule for the administration of tests in a testing programme. This increases the efficiency of the programme and helps to avoid the intrusion of personal preferences of the individual teachers. When the time for giving tests is left to the choice of the individual teacher, it is advantageous to require that the testing be completed within a specified number of days. Otherwise, there may be delays and postponements which will hold up the entire programme.

Place of Testing

The choice of the place for testing will depend on circumstances. With younger pupils it is generally best to administer the tests to the pupils in their usual surroundings, if they provide proper conditions for testing. It is also better, if possible, to test very young pupils in small groups of fifteen or less. With older pupils location is probably not so important. Testing pupils in their own homerooms eliminates the problem of working out a room-assignment schedule and considerably simplifies this aspect of the work. On the other hand, if large numbers are to be tested, it is more efficient to test as many pupils at one time as facilities will permit. It is obviously more efficient to test two hundred pupils at once than to test five groups of forty separately. The number that can be tested properly at one time is limited by the facilities available and by the organisational ability of those in charge. With the necessary facilities and assistance, one thousand pupils can be tested just as easily as one hundred or fewer.

The place of testing should provide conditions and facilities necessary to the correct and most satisfactory administration of the test. In part, the choice of location will depend upon the factors of accessibility and availability.

Administering the Tests

It is essential that standardised tests be given exactly according to directions, which may be long and complicated. No one should expect to be able to pick up a manual just before the test is to begin, and, without previous experience and study, step into the job with complete assurance. Time and study are a necessary part of the preparation for giving a standardised test, even for the experienced examiner. The inexperienced examiner may profitably have a more experienced person help him review instructions and procedure beforehand.

If a considerable amount of testing is to be done, the best plan may be to have all of the administration handled by only a few people. They can be given fairly intensive training by the person best fitted to do it—the school psychologist, research director, counsellor or other qualified person. This small group of specially trained teachers can then administer all the tests. Such a plan is almost sure to increase accuracy, uniformity and efficiency.

With very young pupils it is sometimes preferable to have the testing done by their own teacher, for children frequently will be more at ease and will respond better with someone they know and like than with a stranger. However, when teachers administer tests to their own pupils it is important that the testing be done objectively and that the instructions for administering the tests be adhered to.

Qualities of a Good Examiner

Most teachers and counsellors can learn to administer standardised tests successfully, yet a few seem constitutionally unfitted for the task. A list of qualities which the successful administrator of standardised group tests should possess would almost certainly include the following.

1. ***Ability to understand and follow directions***: The person who is to give a standardised test must have the ability to follow directions exactly. Sometimes test directions require the performance of complicated activities by the pupil and accurate

timing by the examiner. Not every person likes to undertake involved procedures of this nature, and not everyone is qualified to perform these tasks and supply students with the needed guidance and assistance. The examiner must be willing to read and study the directions until he understands them thoroughly. He should work through the entire test himself before he attempts to administer it so that he will be thoroughly familiar with every part of it.

Once in a discussion among teachers about the uses of tests in the classroom, one member of the group, a middle-aged teacher, raised a problem: she stated that on a certain English test which she had used for a number of years her pupils invariably made scores well above the norms for the grade. This puzzled her, since the pupils were not otherwise unusual or exceptional, and she was unable to account for their very high attainment on this test. No one in the group was able to explain it, and the matter was dropped for the time being. The conference proceeded to other matters, but sometime later the same teacher brought up the problem again. This time, however, she happened to mention that when she administered the English test she ignored the time limits set in the directions and permitted her pupils to work on the test as long as they wished! The teacher seemed quite innocent of any notion of error on her part!

Thorough study of the test and directions for its use, and careful adherence to instructions in every detail are the essentials for successful administration of a standardised test. Most teachers and school personnel can meet these requirements without undue difficulty. As teachers gain in experience and confidence, the administration of standardised tests becomes fairly easy and often stimulating and enjoyable.

2. ***Ability to maintain the attention and whole-hearted cooperation of a group :*** The administrator of a standardised test must be able to command the attention of a group and draw from each member his best efforts. If the test is a good one the tasks it involves and the instructions to the pupils will help the examiner hold the pupils' attention. Perhaps most important, the examiner himself must give an impression of serious attention and an attitude of regard for the importance of the task at hand. Many a well-meaning examiner, in his attempt to set pupils at ease, has spoiled the entire effort by such remarks as, "Don't take this too seriously", or, "It doesn't mean anything". Certainly children should not suffer unnecessary emotional strain in taking a test, yet a test is a test and if the child is to do as well as he possibly can, he must be urged to give his undivided attention and cooperation. The examiner must avoid instilling in his pupils either an attitude of extreme emotional tension, which may prevent a child from doing his best *or* an attitude of careless indifference, which will defeat the very purpose of the test.

3. *Ability to read directions aloud clearly and distinctly:* Reading aloud is something of a lost art for the emphasis in the teaching of reading has shifted almost completely to silent reading. The administration of a group test usually requires that the directions be read aloud, clearly and distinctly. This requires a good voice and the ability to use it effectively. It is highly desirable for every examiner, even the experienced one, to practice reading the directions aloud before given a test for the first time. Through such rehearsal he will learn the proper inflections, pronunciations and phrasing. Sometimes the wrong intonation can change the meaning of a sentence and cause confusion or misunderstanding.

By practicing reading the directions aloud the examiner can also gain sufficient familiarity with them so that he can make the reading more pleasant and meaningful to his audience. He should be able to take his eyes off the printed page occasionally, not only to see if all the pupils are paying attention and following him, but also for the good effect this will have on his audience. It may be necessary for the examiner to interrupt his reading occasionally in order to explain an example given in the directions or to make sure that all pupils understand what they are to do. A thorough mastery of the directions helps to smooth such breaks and avoid awkward pauses.

4. *Ability to be objective:* A teacher measuring her own pupils with a standardised test may find it very difficult to be objective because she is aware that the test results may often seem to conflict with her own judgment. She observes Johnny struggling unsuccessfully with a test problem and feels that she must give him "just a tiny hint to help him solve it", for she has seen him solve similar problems many times. The "tiny hint" may not even be expressed in words. As she looks at Johnny's answer sheet over his shoulder, a frown or a surprised expression may be all that is needed to set him on the right track. This may make both Johnny and the teacher happy at the moment, but it destroys the objectivity of a good testing situation and it may later prove harmful to all concerned.

If one is having the antifreeze solution in the radiator of his car tested when the temperature is below freeing an falling rapidly, he does not ask the service-station attendant to make the measurement sound better than it actually is in order to save the cost of a quart of antifreeze. To do so might prove very expensive and even disastrous. In a situation of this sort we want as objective and accurate a report as possible so that we may know what to do to be safe. In the same way, we should seek objectivity and accuracy when using standardised tests. To say that the hydrometer the garage mechanic uses or the tests that educators use are not exact instruments merely beclouds the issue. We do not disregard the report on our antifreeze because the mechanic's instrument is not as accurate as those of the scientist who is dealing with very minute quantities in theoretical physics, or because there is some variation in the grades of antifreeze manufactured by different companies. We know that any instrument—mechanical or educational—that is properly selected and used will give results which are reasonably accurate, or which are at least more dependable and accurate than subjective opinion or plain guessing. The point here is that educational tests should be used as objectively and carefully as possible, with full realisation of their limitations and with regard for the fact that using them carelessly or inaccurately may make the results quite valueless or misleading. Of course, the person administering standardised tests or other measuring instruments should demonstrate warmth, understanding, and every attitude calculated to encourage pupils to enjoy taking tests and to do their very best; yet the examiner in his desire to see his pupils do well must do nothing that will invalidate the results of the testing, and he must not deviate from the test instructions.

Physical Conditions of Testing

The examiner should observe a few simple rules concerning the physical conditions of testing. First, the room should be comfortable. It should be well-lighted, well-ventilated, and well-heated. The seats should be comfortable and of appropriate height. It is not uncommon to enter a room where testing is going on to find it crowded, the temperature too high or too low for comfort, all windows tightly closed, and the air almost unbearable. Frequently, the occupants of the room are entirely unaware of these conditions. Again, when pupils are shifted to a different room for testing, the desks in the new room may be totally unsuitable for them—too large or too small, for example. Such conditions can usually be avoided by calling them to the attention of responsible persons before the testing begins.

It is also a good idea to place a sign on the door of a room being used for testing. This will keep out those whose business is not urgent and will reduce the number of interruptions.

The room should be large enough to permit the spacing of pupils in such a way that the temptation to copy will be minimised. If the desks are movable they can usually be placed at a suitable distance from each other without much trouble. If there are too many pupils to be properly accommodated in a single room the teacher or examiner should try to divide the pupils so that the test can be given in two or more rooms. If the desks are fixed it is desirable to seat pupils at alternate desks and, if possible, in alternate rows. If tables and chairs are used pupils should be seated so that there is no temptation to compare papers. Such measures do not reflect on the honesty of pupils; rather, they are intended to reduce to a minimum the opportunity and temptation to cheat.

Duties of the Examiner

The person in charge of administering a standardised test is responsible for the proper conduct of the examination. He should have one or more proctors or assistants if the group is large, but the over-all responsibility is his. He needs a good stop watch or at least a watch with a sweep second hand. Many standardised tests require timing and this is always the examiner's responsibility. If he has a stop watch he should know exactly how to operate it beforehand. Stop watches of different makes and quality vary somewhat in technique of operation. After the testing has begun, it may be impossible to correct an error in timing resulting from faulty manipulation of the watch controls.

If the examiner has only a watch with a second hand the following procedure is recommended:

1. The examiner should synchronise the second hand and the minute hand so that both are together, that is, at the end of a minute at the same time.
2. At the moment he finishes reading the directions for a timed test and says "begin", or "go", he should glance at his watch, looking at the *second hand first,* and then the minute hand, immediately *writing down* the time, thus: 9-42-21, which means that the pupils began work on that part at forty-two minutes and twenty-one seconds past nine o'clock.
3. Then, if the time allowance for that part of the test is two minutes and thirty seconds, he adds that to the starting time, thus:

9-42-21
2-30
9-44-51

4 Forty-four minutes and fifty-one seconds past nine is the time when he should give instructions to stop, turn over the page, or whatever may be indicated.

No examiner should rely on his memory for the time of beginning, or attempt to figure out by mental arithmetic the time of stopping. It is impossible for most persons to do this accurately. Furthermore, during the administration of a standardised group test there are many things to do which are more useful and important than trying to calculate and remember times of starting and stopping

The examiner should be alert to everything that goes on in the room during testing. It is his responsibility to see that proper conditions for testing are maintained and to note and record any unusual happenings such as extreme nervousness, accidents, or illness. If the group is large these responsibilities are discharged with the help of his assistants or proctors, but the examiner is still the person ultimately responsible for the proper conduct of the test.

Proctors

Thirty or fewer pupils in a standardised testing situation can usually be handled by one person if the physical conditions, such as seating arrangements, are right. If the number being tested is between thirty and sixty, one proctor will be needed, from sixty to ninety, two, etc. The duties of proctors are to see that the pupils follow the directions given by the examiner, to see that pupils have pencils and other necessary equipment, to distribute and collect test blanks, answer sheets, and other necessary materials at the proper time, and to help the examiner in every way to carry out his job as effectively as possible.

The examiner should assign his proctors or assistants to definite sections of the room or to specific parts of the group being tested, and each proctor should be held responsible for his section or part throughout the test. The proctor should stay with that portion of the group and be available to its members at all times for any legitimate assistance. Inexperienced proctors occasionally make mistakes which can easily be avoided. For example, they sometimes line up at the front of the room while the examiner is reading directions. They should avoid this, remaining as much as possible at their stations or in the background. The examiner should be the sole focus of attention when instructions are given or directions read. As far as possible, nothing should divert the attention of the pupils from the task at hand.

If the testing is not being done by the pupils own teacher, he should endeavour to be as inconspicuous as possible; he should either leave the room or sit quietly at the back while the testing is in progress. This may sometimes create a little awkwardness, but it can usually be handled through the principal of the school a day or two before testing begins. The presence of the teacher in the formal testing situation may have effects which are not conducive to the best efforts of the pupils.

Finally, proctors should remain alert and interested in what is going on during the entire test. Sometimes they tend to feel that once the test has successfully gotten under way no further attention on their part is needed. That may be just the time when they should be most alert; a pupil breaks his pencil, his pen runs dry, he turns two pages at once, or something else happens which the alert proctor can remedy immediately. To be most useful, the good proctor should also be thoroughly familiar with the test and the details of its administration. Without this knowledge he cannot actively and properly assist in carrying out the administration of the test.

In connection with the administration of standardised tests the question of how far one may go in giving help often comes up. A good rule to follow is to *allow no assistance of any kind with the problems or tasks of the test proper.* Also, it is generally considered good practice not to answer any questions regarding the test after work on it has actually begun. Though everyone is anxious for each pupil to do his best, the ideal standardised test situation requires uniformity of conditions for everyone being tested. Any act that gives one pupil more help or explanation than is given to all is not permissible. In some tests understanding and following directions are *part of the test,* and in such cases no explanation of directions other than what is provided by the manual is allowed. The manual of a well-standardised test is usually quite explicit regarding what to say and read in giving the test, and it is not permissible to add to or depart from such instructions *in any way.*

Scoring the Tests

Who shall Score the Tests?

After the tests have been given, the next task is to get the scoring done. If arrangements can be made for having the tests scored by machine there is usually no problem. In many situations, however, hand-scoring is still the common procedure. The labour involved in scoring by hand has been greatly reduced by the better arrangement of test items on the page, by the use of separate answer sheets with scoring stencils, and by the development of self-scoring techniques and other aids. However, we are still a long way from entirely relieving teachers of this job. If funds are available some of the work may be done by clerks, but of course this adds to the cost of testing.

If teachers do the scoring it is very desirable to make some adjustment in their regular duties to give them adequate time for the work. Some of their classes may be dismissed or assigned temporarily to other teachers or substitutes, or they may be excused from some of their non-teaching duties for the time.

These adjustments will not only help to get the scoring done quickly, but will also help to create favourable attitudes toward the testing programme. Furthermore, there is the advantage that the scoring task will thus not become an extra burden on busy teachers.

Suggestions for Efficient Scoring

In hand-scoring standardised tests there are certain methods and principles which can contribute much to the speed and accuracy with which the work is accomplished.

Although the suggestions which follow are particularly appropriate where large numbers of tests are to be scored, most of them are applicable to every test-scoring task or situation.

In the first place, it is well to divide the task so that each person may develop speed and accuracy on a particular part of the scoring. For example, if there are eight pages or parts of a test it is more efficient to have one individual score one page or part on all the tests than to have him score each test in its entirety. If there are enough workers to assign one page or part to each, an assembly-line procedure can be set up to good advantage. If not, each scorer should concentrate on one page or part at a time and then go on to the next, as each is finished. By this method the scorer sometimes is able to quickly memorise the scoring key so that he can dispense with it entirely. This contributes to both speed and accuracy since the scorer can concentrate on the scoring without the necessity of manipulating scoring keys or comparing the keys with answers written on the paper. Moreover, with this system the scorer does not need to constantly shift his attention from one part of the test to an entirely different part. He concentrates on the one until it is finished.

The task of arriving at part scores and adding them to get the total score should also be done by one person. The transforming of raw scores into percentiles, or standard scores should be the separate responsibility of another individual, or, if it seems convenient and efficient, the one who works out part scores and total scores can also do this, but again, it is probably more efficient for him to do one part of the job at a time.

The assembly-line procedure should be planned and carried out so that test blanks can move along the line smoothly without piling up at any one point. This requires that the work be assigned according to the difficulty of the separate tasks and the particular skill of each individual. A slow worker will necessarily be given a smaller or easier job; otherwise, he may delay others. The person in charge of the scoring must experiment with his helpers and the task at hand until an efficient and agreeable procedure worked out.

Second, it is generally better to do the work of scoring in a group than to let individuals take tests away with them to score at their convenience. When the scoring is done in a group it is possible to settle questions about procedure, allowable answers, etc., on the spot. Also the scoring is more interesting and stimulating for those participating and delays are avoided. On the other hand, it is sometimes difficult to find the time or a suitable place for assembly-line scoring. However, it is often possible to find time when six or eight teachers can work together if, as has been suggested, the work is done during schools hours.

The place for the scoring of tests should be relatively quiet and free from interruptions, and the workers should be able to talk with each other freely without fear of disturbing others. If possible, there should be a large table or several smaller ones that can be put together so that all the scorers can work comfortably in a group.

Third, all hand-scoring—the entire operation, from beginning to end—should be carefully checked for accuracy. Every step should be systematically checked, and the person in charge should also check the accuracy of his individual workers. Wide variations will nearly always be found in the work of particular individuals; some will perform their tasks with few errors, others will seem unable to score accurately no matter how much they practice.

Checking the scoring is best done by re-scoring a sampling of papers. It may be desirable at the beginning to re-score entirely the first few papers, perhaps five or ten, to see what mistakes are being made by individual scorers and to help correct these mistakes. After this, a sampling of every fifth paper or perhaps every tenth paper should be completely re-scored as a continuous check on the accuracy of the work. If it is found that errors are frequent in all parts of the tests, it will often be necessary to re-score all papers. If errors are consistently found only in certain parts of the test or in certain phases of the work, it will suffice, as a rule, to re-score only those parts where error is found.

There is one basic fact often overlooked by users of standardised tests, namely, that errors occur in all such work, and it is, therefore, absolutely essential that continuous and systematic checking take place. The less experienced the workers, the greater the probability of error, but regardless of the experience of the scorers, the scoring should not be accepted as final or the results recorded until every step of the process has been checked. The permit inaccurate scoring is a waste of time and money, and it may cause grave injustice to the pupils.

Finally, it is important to train workers in the scoring process. One does not usually put scorers to work until they have had some prior instruction. It is usually desirable first to have prospective scorers read the manual, or at least the part dealing with scoring, so that they will understand what they are to do and how to do it. Then the person in charge should help score enough papers so that there is no doubt that the work is being done correctly. In this way one may be reasonably sure that the correct procedure is being followed.

Recording and Analysing Results

Recording Test Results

After the tests have been scored and checked, the results must be made a part of the permanent records of the pupil and the school. Most schools have some sort of permanent record for each pupil, usually in the form of a folder providing for the recording of information such as personal and home background data, schools attended, marks, honours, disciplinary or other special actions, and results of various tests. Many such record systems have been devised, some by national agencies, some on the state level, and some by the larger city school systems. In Figure 8.2, one such sample permanent record form is reproduced. Although the data in the sample record were gathered some time ago, they exemplify the full and complete use of the form and, except for one or two items, are as appropriate for illustrative purposes as though they had been gathered yesterday.

Whatever the type of permanent record, it is important that there be one, that the test results be recorded as soon as possible after they are available, and that this record be readily accessible to those entitled to use it. The entering of test data upon the record form may be done by teachers for their own pupils, or by clerks if such help is available. These records are confidential and should not be available to pupils or other unauthorised persons.

It is probably most advantageous to keep the permanent cumulative records of pupils in some central place such as the principal's office. In some schools records are distributed to teachers so that each will have in his custody the records of his own pupils. It may also be found desirable to have the records filed in the office of the counsellor, if there is one. There are arguments for and against centralised and distributed record systems, but they need not be reviewed here. The important thing is that the records be used—not just filed—and it should be determined in each situation what arrangement is best for all concerned.

Analysing Test Results

Before anything can be done as a follow-up of testing there must be an analysis of the results. The analysis may be very simple in nature, as when a pupil's rank in the class is determined, or it may be more complicated, as in the case of large-scale testing programmes involving hundreds of schools and thousands of pupils in a large city system. Whatever is done, the basic procedures and techniques are usually statistical. By the application of these techniques a teacher or counsellor can make all of the usual types of analysis without going too far into technicalities. For analysis of a more advanced nature one of the standard works in statistical methods should be consulted.

It may be appropriate to say a word here on profiles and other graphic methods. It is sometimes erroneously assumed that when we make a profile, a percentile curve, or some other graphic record of test results, we are making further statistical analysis of test results. It is possible that a graphic representation of data may clarify a statistical situation or even give new insight into its meaning, but a graph or chart simply expresses statistical data in another form. A profile is merely a graphical representation of data which are already known. By extending or extrapolating a curve we may extend the data, but the results of such procedures are always hypothetical. Moreover, the same results may be determined statistically as well as graphically.

The reason for emphasising this matter is that users of tests and test results sometimes are led to believe that profiles, distribution curves, and other graphic methods add something which statistical data do not yield. Profiles and other graphic methods are often very helpful but principally because they express findings in a way more readily grasped than mere statistics. They do not, as a rule, tell us anything about John or Mary which the numbers do not already say.

Before proceeding to descriptions of specific testing programmes it seems pertinent to present some findings of a recent survey of such programmes in Michigan schools. This is the third survey of this nature conducted in Michigan, the two previous ones having been made in 1958-59 and 1963-64. Much of what was revealed in all three is relevant to our discussion, but limitations of space prohibit a detailed review. However, a few of the many important findings of the 1970 survey should be interesting and significant as indicative of present practices in one state in relation to principles and practices recommended in the preceding section of this chapter.

The survey was based on the responses of 464 school districts in Michigan, both public and private, enrolling pupils in grades K-12. This represents an 84 per cent return.

1. In at least three-fourths of the districts committees working with test specialists are in-charge of testing programmes. These committees usually include principals, counsellors and teachers. In most districts (84 per cent) such committees function for the entire district.

2. Test results are recorded in pupil's cumulative folders, which are most often kept with the counsellor or pupil personnel specialist, in the principal's office, or with the grade or homeroom teacher.

3. Test data are available in most situations to teachers, principals, counsellors, consultants and chief school officers. In about one-third of the districts such data are also available to members of the board of education.

Fig. 8.2 : Typical Permanent Record Form.

Anaerson	MARY	MARGARET	MAE	BAPTIST	Amden, Mass. Feb. 12, 1923	M (F)	(W) C Y
LAST NAME	FIRST	MIDDLE	NICKNAME	RELIGION	DATE AND PLACE OF BIRTH	SEX	COLOR

ADDRESS AND TELEPHONE	25 Irving Terrace Circle 5600	Same	Same	Same	2104 Revere Ave. East 6415	Same

PHOTOS (Dated)

PREVIOUS SCHOOL RECORD: Names and Types of Schools Attended, Achievement in Subjects and Activities, School Difficulties Encountered, Summary of Test Results

Attended Parmount elementary school including Kindergarten. Very good record throughout. Citizenship always marked excellent. Work has always been commensurate with mental test scores which indicate intelligence quotients above 130. Tested reading performance above eighth grade level while in sixth grade. Superior performances in Art, Music, and Arithmetic. Family very cooperative with school and much interested in achievements of children. Excellent health and attendance records. Mary should wear her glasses in school.

PHOTOS (Dated)

Name and Type of School Attended	West Jr. High	Same	Same	Amden Sr. High	Same	Same
COUNSELOR	Miss Watson	Mr. Robinson	Mr. Robinson	Mr. Rones	Miss Cowan	Miss Cowan
AGE (As of Sept. 1)	12-7	13-7	14-7	15-7	16-7	17-7
SCHOOL YEAR AND GRADE	1936 7	1937 8	1938 9	1939 10	1940 11	1941 12

ACADEMIC ACHIEVEMENT — These columns are for analyses of development in fields indicated. Headings might include work habits, ability to think logically, mastery of techniques, oral and written communication and some estimate of achievement. In this school S indicates satisfactory and U unsatisfactory progress in consideration of ability of pupil. An X indicates serious lack of progress.

Subject	WH	T	Tech.	Comm.	Mark	WH	T	Tech.	Comm.	Mark	WH	T	Tech.	Comm.	Mark	WH	T	Tech.	Comm.	Mark	WH	T	Tech.	Comm.	Mark	WH	T	Tech.	Comm.	Mark
English: L.T. and Comp.	S	S	S		B	S	S	S		B	U	S	S		B	U	S	S		B	S	S	S		A	S	S	S		A
Oral																S	S	S		B	S	S	S		A	S	S	S		A
Grammar	S	S	S	S	A	S	S	S	S	A	S	S	S	S	B															
Lang.: French											S	S	S	S	B	S	S	S	S	B	U	S	U	S	B	X	X	X	Dropped	
Latin						S	S	S	S	B	U	S	U	S	B	X	U	X	S	C										
Math.: Arithmetic	S	S	U	S	B	S	S	S	S	A																				
Algebra											S	S	S	S	B						S	S	S	S	A					
Geometry																S	S	S	S	A										
Advanced Math.																										S	U	S	S	B
Science: Chemistry																					U	U	X	S	C					
Social Studies: Soc. Studies	S	S	S	S	A	U	S	S	S	B	S	S	S	S	A															
American Hist.																										U	S	S	S	B
Other Subjects: Practical Arts	S	S	S	S	A																									
Drawing	S	S	S	S	A	S	S	S	S	A																				
Music	S	S	S	S	A	S	S	S	S	A														Chorus		S	S	S	S	A
Spelling	S	S	S	S	A	S	S	S	S	\																				
Physical Education					B					A					A					A					A					A

TEST RECORD	TEST	No.	Score	%ile	TEST	No.	Score	%ile	TEST	No.	Score	%ile	TEST	No.	Score	%ile	TEST	No.	Score	%ile	TEST	No.	Score	%ile
ACADEMIC APTITUDE (Use M. A. and I. Q. if Preferred)	Henmon-Nelson	S	IQ	119	Kuhl-Anderson	S	IQ	133	Kuhl-Anderson	S	IQ	130	Kuhl-Anderson	S	IQ	130	Kuhl-Anderson	S	IQ	136	Kuhl-Anderson	S	IQ	[illegible]
									Stan. Binet (L)	N	IQ	142					ACE Psych	N	117	85	ACE Psych.			
																					(College Form)	O	154	96
READING	Stanford Ach.				Stanford Ach.				Stanford Ach.	S			Iowa Reading (A)				Iowa Reading				Coop Reading	O		
	Paragraph M	S	113	98	Paragraph M	S	115	89	Paragraph M.	S	115	84	Comprehension	S	140	81	Comprehension	N	185	94	Level	O	46	90
													Speed	S	[illegible]	[illegible]	Speed	N	[illegible]	89	Speed	O	48	93

ACHIEVEMENT AND OTHER TESTS																								
		S	107	71					Minnesota Clerical	N														
		S	100	65					Names	N	136	87	Coop. French	S	52	76	Coop French	N	66	74	Minnesota Clerical	O		
	History-Civics	S	90	50	History-Civics	S	93	53	Numbers	N	156	92	Coop. Latin	S	65	62	Coop. Chemistry	N	64	77	Names	O	148	85
	Geography	S	89	32	Geography	S	96	36													Numbers	O	169	87
	Phys-Hygiene	S	95	80																	Coop. Am. History	O	53	51
	Arith-Reasoning	S	100	72	Arith-Reasoning	S	105	70	Arith-Reasoning	S	110	77	Coop Math.	O	30	80	Coop. Math	N	40	85	Coop. Math	O	51	95
	Arith-Computation	S	95	47	Arith-Computation	S	101	57	Arith-Computation	S	105	54												
					M-S Art Judgment	S	102	85	Minn P. Form Board	S	4-	79					Minn. P. Form Board	N	47	75				

INTERPRETATION OF TEST RECORD AND ITS RELATION TO ACADEMIC ACHIEVEMENT (In the interpretation of test scores consider differences in norms used. In transferring records indicate basis of norms)	Superior in ability to do school work and frequently finds that work is not challenging enough for her. When this occurs she keeps busy with so many out-of-school activities that she neglects some school assignments		Enthusiastic and exceptionally efficient reader. Can work accurately and fast on objective tests but finds teachers' tests based on cumulative drill work very difficult. Could do much better in languages if she could see more reason for doing them.		Although Mary continues to make high scores on objective tests of ability she has difficulty with cumulative subjects where her background work is irregular and spotty. Finds it hard to settle down to drill which teachers recommend. French teacher says she could be an 'A' student if she would do assignments. Performance in advanced Math. very good despite fact that she had not covered all prerequisites. Mother advised her to carry on all co-curricular activities and have a full pleasant senior year.	
ATTENDANCE (Reasons if irregular)	Absent 10 days – colds	No Absences	← Same	← Same	← Same	Missed occasional classes for rehearsals and clubs
	SIGNIFICANT ACTIVITIES AND ACCOMPLISHMENTS THAT GIVE EVIDENCE REGARDING INTERESTS AND POWERS					
INTERESTS REPORTED BY STUDENT	Art- Lettering, drawing Group sports Vocal music	Art - copy Baseball + hockey teams Music	Art Any activity which brought contact with other people	Art ← Same Said she had read "all the books in the library".	Any opportunity to work or play with others	← same clubs, dates, games
EXPERIENCES IN SCHOOL	Choir	Art editor school paper Glee club Chorus	Designed cover for annual Glee club Chorus	Glee club	Glee club- president Lead in Gilbert + Sullivan	Glee club - chorus Duchess in Gondoliers
OUT OF SCHOOL AND SUMMER EXPERIENCES	Sunday school regular attendance Scouts Played at home in summer	Church choirs	Church choir Designed original greeting cards	Church choir Leader church student group	Church choir ← same	Church choir Chairman missionary group in church
	NOTE TYPE, DURATION, HOURS PER WEEK, EARNINGS AND OTHER SIGNIFICANT FACTS					
WORK EXPERIENCES	NONE	NONE	Assistant to secretary of school. No pay. Efficient worker	NONE	Care of children in evenings. Paid $4 for 12 to 16 hours per month Demonstrator food show one week $15	← Same
FINANCIAL AID (Type and Amount)	NONE	NONE	NONE	NONE	N.Y.A. clerical $6 monthly 20 hours	NONE
Educational and Occupational Plans by — Pupil	Go to college - then get married	Many vague ideas	Commercial artist	Commercial artist	Teaching math. or work in statistics.	Secretary in position where math. is used and then marriage.
— Parents	None stated	None stated	Father discouraged choice of career in comm. art	← Same	Free to choose own career but financial support limited.	Parents agree with above
— Counselor	Wait till school performance observed	Encouraged to continue many activities as try-outs	Consider any career requiring college training	← Same	Further study of colleges and professions recommended	Good compromise
HEALTH AND PHYSICAL CHARACTERISTICS (Vigor or lassitude; assets, disabilities or limitations)	Should wear glasses for reading No marked presence or absence of vigor Rather plump ←	Vigorous - peppy Radiant health Beautiful blonde hair and fine color of complexion Same ←	Stopped wearing glasses because she thought they detracted from appearance. Nurse says she should wear them. Same ←	Will not wear glasses. Excellent health and much vigor SAME ←	← Same ← Same Same ←	← Same ← Same Same
DISCIPLINE — Academic, Personal	NONE	NONE	Some make-up time required to get home-work done.	NONE	NONE	

Reproduced by permission of the National Association of Secodnary School Principals, National Education Association and the American Council on Education.

4. The most common methods of interpreting results of testing are conferences with individual pupils and individual parents, and summaries to administrators and teachers. Somewhat less frequently employed are group analyses with pupils, analyses in teachers' meetings, and written reports to parents.

5. Methods used for in-service education of teachers and other personnel to use test results most effectively are—in order of frequency—building faculty meetings, departmental, grade, divisional or other sub-group faculty meetings, in-service training other than faculty meetings, and general faculty meetings. Each is used, if at all, at least annually.

6. In most situations in the elementary grades, tests are administered once each year (usually in the fall or spring) by the classroom teacher in the classroom to all pupils. In secondary grades, tests are generally administered once a year in the fall or spring by the guidance counsellor, about equally often in the classroom or in large groups, to nearly all pupils.

7. In elementary grades tests are scored in one-third of the districts by classroom teachers and in about one-half by outside agencies such as publishers' or other scoring services. In secondary grades tests are scored most often by such agencies and only rarely by classroom teachers.

8. Test results are seldom reported routinely to pupils in elementary grades. This is true in the case of both ability and achievement tests. In about one-third of the districts results are explained in some cases and in about the same frequency results are regarded as confidential. This is true in 39 per cent of the districts with respect to tests of ability but only 21 per cent with respect to achievement test results. In nearly one-half of the districts test results are reported routinely or in some cases to individual pupils; in only 12 per cent (ability) and 7 per cent (achievement) are test results in secondary grades regarded as confidential.

9. The predominant uses of test results in elementary grades are diagnosis of learning difficulties, counselling parents, evaluation of curriculum, ability grouping, counselling pupils, and evaluating teaching effectiveness in order of frequency of mention. In secondary grades they are counselling pupils, diagnosis of learning difficulties, counselling parents, evaluation of curriculum and ability grouping in order.

10. At both elementary and secondary levels, national norms are used in more than 90 per cent of the districts. Local norms are also used by approximately one-fourth.

11. The most commonly employed test terms are percentile rank, I.Q., and grade equivalent. Much less frequently used are stanine, standard score, age equivalent and band scores. (It is interesting to note that profiles are mentioned almost not at all.)

12. Test results are available to teachers almost without exception, either directly or in consultation with the principal. This is rarely so with parents where the mode is rather an explanation to parents if they request one and the school approves.

In elementary grades test results or explanations of results are generally provided by classroom teachers. In secondary grades in most cases this is done by the guidance counsellor.

13. The pattern of tests given most commonly appears to be:

(a) Reading readiness—once, kindergarten or first grade.

(b) Group intelligence test—twice in elementary grades, once in secondary grades.

(c) Achievement battery—twice in elementary grades, once or twice in secondary grades.

(d) Scholastic aptitude—once in secondary grades (e.g., algebra).

(e) Interest inventory–once in secondary grades.

14. The findings of the survey support the conclusion that the schools of Michigan are making increased use of structured testing programmes and professionally trained assistance, particularly at the secondary level, in implementing the results of such programmes in the improvement of instruction and communicating with parents and the public.

The results also suggest that practices in administering testing programmes in these schools are generally in accord with many of the principles we have recommended. There are none reported that are seriously at variance with these recommendations, though by no means all were touched upon by the survey.

Illustrative Measurement Programmes

To complete this discussion of measurement programmes we shall offer two illustrations representing actual practice in school systems of different sizes. Both programmes have been developed through local leadership and experience. Therefore, they are practical, and their scope is such that they can be managed at the local level without undue expense or labour. Included are programmes for (1) a small community school with no secondary grades, and (2) a city system comprising a number of elementary schools, plus junior and senior high schools.

A Typical Programme for the Small School

The first measurement programme to be described is one which any small elementary school enrolling three hundred or fewer pupils can manage without outside help. It follows closely the minimum programme presented earlier in this chapter; it has been successfully administered for a number of years at the Stoner School near Lansing, Michigan. Some of the students in the writer's classes in educational measurement have participated in the programme, have helped administer and score the tests and analyse the results, and have had the opportunity to discuss with the teachers ways of putting the results to use. This has helped the teachers and the school and has provided important practical experience for a number of university students.

Table 8.1
Stoner School Testing Programme

Grade	*Test*	*Time*
K	Reading Readiness	May
1 or 2	Intelligence	February
3 or 4	Achievement Battery	October
5	Intelligence	February
6	Achievement Battery	October

This programme is simple and it is limited enough to be managed by the regular staff of the school without outside assistance. The results are used in various ways, including identifying exceptional children, both the slow-learning and gifted, counselling with parents, sectioning or grouping, diagnosis and comparing test results with national norms.

The programme gives information of several types, all useful in improving instruction. It reveals the stage of development or readiness of beginners for learning the fundamentals, it gives several appraisals of each child's general capacity for school work, and it provides a reasonably adequate survey of each pupil's progress in the common branches of the elementary school curriculum. The entire cost of the programme, including test material and some clerical assistance for recording the results, can be kept to about twenty-five cents per pupil per year. This allows nothing, of course, for the time of the school staff or for any outside help. However, when teachers become educated to the value of the results of their work and feel that they have a real part in the programme, they are usually glad to contribute a reasonable amount of time and energy to the work of carrying it through.

A Typical Programme for a City System

The second programme to be described is one that has been developed by the Long Beach, California, school system enrolling approximately seventy thousand pupils in elementary schools and in the junior and senior high schools. Altogether, seventy-three schools are involved, of which fifty-four are elementary, Grades K-6; fourteen are junior high schools, Grades, 7–9; and five are senior high schools, Grades 10–12.

The basic programme followed throughout the district is shown on Table 8.2.

Table 8.2
Long Beach Public Schools
Elementary Schools

Grade	*Test*	*Week*
5	Achievement battery	4–6
6*	Intelligence	6–7
6*	Achievement battery	8–10
3	Intelligence	13
3	Arithmetic	21

Grade	*Test*	*Week*
1, 2, and 3*	Reading	34–35
K	Readiness	36–37
	Junior High Schools	
7	Intelligence	3–4
8	Achievement battery	5–7
9	Reading; Arithmetic; Study skills	23–26
	Senior High Schools	
10	Intelligence	3–4
10	Reading	5
12*	Intelligence	6
12*	Achievement battery	8–10
10	English, Mathematics	31–32

* California law requires the giving of intelligence tests and achievement tests in selected grades at selected times of the year. For the school year 1970-71, the pattern of state-required testing consists of intelligence tests and tests of reading, arithmetic or mathematics, and language or English in Grades 6 and 12; and tests of reading in Grades 1, 2 and 3.

The tests in the basic programme are administered to all pupils at the levels and at the approximate times indicated. Tests are usually administered by counsellors or by teachers, though sometimes in an elementary school they are administered by the principal. The few tests which require hand-scoring—mainly tests for pupils of the lower elementary grades—are scored by the clerks, teachers and counsellors at the individual school sites; where machine-scorable answer sheets are used, the scoring is done in a central office and the scores are returned to the school for a tabulation of results. In general, tabulations of all test results are sent to the office of the Director of Research, but the scored tests are kept at the school. Test results are recorded in each pupil's cumulative record.

The Long Beach Director of Research has developed a series of mimeographed instruction sheets which supplement the manuals for the various tests, and these instruction sheets provide examiners with practical suggestions on administering and scoring tests, tabulating, analysing, and recording results, and reporting them to the office of the Director. Such carefully worked-out instruction sheets are essential in a large programme such as this where personal contact with all cooperating personnel is impossible.

In addition to the district-wide or required programme of testing, each school has an opportunity to select additional standardised tests for optional use in any grade or classroom. These tests are selected by the personnel of the individual schools, and vary considerably from one school to the next. Test requests by teachers of a school are channeled to the offices of the counsellor and school principal; they are then forwarded to the district's Research Office for final review before the materials are delivered or requisitioned for later delivery.

By common agreement among the junior high schools, ninth-grade students are given a vocational interest test and a battery of differential ability tests. In the senior high schools those seniors who are not planning to enter college are given another battery of multiple-aptitude tests. General ability and achievement tests that are part of national testing programmes are given to a high percentage of those juniors and seniors who plan to enter college.

Many of the junior and senior high schools elect to give standardised achievement tests that are not required on a district-wide basis, particularly in the fields of foreign language, Mathematics and Science. Schools that are making unusual efforts to develop reading skills often request standardised reading tests that help measure gains during a specified instructional period. Those schools that receive special funding because they are serving concentrations of "educationally disadvantaged" pupils require before-and-after achievement tests in order to provide some of the data needed in the evaluation of special programmes. Teachers make frequent requests, too, for reading tests (and sometimes for tests in other areas of skill) that are designed to offer clues concerning the specific learning deficiencies of individual pupils.

The Research Office does not purchase the pencil-and-paper personality tests or adjustment inventories which may occasionally be requested by a school. This is the only broad limitation on the selection of tests by school personnel except for the restrictions imposed by the status of the district's test supply budget.

The programme of testing in Long Beach—the required or district-wide schedule and the near-uniform testing by common agreement—may be summarised as follows:

Table 8.3
Grade in which Tests are Given

Test	*K*	*1*	*2*	*3*	*4*	*5*	*6*	*7*	*8*	*9*	*10*	*11*	*12*
Readiness	X												
Intelligence				X			X	X			X		X
Multiple Aptitude										X			
Vocational Interest										X			
Study Skills										X			
Merit and Pre-College											X		X
Reading		X	X	X		X	X		X	X	X		X
Language–English						X	X		X		X		X
Arithmetic—Math				X		X	X		X	X	X		X

A pupil attending the Long Beach public schools from Kindergarten through Grade 12 will take six different measures of general scholastic ability as he moves through the grades. In Grade 9 he will be given some assistance in his early search for a career choice by taking both a multiple-aptitude battery and a measure of his vocational interests. Toward the close of his high school career he will take a second battery of aptitude tests if he does not plan to attend college; if he does plan to attend college, he will probably take one or more tests of the usual pre-admission type. Skill in locating needed information and in handling common references is checked in the latter part of the ninth grade, shortly before admission to senior high school.

In line with the existing pattern of required testing throughout California in the early 1970's, the Long Beach public schools give a battery of achievement tests covering the "three R's" in Grades 6 and 12. In addition, there is state-required testing of reading in each of the primary grades. The bulk of the achievement testing that is not state-required is concentrated in

Grades 5, 8 and 10. Each of the grades in which several achievement tests are given is a crucial year, and the information derived from the measurement programme thus becomes available at a time when it will be most useful. By the time a Long Beach pupil finishes high school, he will have had at least nine standardised measures of reading achievement, five measures of language or written English, and seven tests of arithmetic or mathematics.

Such a programme requires the leadership and assistance of a central co-ordinating agency; in the case of the Long Beach school system the supervisor of the programme is the Director of Research, though the major share of the work is divided among the teachers and counsellors so that no one will be overburdened. The results are reported to the central office, but the scored tests are kept in the respective schools where they may be interpreted and put to use. This programme, moreover, is not an expensive one.

The results of the Long Beach testing programme are used in various ways including the following:

1. *To assist the central office staff—particularly those in the Division of Instruction—in identifying curricular fields of strength and weakness for the total district.* If the district-wide test results in a given field are not satisfactory, special effort must be made to analyse the causes and then to correct conditions believed to be responsible for the weakness in pupil achievement.

2. *To provide school administrators with one basis for evaluating pupil achievement in individual schools of the district.* For example, each principal is expected to maintain a six-year record of the test achievement of pupils in his school. By examining these records, a newly-appointed principal can see what the past performance of his school has been on reading tests, for example, and he has a basis for judging whether the current year's test scores are in line with those of previous years.

3. *To identify those pupils in the district who rank in the upper 2 per cent of general scholastic aptitude, so that these "mentally gifted" pupils can be given individual counselling and instruction adapted to their abilities. Similarly, to identify those pupils in Grades 9 to 12 who rank one standard deviation above the mean*

in general scholastic ability, so that these "academically talented" students may be counselled concerning the kinds of high school courses best suited for those planning to take four years of college. Another related use: to identify those who may be admitted to certain elective courses designed for pupils in accelerated programmes.

4. *To identify pupils who should be re-tested individually in order to determine whether they should be placed in special classes for the slower learners.*

5. *To furnish teachers and counsellors with test data needed for student counselling.*

6. *To provide data needed by counsellors and administrators in grouping high school students by ability and achievement in certain required subjects such as tenth-grade English.*

7. *To give teachers an objective basis for judging student progress in achievement.* For example, the senior high teacher of English can compare the achievement of his students with that of other students in the nation who were in the norm group.

8. *To supply teachers with certain instructional clues.* Following some surveys, an analysis of the pupil's answers (an "item-count") in a sample of test papers is made. A report is then prepared so that teachers can learn which types of skills and understandings seem to have been satisfactorily mastered, and which types appear to be in need of strengthening.

9. *To maintain public confidence in the local schools.* During a given week thousands of pupils tell their parents that they have just taken a standardised reading test. Many parents are impressed with the fact that the school system not only teaches reading (and the other basic skills), but also checks up on its teaching efforts. Another important use in public relations: the district-wide data can be used by school administrators to provide a factual answer to an occasional critic making an unfounded charge concerning the general level of achievement of local pupils. A citizen sometimes bases his criticism of a school's educational programme upon extremely limited evidence, perhaps on his subjective judgment regarding the academic accomplishment of a few pupils or graduates he has met. In such circumstances a skilful administrator can use the results of the district's testing programme to build and maintain public confidence. He might

tactfully show the critical citizen (assuming the critic is a reasonable person) that according to the results of a recognised achievement test given to the total school population of many thousands in a grade, the district median represents a satisfactory level of accomplishment.

Other testing programmes in similar-sized communities could be described, and these would differ in such details as grade placement of tests, and areas tested. However, the two programmes we have described have been found workable and useful in their respective communities. They are not extremely elaborate, and they are modest in cost. They serve to illustrate the principles discussed in the first part of this chapter and should be suggestive of what can be done by other communities with similar needs and purposes.

It is probably unnecessary to state that in any measurement programme the teacher or supervisor should anticipate the necessity for re-testing in doubtful cases and tht provision should be made for this on an individual basis. Accidents will happen to prevent pupils from finishing a test; there will be surprisingly low, or sometimes surprisingly high, scores and, of course, there will always be absentees. Wherever a child misses the testing, or when there is good reason to believe that he has not been adequately or accurately measured, a make-up test is in order. Whenever an alternate form of the same test is available, it should be use in such cases, especially when a child has started a test, but has been unable to finish. It is usually more satisfactory to have him take the entire test in another form than to have him attempt to go on from the point where he stopped.

It should be understood that the discussion in this chapter has been concerned entirely with group tests. It is recognised that in some cases an individual examination like the *Binet,* the *Wechsler,* or other individual tests may be used. However, such examinations must be administered by a person with special training since most classroom teachers have not had the necessary instruction in the use of these instruments. Where such tests are needed and used it is assumed that qualified persons are available to administer them, and that tests will be given as necessary.

9

Using the Results of Measurement

In preceding chapters many kinds of measuring instruments have been described and evaluated. We have suggested or discussed the uses of these instruments in many instances. In Chapter 8 we emphasised that measurement programmes should be planned and carried out in the light of definite purposes. In that chapter also, a number of broad objectives or purposes for a measurement programme were cited, and it was stated that these would be discussed in some detail later. Listed below are the objectives mentioned there:

1. Placement and promotion
2. Homogeneous grouping
3. Diagnosis and remedial work
4. Counselling and guidance
5. Marking
6. Curriculum evaluation
7. Motivation
8. Identification and study of exceptional children
9. Interpreting schools to the community
10. Improvement of school staff
11. Educational research

These are probably the main purposes for which tests and other measuring instruments are used in the schools today. Certainly they seem important and worthy of careful consideration. It will be the aim of this chapter to discuss these purposes and to show how measurement can contribute to the attainment of each.

Interpretation of Test Results

Basic to using the results of measurement is the interpretation of scores. A test score is merely a number, devoid of meaning in and by itself. Not until it is related to something does it become meaningful and thus useful. Before we proceed with a discussion of the various uses of test results, it would be well to take another look at a device which facilities interpretation. This is the *profile,* a graphic method of depicting the results of the testing of individuals and of groups. The profile typically shows the results of an achievement battery such as the *Stanford,* an aptitude battery such as the *Differential Aptitude Tests,* or scores on an interest inventory for various occupations such as the *Strong.* Although a profile actually adds nothing to the information given by scores, norms and statistical interpretations, it does facilitate comparisons and interpretations by presenting results graphically and all in one package for a given individual or a group. Several examples of profiles are shown here as illustrations.

Figure 9.1 shows the scores of an individual pupil on the sub-tests of the *Stanford* battery and his median score. His profile shows the comparative score on each sub-test. The chart also shows his standing on each sub-test in terms of grade equivalents, age equivalents and percentile ranks and in relation to the grade norm. The median for the class on each sub-test could also be added to produce a group profile, if desired. Additional profiles and class analysis charts are shown in Figures 9.2 and 9.3.

Figure 9.2 depicts results on the *Metropolitan Achievement Test* for a homogeneous second-grade class. Individuals' scores on the sub-tests of the battery are located by numbered circles; results on a learning capacity measure are shown in column 8; all scores are expressed in stanines; and median stanines for each sub-test and the capacity measure are shown at the bottom. It will be apparent that this class is quite homogeneous in both ability and achievement: no pupil is below the fourth stanine. Median stanines on the *Metropolitan,* based on national norms, are all 7 or 8. The median stanine on the *Pintner-Durost* is 6, suggesting that the achievement of this class is consistent with its measured capacity to learn.

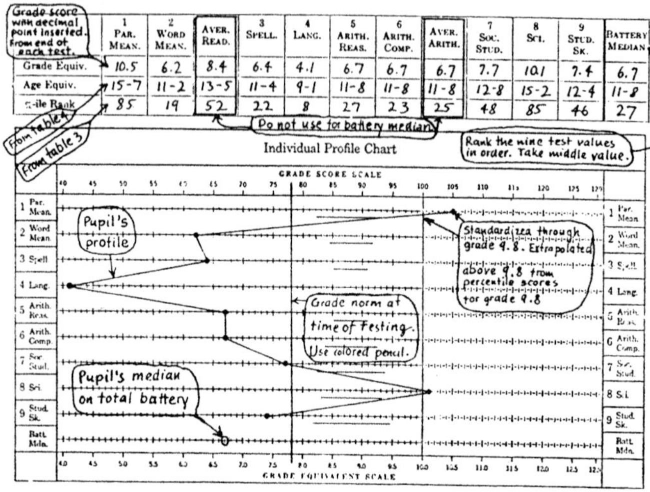

Fig. 9.1 : A Pupil's Completed Profile Chart, Based on His Scores on the *Stanford Achievement Test, Advanced Battery.*

From *Stanford Achievement Test: Forms J-N* by Truman L. Kelley, *et al.* Individual Profile Chart from *Direction for Administering Intermediate and Advanced Complete Batteries.* Reproduced from *Stanford Achievement Test,* copyright 1952–1956 by Harcourt Brace Jovanovich, Inc.

Figure 9.3 shows results for a Grade 6 heterogeneous class on the *Metropolitan* and the *Pintner Intermediate* tests. The first and most obvious difference from the Grade 2 chart is the much greater range in ability and achievement. Pupils range in both from the first stanine to the ninth. Median stanines are all 5's. Individual profiles for a few pupils are again shown by connecting lines revealing, in some cases, wide fluctuations from one sub-test to another, in other cases, extremely consistent performance.

Such class analysis charts and profiles provide teachers with valuable information and facilitate interpretations of test results for most of the purposes for which tests may be used.

Fig. 9.2 : Class Analysis Chart–Homogeneous Second-Grade Class.

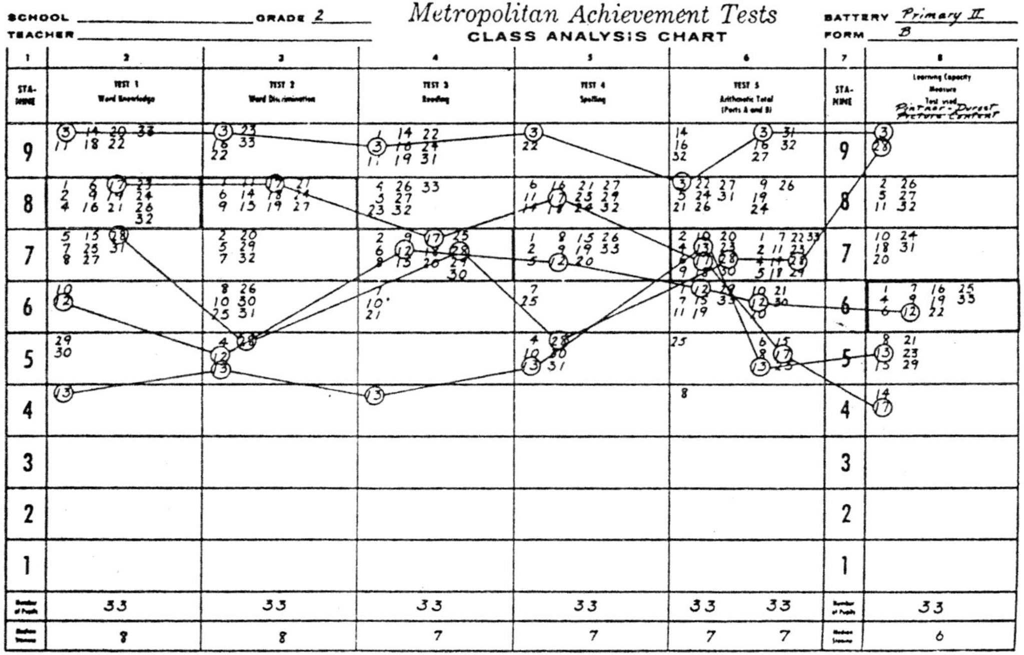

Reproduced from *Metropolitan Achievement Tests, Manual for Interpreting* by Walter N. Durost, copyright © 1958-1962 by Harcourt Brace Jovanovich, Inc.

Fig .9.3 : Class Analysis Chart—Heterogeneous Sixth-Grade Class.

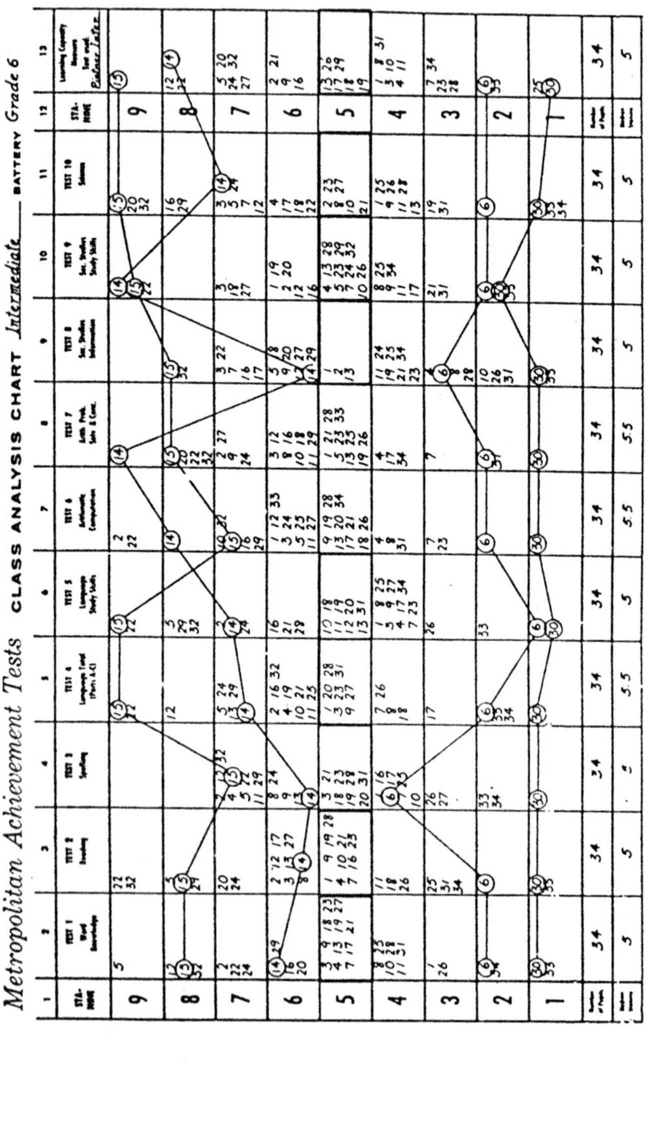

Reproduced from *Metropolitan Achievement Tests, Manual for Interpreting* by Walter N. Durost, copyright © 1958-1962 by Harcourt Brace Jovanovich, Inc.

Placement and Promotion

One of the primary uses of test results is placement of pupils at particular grade levels, promoting, accelerating, or holding them as may be judged appropriate. Ideally, pupils should be placed at levels where they can learn without being unduly discouraged, overworked, or bored. Placement at particular grade levels may be thought of as *vertical* classification, as contrasted with *horizontal* grouping which will be discussed shortly. The most useful test for such classification or grade placement is probably a general school achievement battery. As noted above, these batteries have grade norms for the separate subject tests, norms for the battery as a whole, and norms for converting the scores into age levels. With these three types of norms it is possible to determine fairly accurately a pupil's grade level with regard to achievement in school subjects.

When a pupil transfers from one school to another, particularly when he moves to a different school system or state, a standardised achievement battery is one of the most dependable tools for determining his level of achievement. It is probably more accurate to speak of *levels* of achievement, since these will not always be the same in different subjects or parts of the test battery, and, as we have seen, the profile, based on scores on the different subject tests, will generally not be a straight line.

It is usually desirable in classifying pupils to give a general intelligence test in addition to achievement tests so that both educational and general mental development can be taken into account in placing the pupil. Then, knowing his grade level of achievement, his chronological age, his mental age and his I.Q., it is possible to arrive at a decision based on objective data rather than guesswork. If the pupil's previous school record is available, this too should be taken into consideration, though for grade placement with respect to subject-matter achievement the test battery is probably the more accurate measure.

Thus, for example, if a pupil is nine years, six months of age, with an over-all achievement of the seventh month of the fifth grade, and a mental age of ten years, eight months, we can form a fairly accurate estimate of his level of development and achievement. His I.Q. is 10–8 (or 128 months) divided by 9–6 (or 114 months) $\times$ 100, or 112. Assuming school entrance was between

5–6 and 6–0 (which can usually be checked), we have the following data:

Age	M.A.	Grade Level	I.Q.	Year in School
9–6	10–8	5–7	112	5th

In this case the picture is fairly clear. The pupil is somewhat above average in mental age and intelligence, and is at grade for his age and years in school. He could properly be placed in the fifth grade and encouraged to do extra work and outside reading to satisfy his accelerated mental development.

In cases involving retardation or acceleration the same types of information about the individual will be useful. The weight of evidence and opinion seems to be against holding pupils back, particularly at upper grade levels. Studies show that most pupils repeating a grade do just as badly or worse than they did the first time. If this is generally true, there seems little to be said in favour of holding back over-age pupils. However, tests can be very useful in determining a slow-learner's level of achievement and his mental level. A pupil aged twelve years with a reading level of third grade, a mental age of nine, and an I.Q. of 75 will almost surely flounder hopelessly if he tries to do sixth-grade work. He may never go beyond the eighth grade and can hardly be expected to do satisfactory work as compared with average pupils; yet he can be helped through special instruction in reading, arithmetic, and other subjects by the use of material at the third-grade level in difficulty, but suitable in content for a twelve-year-old. The necessary preliminary information for the proper adjustment of a programme to individual differences in ability and achievement is provided most quickly and efficiently by standardised tests.

The question of acceleration is related to that of non-promotion. If it is undesirable to hold back slow pupils, the same argument applies in the case of bright ones. When a very able pupil is kept *at grade* for his age we are in effect not promoting him just as surely as when we make a dull pupil repeat a grade. Pressey has made a thorough review of the substantial evidence on this point. The evidence shows clearly that students who are accelerated by extra promotions in school, or who are permitted to finish college in less than the usual time, seem to do well in their studies and are well adjusted socially; they seem not to suffer in health, and not to be handicapped otherwise as a result of their acceleration. Nevertheless, many school authorities are reluctant to adopt such practices. Parents also often wish their children to remain with "their group", and are fearful of what acceleration might do to their children's social adjustment. It is unfortunate that high school and college students who are both mentally and physically advanced for their age are generally required to sit through all the regular lessons and classes when they could proceed much faster in the environment of a more advanced grade or level. Not only would acceleration save much valuable time, but it would also help to avoid the boredom and the bad study habits which may be developed by a bright pupil who is required to wait while the slowest in the group catches up.

When achievement tests and mental tests reveal that a pupil is accelerated in achievement and mental development, and if he has no physical or social handicaps, he should be carefully considered for extra promotions and adjustment of work to his level. Moreover, he should be encouraged to progress through school and college as rapidly he can, and at every level the tasks presented him should be in keeping with his abilities and should require appropriately high standards of work. Able students are needed in the world of today, perhaps more than ever before. To hold them back on the basis of fears which seem quite unsubstantiated by the available evidence is an injustice to them and to society.

Homogeneous Grouping

Various methods of grouping pupils according to ability are widely practiced, particularly in the elementary grades. The grouping may be done informally and more or less subjectively, as when a teacher of second grade forms her thirty pupils into reading groups of ten to fifteen on the basis of reading ability. Or it may be done formally, as when a hundred pupils in the fifth grade are divided into three classes according to general mental ability.

This type of classification, by which pupils in the same grade are grouped according to ability, may be thought of as *horizontal*, in contrast with the *vertical* grouping already discussed. Ability classification, or homogeneous grouping in one form or another is common in the elementary schools where pupils read, recite, and do other academic work in groups whose members are usually judged by the teacher to be somewhat alike in ability. However, in the elementary school pupils are not sectioned and separated as high school pupils usually are, and therefore the objection that grouping at the elementary level is undemocratic does not apply, or at least seems less important. There is ample opportunity in the elementary classroom for social intercourse among all pupils in a class, even if they are grouped according to ability in reading, arithmetic and other academic work.

Grouping has been a somewhat controversial practice. Its opponents have charged that pupils placed in fast groups are likely to become "conceited", while those in the slow group are stigmatised as "dumbbells". They have also held that there is no such thing as a homogeneous group and that when pupils are grouped on the basis of one criterion, such as I.Q., they are still heterogeneous with respect to other, perhaps equally important, criteria, such as achievement. Furthermore, it is said that individual pupils vary widely in different skills or abilities. The profile Figs. 9.1, 9.2 and 9.3 throw some light on this point. It is apparent that, while a given pupil does not perform at exactly the same level on each sub-test of the achievement battery, there is much consistency of performance in many cases. It is also clear that the range of performance on the *Metropolitan* is much smaller in the homogeneous class than in the heterogeneous class.

Recent years have seen a greatly increased emphasis on quality in education and greatly increased interest in providing stimulating and challenging opportunities for the superior pupil. It is felt that we have permitted the most able pupils to go along at "half speed" as it were, with a resultant loss of interest and accomplishment. Advocates of homogeneous grouping believe that providing a more rewarding and challenging education for gifted pupils can be done more easily and successfully if such pupils are grouped or sectioned so that they can have an enriched programme and can also proceed at an accelerated pace. It is also maintained that homogeneous sections for slow learners are advantageous for them in that the instruction can proceed at a pace more suited to their abilities. Furthermore, it is felt that the slower learners in a class of similar capacity and interests avoid the discouragement and failure that are often their lot when they are instructed in classes with pupils who are much more able academically.

A great deal of research has been done on the question of homogeneous grouping. One of the earliest reports dealt largely with the question of reactions to the practice. The conclusion on this point was that where such grouping was practiced, the majority of parents, pupils and teachers were happy and satisfied with it. Similar reports seem to indicate that the slow learners, who are quite often the main concern of opponents of the practice, prefer homogeneous to heterogeneous classes. A study in point was conducted by Drews. This was a carefully designed, controlled experiment involving 432 ninth-grade pupils enrolled in English classes in four junior high schools. The pupils were sectioned into Superior, Average and Slow groups on the basis of (1) achievement in reading and language, (2) I.Q., (3) school marks, and (4) teacher judgment. The performance of homogeneous classes was compared with that of equivalent heterogeneous classes. Each of the latter classes included the full range of abilities represented in the three levels of homogeneous groups.

On a questionnaire of attitudes toward homogeneous and heterogeneous classes, 83 per cent of the slow students in homogeneous classes gave positive reactions toward homogeneous classes as against 60 per cent positive reactions toward heterogeneous classes by slow students in such classes. One the same questionnaire superior students in homogeneous classes gave 73 per cent positive reactions toward such classes as against 33 per cent positive reactions of superior students in heterogeneous classes toward such classes.

Summaries of research studies of homogeneous grouping indicate that the results, taken altogether, are inconclusive. The findings in about half the studies are favourable to the practice and an equal number are unfavourable. In any case, wherever homogeneous grouping is used several factors have a most important bearing on the success of the practice. First, it must be recognised that what teachers do in adapting content and method to different ability groups largely determines how effective the grouping will be in terms of increased learning and attainment of goals. To form different groups according to ability without making modifications in the methods and materials used with those groups is not likely to result in any advantage.

Second, in any scheme of grouping there should be provision for the shifting and adjustment of individual pupils. No pupil should feel that he is finally and permanently attached to a particular group. The able pupil must demonstrate his ability to stay in a faster group, while the slow pupil should always be made to feel that he can change his status by doing better work. Such flexibility, though perhaps difficult from the administrative standpoint, would go far toward meeting one of the most frequently-voiced objections to ability grouping, namely, that it is not democratic. Moreover, it would provide excellent motivation for pupils at all levels and in every group.

Third, as the previously presented profiles have clearly shown, a pupil's achievement in different academic areas is often uneven. Consequently, it may be appropriate to have him in a fast section in one subject, an average section in another, and perhaps even in a slow section in a third subject. For example, the pupil whose profile is shown in Figure 9.1 is above the grade norm in Paragraph Meaning and Science, at the grade norm in Social Studies and Study Skills, and far below in Language. If ability grouping were practiced he would presumably be in fast, average and slow sections in these respective areas. To be effective any system of grouping should take such differences into account in the placement of pupils.

It seems reasonable to assume that such flexibility would help to eliminate or at least reduce any tendency to stigmatise pupils, since the same pupil would probably be in different groups for different subjects or activities.

Diagnosis and Remedial Work

In contrast to the two areas of usefulness just discussed, the employment of tests for diagnosis is an instructional function rather than an administrative one. The purpose of a diagnostic test is to find the specific weaknesses and strengths of a pupil in a particular area of study or subject-matter. In the survey of measurement practices and preferences of high school teachers it was found that diagnostic testing and remedial work are the most frequently mentioned uses of standardised test results. Between 40 and 50 per cent of the teachers using standardised tests reported these as their purposes in giving such tests. It will be recalled from Chapter 8, also, that these uses of test results were the most frequently mentioned by Michigan teachers in elementary grades and the second most frequent in secondary grades.

The process of diagnosis in education may be thought of as a progression from broad, general areas to narrower and more specific knowledges or skills. For example, one might begin by giving to a class of seventh-grade pupils a survey battery including tests of Language Arts, Social Studies, Mathematics and Science. After these tests are scored and the results analysed, it might appear that the class as a whole is up to or above acceptable standards in all areas tested except language arts. Further testing in the language arts might show that vocabulary, reading and spelling are acceptable, but that there are serious weaknesses in fundamentals of grammar, sentence structure, punctuation and capitalisation. Knowing of these weaknesses, one can then proceed to give diagnostic tests in these areas to determine which fundamentals have been inadequately mastered and are in need of further study and drill. The real diagnosis is done only at this last level of measurement, although all that precedes it is basic to the last step. However, a teacher may begin at this point without going through the earlier steps. That is, he may give his pupils a diagnostic test at any time to discover strengths and weaknesses in pupil learning so that he may review and improve points not mastered through previous teaching and study.

A truly diagnostic test should be planned and constructed with this function in mind. Many achievement tests may be used for diagnosis, but much time and energy is saved and a more systematic analysis is possible when a test is designed and built with diagnosis in mind, if that is to be its function. There are several important steps to be followed in the diagnostic testing procedure.

First, *there should be a careful analysis of the rules, principles, knowledges, or skills which the test is intended to measure:* In the example cited above, this would mean analysis of the rules or principles of good usage with respect to grammar, sentence structure, punctuation and capitalisation in English. The Pressey *Diagnostic Tests in English Composition* are good examples of tests based on this kind of analysis. The test in each of the four areas covers the basic rules in that area. For example, the punctuation test covers such rules as, "Every declarative sentence should be followed by a period." The capitalisation test covers such rules as, "Begin every proper name with a capital letter," and similarly appropriate rules are covered in the tests of grammar and of sentence structure.

Second, *a good diagnostic test is planned and constructed so that every rule or principle is adequately and equally tested by objective items.* For example, in the Pressey test on capitalisation each of seven basic rules is covered by four objective test items. By this method, no point of importance is slighted or over-emphasised, and the user of the test can be sure of reasonably adequate and systematic coverage.

Third, *the test items are generally arranged in groups to facilitate analysis and diagnosis.* That is, if there are four items on each rule, those dealing with the same rule will be placed together rather than scattered throughout the entire test. This makes it simpler, in analysing the results, to determine specific areas of strength and weakness.

In addition to the above-mentioned principles, diagnostic tests are usually accompanied by a chart similar to the one reproduced in Figure 9.4. This permits the diagnosis of strengths and weaknesses of the class or group as a whole, as well as of individuals.

The diagnostic chart for Miss Jones's seventh-grade class reveals the standing of individuals and of the class. Reading across the page, it is possible to determine individual needs in capitalisation. Jane Allen, for example, misses only five items out of twenty-eight, and these deal with Rules 4, 5, 6 and 1, respectively. On the other hand, Mary Brady appears to be very weak on capitalisation, for she has answered correctly only eight out of twenty-eight and has missed most of the items relating to every rule except No. 2.

Reading the chart vertically, by groups of items relating to each rule, we see that the class as a whole is strong on Rules 2, 7 and 1, and is comparatively weak on Rules 3, 4, 5 and 6—especially the latter two. This gives Miss Jones information which will be useful in planning remedial work and drill for the whole class.

At the side of the figure chart the individual scores are tabulated and the median is determined. By comparison with seventh-grade norms it is evident that this class is quite deficient in knowledge and understanding of the rules of capitalisation and will need thorough review and practice on fundamentals. Sometime later, another form of the test may be given to measure improvement. Since there are four forms of the test, the teacher may test and teach, test and teach, several times without giving the same test twice.

Equivalent forms are very advantageous in diagnostic tests, perhaps even more for standardised tests in general. The most widely accepted method for the use of diagnostic tests calls for testing, remedial instruction, retesting, further remedial instruction, etc., until adequate mastery is attained. For this process it is highly desirable to have available several equivalent forms of each test so that the second and subsequent testings may be done with different forms covering the same objectives. This avoids the repeated use of exactly the same questions, and thus greatly reduces or practically eliminates gain in scores due to familiarity with the questions.

Another example of a truly diagnostic test is the *Doren Diagnostic Reading Test,* designed for use at the end of the second grade or beginning of the third grade. It is based on the theory that reading difficulty occurs mainly because of deficiency in skills of word recognition. Unless a child possesses these skills to an acceptable degree he will not be able to develop the higher level skills of understanding or comprehension necessary to acquire information, apply it as in study, or read for enjoyment.

The test is based on the analysis of word recognition skills as found in five basic reading programmes. The skills arrived at through the analysis are the following:

1. Letter recognition
2. Beginning sounds
3. Whole word recognition
4. Words within words
5. Speech consonants
6. Ending sounds
7. Blending

Fig. 9.4 : Analysis Chart Showing the Results of a Seventh-Grade Class on the *Pressey Diagnostic Test in Capitalisation.* Reproduced by permission of the publishers, The Bobbs Merrill Company, Inc.

CAPITALIZATION TEST RULES COVERED BY TEST

1. Capitalize the first word of every sentence. Capitalize also the first word of every line of poetry, and the first word of a direct quotation. However, if the quotation is indirect do not use the capital.

2. Capitalize the names of persons, with their titles; however, do not capitalize titles when they are not part of a name.

3. Capitalize the names of countries, states, cities, streets, buildings, of mountains, rivers, oceans, or any word designating a particular location or part of the world; however, do not capitalize the points of the compass, or such terms as street, river, ocean, when not part of a name.

4. Capitalize the names of business firms, schools, societies, or other organizations; however, do not capitalize such words as company, school, society, when not part of a name.

5. Capitalize words derived from the names of countries, places, organizations or persons.

6. Capitalize the days of the week, the months of the year, and holidays; however, do not capitalize the seasons.

7. Capitalize the first word, and all other important words, in titles (and sub-titles and headings) of themes, magazine articles, poems, books, of laws or governmental documents, and the trade names of commercial products.

Grade 7th School Roosevelt City Smithport State Pa. Date 11/15/55 Examiner Miss Jones

Form of Test 1 (1, 2, 3 or 4)

Capitalization Test

	Pupil's Name / Sentence →	1	2	3	4	5	6	7	8	9	10	11	12	13	14	15	16	17	18	19	20	21	22	23	24	25	26	27	28	Total
1	Allen, Jane	X	X	X	X	X	X	X	X	X	X		X	X		X	X	X	X	X	X	X		X		X		X	X	23
2	Bedford, Jim		X	X				X		X		X	X		X	X		X	X				X			X	X		X	14
3	Brady, Mary	X	X		X		X									X				X							X		X	8
4	Clark, Mary Jane	X		X	X		X	X	X			X			X			X			X		X		X		X	X	X	15
5	Cole, Harry	X	X		X	X					X			X			X			X				X		X	X		X	12
6	Drake, Alice	X	X		X		X					X				X			X		X		X			X	X	X	X	13
7	Ferguson, Charles		X	X			X				X				X			X		X		X					X	X		10
8	[illegible], Marjorie	X		X	X		X	X		X		X	X	X		X			X	X	X		X		X		X		X	17
9	Gray, Bob			X		X			X						X			X	X					X			X		X	9
10	[illegible], Elmer	X	X		X			X			X									X	X					X		X	X	10
11	Holt, John	X	X	X					X			X			X		X	X		X						X		X	X	12
12	Jones, Albert	X		X	X		X				X			X				X		X			X	X			X	X		12
13	Lane, Kenneth	X	X	X						X			X							X					X	X		X	X	10
14	Lane, Susan	X	X	X	X	X							X			X		X			X			X		X		X	X	13
15	Miller, Paul	X	X	X	X		X	X			X	X		X			X	X	X	X	X	X	X		X	X	X	X	X	21
16	Nelson, Jim	X		X	X	X					X		X		X					X				X		X		X		11
17	Reed, Henry		X	X			X		X	X									X					X			X		X	9
18	Ross, Ruth	X		X	X			X			X		X			X					X					X	X		X	11
19	Scott, Bill	X	X	X		X				X								X					X			X	X	X	X	11
20	Watson, Ann	X	X		X				X			X		X			X		X		X				X	X	X		X	13
21	White, Frank	X	X	X			X				X	X			X	X			X		X	X		X		X		X	X	15
22																														
23																														
24																														
25																														
26																														
27																														
28																														
29																														
30																														
31																														
32																														
33																														
34																														
35																														
36																														
37																														
38																														
39																														
40																														
	Total right—each sentence →	17	15	16	13	6	10	7	6	6	9	8	7	6	7	8	5	10	9	11	10	4	7	8	5	14	14	13	18	
	Rule illustrated (Forms 1 and 3)	Rule 2				Rule 3				Rule 4				Rule 5				Rule 7				Rule 6				Rule 1				
	Rule illustrated (Forms 2 and 4)	Rule 6				Rule 2				Rule 3				Rule 5				Rule 4				Rule 1				Rule 7				

Compare with rules in column to left. • Notice what rules are most frequently violated • Teach each child what he does not know.

Norms (November testing)

Grade	Medians: Forms 1 & 2	Medians: Forms 3 & 4
7	18.8	18.0
8	20.4	19.7
9	21.5	20.5
10	22.8	21.3
11	23.3	22.1
12	23.8	22.5
College	24.0	23.0

Class Record

Score	No. of Pupils
28	
27	
26	
25	
24	
23	/
22	
21	/
20	
19	
18	
17	/
16	
15	//
14	/
13	///
12	///
11	///
10	///
9	//
8	/
7	
6	
5	
4	
3	
2	
1	
0	
Total	21
Median	12

8. Rhyming
9. Vowels
10. Sight words
11. Discriminate guessing (ability to supply missing words from a clue given by other words in content).

Each of the skills listed is measured by a separate part of the test, thus enabling the teacher to identify for each pupil his specific weaknesses in skills of word recognition. The test is designed to be given to pupils in groups, thereby saving much time over what would be required for individual diagnosis. It may, of course, be given to individual children. The total time required is three hours.

The test has been carefully standardised. Correlations with scores on a reading achievement test range from .77 in Grade 1 to .92 in Grade 4. Mean scores show substantial growth in word recognition skills in Grades 1 and 2 with smaller increments, as might be expected, in Grades 3 and 4. Reliabilities of the eleven sub-tests range from .53 to .83 with most in the .70's and .80's. As sub-test reliabilities go, these are good.

The manual is very complete. It includes a detailed account of the rationale and development of the test, instructions for administering and scoring, and technical data. In addition, there are many practical suggestions for remedial activities in each skill tested and a class analysis chart similar to the one shown in Figure 9.4 for the *Pressey* test.

Although the discussion so far has stressed the value and usefulness of diagnostic tests as such, it is quite possible for a teacher to make diagnosis by studying results of standardised achievement tests. By tabulating responses to individual items on a sub-test of a battery he can determine strengths and weaknesses of individuals and of classes or groups. Although this procedure is not likely to yield as systematic and thorough coverage as a planned diagnostic instrument, it nevertheless can provide the teacher much useful information on which to base remedial instruction. There can be no doubt that the diagnosis so frequently mentioned by teachers as the most important use of results of standardised testing is often of this nature. Producers of standardised tests of achievement, particularly in basic tool subjects, would be well advised to facilitate and encourage such use of their tests by organising them, insofar as practical, with that use in mind. It is also helpful to include table sof specifications and classification of items in manuals accompanying standardised achievement tests. Many publishers now provide this information.

Finally, it should be recognised that diagnostic testing does not necessarily reveal the *causes* of weaknesses. A diagnostic test in arithmetic may reveal certain specific deficiencies, let us say, in the multiplication of two-place numbers by two-place numbers, as 87 × 34. These weaknesses may be the result of a lack of correct knowledge of multiplication tables, or of carrying, or of adding, or of some other process. But knowing that a pupil does not perform one or the other of these operations correctly is no guarantee that remedial work and drill on the specific processes will produce the desired improvement. Deficiencies in learning may be due to various causes, such as defective hearing or vision, poor home conditions, unsatisfactory relations with classmates or teacher, lack of ability, and so on. In all diagnostic and remedial work it is essential to attempt to identify the basic causes of deficiencies, and to work on those. Otherwise, remediation is likely to be a waste of time and energy.

Counselling and Guidance

Broadly stated, the function of the counsellor or guidance worker is to help pupils achieve satisfactory and satisfying solutions to their problems. Darley, as a result of a survey of high school seniors in a large city, classified these problems in a descending order of frequency, as follow: (1) vocational, (2) educational, (3) social or personal, (4) financial, (5) family adjustment, and (6) health. The emphasis might be different at lower grade levels or in different communities, but the categories seem to encompass the major areas of concern to adolescents, as well as to people in general.

The most common problems under these respective categories were: (1) discrepancy between vocational goal and abilities, (2) discrepancy between educational goal and abilities, (3) feelings of inferiority, (4) too much outside work, and inadequate finances, (5) family conflicts over educational and vocational plans, desire for independence, personality and age differences, and (6) poor health. Under educational problems (2) should probably be added those related to the choice of subjects (such problems, for example, as whether to take algebra or homemaking), and those related to the choice of a curriculum or course of study.

Among the "tools" available to and used by the counsellor, tests are often regarded as of central importance. This is recognised in the National Defense Education Act of 1958, which provides financial support for testing in programmes of guidance and counselling. The extensive use and the value of tests in counselling and guidance is also attested by the requirement of courses in tests and measurements in training programmes for counsellors or by the publication of books dealing specifically with the use of tests in the counselling process.

It is difficult to imagine how a guidance programme could function without the use of measures of intelligence, achievement, aptitudes, interests and personality. Where discrepancies between goals and abilities exist, intelligence test results tactfully and confidentially discussed with the pupil may help bring about a readjustment of plans more in line with his talents. Marks and test scores representing the student's achievement in school work will often bring a student to face realities and help him decide that perhaps he does not want to be an electrical engineer after all, in view of the advanced mathematics and physics required. Together with the results of measures of general academic ability, such data, when discussed sympathetically with the pupil and his parents, have great value in bringing about an acceptance of educational and vocational goals that are more consistent with abilities. Such counselling procedures often avoid frustration and unhappiness for those most concerned.

On the other hand, tests of academic ability may reveal a discrepancy of the opposite nature. This occurs when a pupil is not working up to capacity as shown by high level performance on intelligence tests and poor marks in school subjects. Although much has been written about these "under-achievers", not much is known about effective methods of motivating them to close the gap between achievement and ability. However, standardised tests of intelligence serve to identify such individuals and provide the counsellor with facts and insights he may otherwise not have. At least they serve to identify the problem, though they do not provide a solution.

When a pupil seeks guidance in educational or vocational

matters, tests of aptitudes and interests provide useful tools. The nature of such instruments has already been discussed in Chapter 5, and the applications of these instruments in guidance and counselling are obvious, particularly with reference to educational and vocational decisions.

An aptitude test is a useful tool in counselling if the results are properly understood and used. A high score on a test of mechanical aptitude does not guarantee success in an occupation requiring mechanical ability any more than a good score on a test of musical aptitude guarantees that the person who made the score will become a great musician. Many other factors besides aptitude enter into success; interest, effort, persistence and opportunity, for example. Yet the counsellor can encourage the person making a high score on an aptitude test by saying that he seems to have the talent if he will develop it, and can help him to determine whether or not he has the other qualities needed for success in the field in question.

On the other hand, the counsellor can speak with more assurance in the case of a low score on test. It is safe and pertinent, in such instances to point out to the individual that statistics show that perhaps only one person in ten with an equivalent score is successful in this particular vocation.

In this connection the so-called *expectancy table* is a useful device for estimating probabilities of success and for interpreting test scores to the student. An example of such a Table 9.1 is shown.

In Table 9.1, scores on a *General Clerical Test* are plotted against performance ratings. Thus, all of those making test scores of 200 or better are predicted to obtain rating of average or better. Of those making scores of less than 100 only 55 per cent are expected to be rated average or better. The percentages are also shown in the graph to the right.

With information of this nature the counsellor can say to a student whose test score, for example, falls in the 50–99 range that his probability of attaining average or better ratings is on the order of 1 in 2. The accuracy of such predictions depends, of course, on a number of factors including the size and representativeness of the sample, and the reliability of the test and of the criterion (in this case, ratings). Furthermore, the counsellor would want to take into consideration other factors besides test scores, such as personal characteristics and plans, aptitudes, etc. The limitations of expectancy tables are not to be overlooked but they do provide a useful tool for the counsellor in helping students to arrive at sound educational and vocational decisions.

Table 9.1

Expectancy Table and Graph Showing Per cent Expected to Rate Average or Better in Office Clerical Tasks on the Basis of Scores on the *General Clerical Test* (N = 65, mean score = 136.1, S.D. = 39.1, r_{bis}=.31).

General Clerical Tests Scores	No. in Score Group	No. Rated Average or Better	% Rated Average or Better
200–up	5	5	100
150–199	18	15	83
100–149	31	23	74
50–99	11	6	55
Total	65		

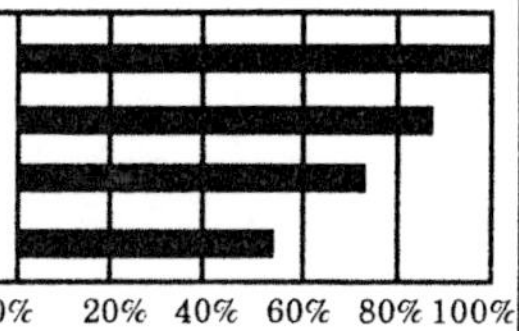

Expectancy Tables—*A Way of Interpreting Test Validity.* New York: The Psychological Corporation. Test Service Bulletin, No. 38 (December 1949).

The interest inventory provides a useful supplement to other kinds of tests. It should be emphasised again, perhaps even more strongly than in the case of aptitude tests, that a particular pattern of interests or preferences is not in any sense a guarantee of success in a given field. All one can say is that the interest score or pattern of the individual tested resembles or does not resemble that of successful persons in a particular occupation or field of work.

Interest tests are widely used, especially at the high school and junior college level. The results of such tests, when carefully studied and discussed with the counsellor, have considerable usefulness, particularly in giving the student more insight into his own potentialities and causing him to think more carefully about his own decisions and choices. Used in conjunction with the results of other tests, with information about home background, financial status, scholastic record, and health, they help to round out the picture of the individual.

Student problems also frequently occur in the areas of adjustment and personality. The survey reported by Darley revealed that feelings of inferiority, lack of confidence, and personality clashes in the home were among the most common problems of high school seniors. The use of personality measures will sometimes reveal the existence of such problems when interviews and other means have failed to bring them to light.

Personality measures of various types may be used with groups to identify more or less serious cases of maladjustment. In every hundred pupils there will be on the average from two to five who need help and who should be referred to a clinic or to someone trained to deal with such cases. Tests of this nature can also be used by counsellors to shed additional light on the cases of pupils who come for advice and help, either on personal, educational or vocational problems. With the pupil who is having difficulties in school or at home, a personality test often gives a helpful insight into the situation. The test may be supplemented by interviews, anecdotal records, ratings, and other information, all of which will usually provide a basis for understanding and help.

Personality tests may be used to help a pupil make the most of his talents, and they may help him get along better with others and attain better adjustment by giving him and the counsellor more insight into his emotional and social behaviour. In short, these tests help to give the individual a better understanding of himself, and thus explain why he behaves as he does in certain situations.

Concerning financial problem and poor health, the counsellor will obtain information about problems of this nature through means other than tests. These difficulties, particularly the health problems, usually require expert advice and treatment, and the responsibility of the counsellor is mainly to identify such cases and refer them to the proper authorities. There may be things a counsellor can do to help a pupil earn money in after-school hours, or to help the one who is working too many hours outside, but these are not matters in which tests will generally play a significant role. Yet a knowledge of a student's I.Q. may be useful in helping the counsellor and the student decide how much work he can take on to earn money without doing an injustice to his school work.

Marking

It was stated early in this book that measurement and evaluation are a part of the job of teaching. Every teacher has the responsibility for making the best judgments he can about his pupils' achievement and development in subject-matter, maturity, citizenship, character, and other areas. These judgments may be expressed in various ways, but marks are the most common. As our schools and educational programmes are constituted, marks are an integral part of the system. Pupils, parents and administrators expect them. They are the terms in which appraisals of a pupil's accomplishments are communicated. It is, therefore, only sensible for the teacher to try to do the best possible job of evaluating and marking, to strive constantly to improve the marking system, and to do his best to keep abreast of improvements in marking practices.

That measurement has an important function in marking is self-evident. Teachers regularly use tests and examinations of their own devising as a basis for marking, especially when measuring achievement in subject-matter. However, tests of capacity such as the intelligence test are also useful in marking in that they provide a basis for judging whether or not a pupil is working up to capacity. It has been suggested that two marks be given, one expressing actual achievement in terms of A, B, C, D or F, and the other in terms of S or U, expressing whether the pupil is doing satisfactory or unsatisfactory work in relation to his ability. Thus, one pupil of high intelligence might get a B and a U in algebra, while another less able pupil might receive a C and an S. In at least one community where this has been tried, the system apparently worked well.

A perennial question in arriving at marks has to do with the propriety of using standardised tests for this purpose. It may be said at once that the use of such tests as the sole basis for marks is seldom justified, since no standardised test is likely to provide adequate measures of all the outcomes of a course in a particular school or community. Few teachers would be satisfied to base the evaluation of their pupils' accomplishments solely or even substantially on standardised test scores. Nevertheless, it is true that such tests may be useful in helping to arrive at a semester's or a year's mark in a given course. That is, when a standardised test is judged by the teacher to be an adequate measure of one or more of the locally determined goals of instruction, there would seem to be no valid reason for not using it, together with other measures, for marking purposes. A standardised test can supplement or contribute to evaluation based on the teacher's own measurement procedures. A goal of every teacher should be the best possible evaluation of each pupil's accomplishments. It is only good sense to make use of every practical device that helps achieve this objective. It may even be that a carefully constructed standardised test will at times provide a better measure of certain outcomes of instruction than the average teacher can make for himself, as, for example, in the case of skills tests in elementary grades. The school assumes some responsibility for the all-around development of each pupil to the extent of his capacity and desire to achieve. This includes not only achievement in subject-matter, but also development of character and personality, physical development and health, maturity in selecting and planning for his future vocation, choosing a life partner, and so on. In any of these areas the teacher may be called upon to express some judgment or evaluation of the pupil's status and development. Every measurement has something to contribute. Personality measures, interest inventories, measures of physical development, and records of health and physical examinations are all useful in making evaluations, whether they are expressed in the form of a mark or in some other manner. Measurement can and should enter in some degree into every aspect of the process of evaluating pupil accomplishment and growth.

The problem of what proportion of various marks to give—how many A's, B's, C's., etc.—is one that is often vexing to teachers. The conscientious instructor tries to do justice to all his pupils and at the same time attempts to conform with good principles of marking. There is no simple method to satisfy both purposes. Recommendations on this point may be based on the concept of the normal curve. In any group or class, unless it is a very small one numbering less than twenty, abilities and achievement are likely to be distributed in a fashion approximating the normal distribution. If this assumption is appropriate, then the distribution of marks should approximate the proportions of the normal curve, which means that the largest proportion should be average, which is usually C. Smaller proportions will be somewhat above and below the average, and these would be marked B and D, respectively. Approximately equal and quite small percentages would be found at the upper and lower extremes, and these would receive marks of A and F, as the case might be.

These principles can be embodied in a number of different systems or proportions, one of the most widely used being based on the standard deviation, which is illustrated in Figure 9.5.

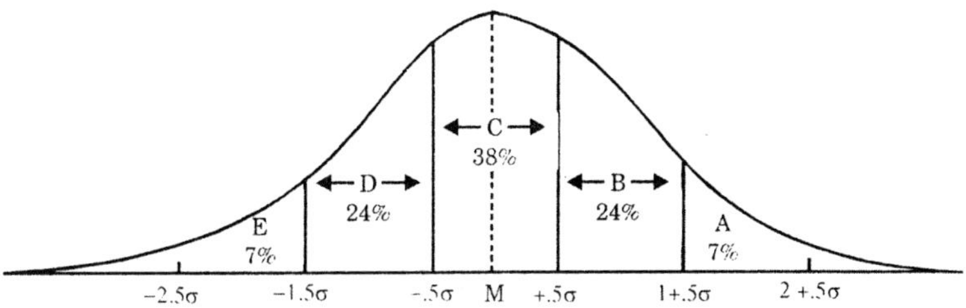

Fig. 9.5. : Distribution of Marks Based on Standard Deviation.

It can be seen that the middle group, or C, extends one half standard deviation on either side of the mean, which area under the normal curve includes approximately 38 per cent of the total. One additional standard deviation beyond these limits on either side will include another 24 per cent in each case; and another standard deviation beyond the $+1.5\sigma$ and -1.5σ, extending to $+2.5\sigma$ and -2.5σ, will include approximately 7 per cent more. The total 38 + 24 + 24 +7 +7 = 100.

Although the results of measurement of most classes will not be distributed in exactly these theoretical proportions, they will quite generally approximate them if (1) the classes are not highly selected, and (2) the measures used are adequate for all levels of ability represented in the group. No teacher will want to force his distribution of marks into these theoretical proportions, particularly if he has reason to believe that the nature of the group or the measuring instruments used do not justify it. Nevertheless, the concept of a normal distribution as applied here can be a very useful guide to a teacher in giving marks and can help him to avoid giving marks that are clearly out of line with sound principles.

What has been said so far and the facts that are known about the distribution of human abilities and achievements provide a basis for some useful generalisations about marking and the use of measurement in marking. A brief statement of these principles is given below. In reading and thinking about them the student is cautioned to remember that no hard and fast rules can be laid down for every teacher to follow in giving marks. Each teacher will have to use his own best judgment in his own situation, since marking, generally speaking, is a responsibility that cannot be shared with anyone else. The one unequivocal principle, if there is such, is that justice be done to *every pupil* insofar as possible, and that none be favoured above any other.

1. *It is generally agreed that marks should be assigned on a comparative basis*. That is, the best pupils should receive the highest marks, the next best, B's, etc. In most school situations this practice is certainly preferable to setting some arbitrary and perhaps unrealistic standard and failing those pupils who do not attain it.

2. *Practice now generally favours the use of a marking system employing a small number of categories such as letters, integers, or stanines*. Letter marks have several advantages: they are easier to use, easier to interpret, and are more realistic. In the first place, it is easier to mark a group with a five-point scale than with one having a hundred divisions. Letter marks are easier to understand for the same reason. It may be said with confidence that not many people can make the fine distinctions of judgment that percentage marks imply. It has been demonstrated that teachers can discriminate among five or six levels of quality or achievement, but not one hundred!

3. *Marks should be based as much as possible on objective measurements*. Enough has been said in earlier discussions to show the unreliability of teachers, judgments of essay examinations. It may be assumed that what was demonstrated in those experiments applies with equal force to other subjective judgments or processes. It may not be possible to find or construct objective measures of all desirable outcomes, but the aim should be to move constantly in this direction and to increase the objectivity of our measurements as much as possible.

4. *As far as possible, marks should express accomplishment of specific goals rather than the results of global or omnibus*

appraisal. A marking system which does not provide for some precise differentiation as, for example, between knowledge and skills, is less informative than one which does. Also, one should not attempt to combine in one mark achievement in subject-matter and such other traits as courtesy, punctuality, or effort. The measurement of these traits is important, but if the pupil is given a B in arithmetic the *mark should denote his accomplishment in that subject.* If desired, he may be given credit for courtesy, effort, and other important matters, but this should be expressed in *separate marks.* Otherwise, two pupils may receive B's in arithmetic, one of the marks representing achievement of A and effort of C, the other representing an achievement of C and effort of A. To give them the same mark of B is an injustice to both pupils as well as to their next teacher, their parents, and any others who have no ways of knowing what the marks really represent.

This principle applies also to the appraisal of growth or improvement. Such outcomes should not be combined in one mark with status or level of accomplishment. To illustrate, let us assume that marks are being given to two girls learning how to type. X starts at ten words per minute and progresses by the end of the year to forty words per minute. Y starts at thirty words per minute and goes to fifty words per minute. X made a gain of thirty words while Y gained only twenty. Yet Y is a more efficient typist than X. Would it be fair to give X a better mark than Y, because she had made a numerically greater gain? It would not seem so. Certainly anyone seeking to employ a typist would be misled if both girls received even the same mark. Here, as in cases already cited, it would be most accurate and fair to use two marks, one for status and another for improvement. Then the picture might be as follows:

Pupil	*Status*	*Important*
X	C	B
Y	B	C

In substance, we are saying that marks should mean and stand for what they are intended to mean and stand for. If a mark is given in English it should represent accomplishment in English and, if possible, should be differentiated to designate accomplishment in composition, American literature, English literature, or some other specific course or part of a course. If evaluations of other important qualities such as effort, citizenship, personal traits, and the like are desired, these should be reported separately with adequate labels so that they will not be confused or misunderstood. The use of objective measurements should contribute to the attainment of this principle in practice.

5. *Finally, better marking can be attained by using a wide variety of measures*. The more measures of a pupil's achievement that are employed and the more varied in approach and design they are, the better the sampling of his behaviour is likely to be. Even if the tests are quite similar in nature the combined results of several of them should give a more accurate appraisal than any one of them alone. This is simply an application of the principle of sampling: the more samples taken the more accurate the measurement will be, always providing, of course, that there is no constant bias operating. Furthermore, by use of a variety of measuring instruments we are likely to obtain a wider sampling than we otherwise would. In measuring the results of instruction in civics, for example, a teacher may find it desirable to use not only tests, but also rating scales, anecdotal records, and systematic observations of behaviour—all of these contributing to the appraisal of achievement in civics.

The principle stated above should not be interpreted to suggest that the assignment of marks is a purely mechanical process. Even with the use of the most objective measurements, judgment by the teacher in translating them into marks is inescapable. This is particularly relevant with respect to decisions on failure or non-promotion. Many factors besides test scores will enter into such decisions, particularly in elementary grades, and it is right that they should. The most important consideration should be the best interests of the learner. At the same time, it should be remembered that "soft-heartedness" and emotionality are inimical to accurate measurement.

An example showing assignment of marks to a college class in tests and measurements will serve to illustrate the principles just enumerated.

There were thirty-six students enrolled in the class, most of whom were juniors and seniors preparing to teach in elementary or secondary schools. The assignments and tests included a set of simple statistical problems; a blueprint or two-way chart showing content and objectives to be measured by an objective test; the test itself, constructed by the student; an objective mid-term test of seventy-five items on the first half of the course; and an objective final examination of seventy-five items covering the second half. The assignments were marked by the instructor personally, either in points (in the case of the statistical problems) or in letter grades. The letter grades were converted to points on the basis of A = 50, B = 40, etc. The mid-term and final were scored on the basis of number right. Thus, in the end, each student's marks or accomplishment were expressed in points. These points were added to obtain a total for each student. The totals were then arranged in a frequency distribution and assigned marks as shown in Table 9.2.

Table 9.2
Distribution of Total Points and Marks Earned by Thirty-six Students in a Course in Educational Measurement

Total	*f**	*Marks*
200–204 ///	3	5A's=14%
195–199 //	2	
199–194//	2	
185–189 ///	3	12 B's=33%
180–184 //	2	
175–179 ////	5	
170–174 //	2	
165–169 ///	3	
160–164 /	1	14 C's=39%
155–159 ~~////~~	5	
150–154 ///	3	
145–149	0	
140–144 /	1	
135–139 /	1	3D's=8%
130–134 /	1	

Total	*f**	*Marks*
125–129	0	
120–124	0	
115–119 /	1	
110–114	0	2F's=6%
105–109	0	
100–104	0	
95–99	0	
90-94 /	1	
N = 36		

* Frequency.

A number of aspects are at once apparent. First, the distribution is not "normal" in the sense of producing, if it were graphed, the bell-shaped curve. It is, in fact, bi-modal because of the fact that some students did additional work on some assignments to obtain graduate credit. Second, the assignments and tests did produce a spread or range. Some students did twice as well, in terms of total points earned, as others. Thus, there is a clear basis for differentiation. Third, it is obvious that the proportions of the different marks assigned are not in accord with any theoretical distribution. There are more than twice as many A's as F's and four times as many B's as D's. Here, the facts that the course is an upper-level elective for prospective teachers and one enrolling graduate students as well as undergraduates have a bearing. This is clearly shown by the top-heavy nature of the distribution and is recognised in the proportion of the various marks given.

It should also be noted that the "breaks" between different marks are placed, insofar as possible, at points where there are gaps in the distribution. This is clearly the case between C and D and between D and F.

It must be admitted that no system of assigning marks is entirely objective. Even if the teacher adopts some arbitrary system such as 7 per cent A's, 24 per cent B's, 38 per cent C's, etc., he is making a decision based on his judgment or belief that

that system is the right one. In the example above, the chief element of subjectivity comes at the choices of division points between marks. In this case, other factors as mentioned above also introduce elements of subjective judgment. Nevertheless, a review of the process illustrated will show that it adheres to and applies each of the principles of good marking enumerated earlier. In larger classes, at lower levels with less selected and more heterogeneous students, and in required courses, it is possible by such a system of appraisal and marking to come much closer to theoretical proportions of marks based on the concept of a normal distribution. However, it must always be kept in mind that the fundamental purpose of marking is not to follow some theory but to communicate as accurate, unbiased and true appraisal of a pupil's achievement as possible.

Curriculum Evaluation

Perhaps one of the most difficult areas in which to measure and evaluate is that of curriculum or programme. Objectives and content are often broad and diverse as, for example, in a year's course in biology or arithmetic; curriculum workers and evaluators often have difficulty in communicating with each other in a meaningful way; and valid methods of measuring and evaluating the outcomes of a course or programme are not always easy to devise or readily available.

Probably no event or action has done more to bring about serious attempts at curriculum evaluation than the Elementary and Secondary School Acts of 1965 and subsequent years. These acts provide billions in federal funds for schools with high poverty populations and they require school districts receiving such funds to evaluate the effectiveness of the programmes or innovations supported by these funds. Although the quality of evaluative efforts thus instigated has sometimes left much to be desired, the effort is being made and the procedures and results seem to be improving.

In general, the curriculum evaluator works in two major areas. First, he tries to evaluate a course or programme as it unfolds or proceeds. Thus, he may find by tests or other means that instruction in fractions is not producing the results desired and he therefore tries to find better methods of instruction. Second, curriculum evaluation may focus on the end product to determine the effectiveness of the course of instruction as a whole. As an example, the evaluator may try to determine by various means how well-prepared graduates of a nurse's course in psychology apply its principles in their relationships to patients.

A pattern for curriculum evaluation has been evolving and is becoming standard practice with but local and generally minor variations. The first step is the identification and clear statement of objectives. As has been frequently emphasised in this volume, all evaluation should begin with this. Objectives should be stated wherever possible in behavioural terms. They should indicate what changes in behaviour are expected as a result of instruction. When objectives have been formulated, test items or other evaluative procedures are developed to measure them. This step is often the most difficult since objectives may be quite broad and diverse and some may not lend themselves to testing by conventional methods. A variety of evaluative procedures including objective and other types of tests, ratings, interviews, observational and anecdotal records, and follow-up may be used as seems appropriate.

One of the most ambitious undertakings in evaluation of instructional programmes is being carried on by the Center for the Study of Evaluation. Objectives and related test items for 16 subject areas (e.g., mathematics, K-3; biology, 10-12, etc.) at elementary and secondary levels have been collected from school districts all over the country. In addition, the Center has participated in the development of additional collections of instructional objectives at the secondary level for nineteen subjects (bookkeeping, woodworking, American history, etc.). To date nearly 25,000 objective test item collections have been distributed to educators in every state and beyond.

Statements of objectives are continuously refined by submission for reactions and criticism to groups of experienced teachers and by soliciting comments from users of the collections in the field. Finally, a small group of ten pilot schools in different parts of the country has been formed to try out and criticise the collections of objectives and test items and, second, to test the usefulness of the products of the Center to the schools. In both respects results have been positive.

Many courses, especially those established with the support of federal funds, are often hastily instituted with little or no advance planning or design; the money is there if something can be started by which to justify a request. In such cases evaluation can help at all stages—planning, trial, revision, further trial and further improvement. In fact, it is essential to the accomplishment of goals. It can also be started that well-established courses frequently have grown without any serious, systematic attempt at evaluation. Indeed, vested interests may strongly resist proposals aimed at subjecting them to any type of objective appraisal, but there is evidence to suggest that attitudes are slowly changing. The impact of the evaluation requirement in Title I may eventually be felt far beyond the limits of the Elementary and Secondary Education Act itself.

Performance Contracting

At this point it seems appropriate to mention an innovation known as *performance contracting*. Briefly, this refers to a plan whereby private firms are employed by a school board to come into a school or district to take over teaching a basic subject like reading or arithmetic, usually to disadvantaged children. The terms of the contract specify that the contractor will be paid according to the "amount of learning" he is able to produce in a given time such as one school year. The funds in most instances come from some federal agency.

Obviously, tests constitute an essential element in such an undertaking as the means of measuring the gains made by pupils. Although standardised achievement tests would appear to be the best measure for the purpose, contractors generally prefer to use tests which they have devised. There are, of course, many difficulties and some dangers inherent in such situations, and experience so far suggests that these are not to be passed over lightly or ignored. One obvious difficulty is that the contractor, in his desire to obtain as much money as he can, will "teach for the test", or even use items from the test as teaching material. There are other problems also which need not be detailed here.

Performance contracting has implications for curriculum evaluation, since it may suggest improvements which will produce better learning materials. It also has implications for improvement of school staff, for the same reason. Finally, if conducted properly with suitable safeguards, it may turn out to be a productive form of educational research for evaluation of different teaching materials and methods.

Motivation

It is generally assumed that the prospect of taking a test motivates pupils to study. There is no doubt that most people make some preparation, if they can, when faced with the prospect of taking a final examination in a course. There are other aspects of the problem of motivation, however. For example, there is the question of whether pupils do better on a final examination if they have had occasional tests during the term or semester than they would without having had such periodic tests. The question is complicated by various factors such as the kinds of periodic tests used in relation to the kind of final examination given, whether students are simply told their scores on the tests or are permitted to go over them afterwards, and whether the tests are announced in advance or are given without warning.

The question of motivation is not a simple one, and it is likely that many teachers and others assume the motivational value of tests without giving much thought to the various problems involved. It is a generally accepted principle of psychology that the practice of a skill with knowledge of results—that is, of errors, successes, and over-all improvement—produces much more progress than practice wherein such information is withheld from the learner. Indeed, there is evidence that the practice of a simple skill such as drawing a straight line just two inches long without knowledge of the accuracy of the preceding efforts or trials does not bring about any real improvement in accuracy. In other words, practice under such conditions does not even result in slight improvement. It is a widely accepted fact that only when the learner knows his errors and knows when he performs well does practice bring about noticeable improvement.

There is considerable experimental evidence on the effect of occasional testing on achievement as measured by success on final examinations. In most such experiments two groups, equal in ability and previous preparation, are formed. Both are taught by the same teacher using the same materials and methods. Both take the same final examination. The only difference is that one group, which may be called the experimental group, is given tests at intervals throughout the semester or term while the control group is not. Any difference in achievement as measured by the final examination can then be ascribed to the single variable of periodic tests.

The results of numerous experiments of a similar nature may be summarised as follows:

First, it appears that the effect obtained differs according to the way in which test results are used. If tests are used as a basis for specific remedial instruction the results seem beneficial. When the tests are returned after being marked, with no indication that they were used for instructional purposes, there is little evidence that this procedure has any great value. Furthermore, most studies on the college level show no effect whatsoever on final achievement when measured by comprehensive objective examinations, even when the test results are discussed with the students or when they are invited to use them for study purposes.

Second, there is a suggestion in one or two reports that less able or below average students are helped more by tests than those who are superior in accomplishment.

There is some indication, in the third place, that younger and less responsible students, as those in secondary schools, are more likely to be motivated and helped by quizzes than older students who are presumably more mature.

Another aspect of the question has to do with the reactions of students to frequent testing. One study is reported in which a college class in introductory psychology was given fourteen weekly objective quizzes in addition to unit tests and a final examination. The quizzes were scored, returned to students, and discussed or commented upon by the instructor. At the end of the semester students responded to a questionnaire asking for their reactions to the weekly quizzes and discussion of test results. Eighty per cent of the students said that the quizzes helped them to learn more, and 20 per cent said no more. Ninety-three per cent reported that the quizzes motivated them to study more than usual. A third question asked students if weekly quizzes caused increased anxiety. Of those who answered in the affirmative, 87 per cent said they still approved the use of weekly quizzes. On the matter of effect on grades, 31 per cent said their grades would be better as a result of the quizzes, 55 per cent said there would be no difference, and 14 per cent said they would be poorer or lower. Also, 89 per cent reported that frequent testing helped to check progress or learning and 11 per cent that it made no difference.

With regard to the effect of class discussion of test results, 31 per cent said it improved subsequent performance, 67 per cent said it made no difference, and 2 per cent said it resulted in poorer performance on succeeding tests. Fifty-three per cent said discussions helped performance on the final examination while 45 per cent reported no difference.

In summary, it may be said that the results of this study show student perceptions of frequent quizzes to be highly favourable. Discussions of test results were viewed as helpful by considerably fewer students, although 75 per cent reported that they helped them avoid foolish or technical errors.

Teachers will probably go on using tests, particularly those of their own devising, at least partly to stimulate pupils to greater achievement, in the belief that the tests function in that way regardless of the findings of experimental studies. In this connection, it must always be remembered that situations and circumstances differ form one teacher and class to another, and that the use of tests for motivational purposes will depend on the individual teacher's judgment and experience of what is effective for him and his students.

The use of tests for motivation is confined largely and quite naturally to achievement tests. There is little that an individual can or should do beforehand in trying to improve his score on tests of intelligence, aptitude, interests or personality. On those, we are interested in motivating the person tested to put forth his maximum effort at the time of testing, and we are interested also in eliminating any coaching, studying, or previous knowledge of the test which might give a pupil an unfair advantage and which might result in an inaccurate and misleading measurement of that pupil's ability. Achievement tests have as their basic purpose the measurement of the results of teaching, and anything that can be done legitimately to improve such learning is desirable. Therefore, if periodic testing serves to stimulate interest and motivate the pupil to greater effort and accomplishment, there is justification for the use of tests for that purpose.

Identification and Study of Exceptional Children

The majority of pupils in our schools fall within what may be thought of as the normal range. However, in nearly every class or group there are those who are outside this range in some respect. They may be exceptionally bright or dull; they may have more or fewer than the usual number of adjustment problems, or their problems may be unusually severe or mild; some may be exceptional in physical qualities—either unusually gifted or perhaps handicapped in some way that interferes with normal participation and success in activities of various sorts. Such children are referred to in educational literature as *exceptional children*.

For those who are exceptional intellectually, tests have been found over many years to provide the best basis for screening and identification of both gifted and retarded. The procedure that seems most effective is to use group tests of mental ability along with nominations by teachers as the initial basis for screening. Those thus located are then tested by a school psychologist or psychometrist with an individual examination such as the *Stanford-Binet*. In the study by Pegnato seven different procedures for identifying gifted children were used and evaluated. The procedure found to be most efficient was an initial screening by the use of group intelligence tests followed by individual testing for actual identification of the gifted.

In recent years much attention has been given to the study of creativity, and there have been attempts to devise tests of creativity. There is some difference of opinion among psychologists regarding the similarity between general mental ability and creativity. Some hold that these are essentially distinct and separate entitles, others that they are very closely related if not the same thing. In Chapters 4 and 5 we have described and discussed tests designed to measure general intelligence and some designed to measure creativity. We need only add here that existing measures of intelligence have been found very useful in identifying intellectually gifted children and that tests of creativity may prove in time to have similar value for identification of giftedness.

Children with obvious physical handicaps such as those who are crippled, those having nervous disorders as a result of brain damage, and the like, pose little problem as far as identification is concerned. The exact nature of the disability will be diagnosed and treatment prescribed by medical means. Less obvious but often equally serious handicaps, as far as school learning is concerned, are defects of vision and hearing. These often go unnoticed by teachers and even parents. Children are apt to try to hide such defects and in rare instances may themselves be unaware of them. They can be detected and measured quite accurately, however, by standard tests.

Visual acuity can be checked by devices such as the *Snellen Chart;* colour vision or colour blindness can be measured by various tests designed for the purpose; and a thorough measurement of all visual functions can be made by such instruments as the *Ortho-Rater, Sight Screener* and the *Telebinocular.*

Hearing acuity or hearing loss can be measured roughly by whisper or watch-tick. The examiner simply determines the greatest distance from which the child can hear a whisper or the tick of a watch. A more accurate and thus more reliable measurement of auditory acuity or defect is made with the *audiometer.* Such instruments as the *puretone audiometer* measure the hearing loss of an individual by determining how much louder the tone must be made for him to hear it than is required with normal hearing.

For use with physically handicapped children the typical paper-and-pencil test of school achievement must often be modified in some way. Larger print for the visually handicapped, oral or Braille instructions for blind children, modification of directions for the deaf or hard-of-hearing, and various adaptations of test procedures for use with crippled children represent ways in which tests have been modified for use with the handicapped child. Individual tests such as the *Stanford-Binet* have also been modified for use with handicapped children.

Tests may also be very useful in measuring results of special programmes. Usually after a handicapped child has been identified and his case diagnosed there is an attempt to do something about his handicap and make adjustments for it. Special schools, special classes, remedial work, therapy of various kinds, and correction of defects by more radical means are used as each case may require. The amount of improvement—educational, psychological, or emotional—may be gauged by the use of suitable tests, either tests designed for the purpose or modifications of existing tests.

In working with exceptional children it is only natural that the handicapped should receive the most attention. A child who is blind, deaf, feeble-minded, or crippled naturally calls forth sympathy and assistance. This is as it should be. However, there is another type of exceptional child, the gifted child, who is often neglected and given even less attention that a normal child. Because a child is gifted it is easy to ignore him or leave him to his own devices while energy and help are directed toward the others. The gifted child can usually be depended upon to "come through" without much help from anyone. Not to give him special attention and encouragement is, however, a short-sighted policy. Our future leaders in science, industry, and public affairs will come largely from the ranks of these gifted children, and it is to society's advantage to help them in every way to make the most of their unusual talents. Not to do so is to risk depriving society of great benefits. There is considerable evidence that schools and society in general are becoming increasingly aware of the importance of giving special attention to gifted children, and that they are now providing rich opportunities for these children to develop their unusual gifts to the fullest.

The development of standardised intelligence tests and, to a lesser degree, standardised achievement tests has made it possible to identify and measure more accurately than ever before these gifted children in our schools. Personality tests have made it possible to study their personal and social characteristics and have demonstrated that, contrary to belief among some persons, children who are gifted intellectually are usually normal and well adjusted, at least as much so as the general population. The use of tests with gifted children has opened a whole new field of study and research which should result in benefits of considerable importance to society as a whole.

The research on creativity referred to earlier, the National Merit Qualifying Examinations, the Advanced Placement Programmes, the testing of high school seniors by selective service, the many scholarships offered by public and private agencies, and loan funds for students are some of the ways in which individuals who have exceptional ability are being encouraged and assisted to obtain as much education as they can take and to develop their talents to the fullest possible extent. Such provisions are advantageous not only to the person who is helped but also to his family, his community, his state and the nation.

Interpreting Schools to the Community

Recent developments in education have included a tremendous increase in the concern, interest and participation of the public in school matter. These developments have affected the work of all school personnel but their effects have been felt most strongly by principals, superintendents, and others in administrative and supervisory positions. They have usually been the ones to answer questions and criticisms, to explain and justify what schools were attempting to accomplish, and to present evidence that these objectives were, in fact, being achieved.

It is with respect to this last point that evaluation and measurement find particular usefulness. When citizens ask for evidence on what their children are learning, the results of testing programmes are naturally among the first lines of evidence to be presented. Likewise, if the question has to do with how well the schools are achieving the objectives set up by and for them, test scores provide evidence on this matter. Evaluation and measurement thus provide one of the best means of interpreting schools to the community.

However, having said this, it is necessary to recognise that this use of test results embodies some problems. One of these is the tendency to react negatively to test results if they do not support or reinforce what the community or individuals want to believe. Reference has been made in an earlier chapter to the reaction to poor scores on a test by faulting the test. If an individual or one's child does badly on a test, the test is said to be biased or unfair. The ultimate result of this attitude would be tests that everyone did well on. This is plainly *reductio ad absurdum*. In some situations there has been a demand that tests such as the *Scholastic Aptitude Test*, an instrument of proven validity in predicting success in college, not be used with certain minority groups because members of these groups typically make poor showings. In some situations the results of such tests have been ignored or those who are well-qualified to interpret them have not been called upon or permitted to do so.

Another problem in the use of the results of measurement in the interpretation of the programme and accomplishments of the schools is the development of understanding by the lay public and even by classroom teachers of the terms and concepts used in measurement and the meaning of the different types of test scores. Unless there is adequate comprehension and understanding of these matters the attempt to explain and interpret the results of measurement may mislead more than inform. In one community a detailed outline of a programme to explain test results to community groups was developed to provide information on the nature and scope of the testing programme, the kinds of tests being given, the skills being tested, and the types of norms and scores used. When such an effort is made parents and teachers will have a much better understanding of the goals and accomplishments of their schools and a sounder basis for interpreting test scores of individual pupils. It seems reasonable to generalise that the results of standardised tests and other measures, when properly presented and understood, can be extremely useful in interpreting schools to the community.

Improvement of School Staff

The use of tests and other measuring techniques can contribute substantially to the professional development of teachers in several ways. In the first place, putting on a measurement programme can result in professional growth through cooperative planning, organising and conducting of such a project. In order to participate actively, teachers must learn something about available tests, the characteristics of good measuring instruments, methods of determining how good a test is, and sources of information which will provide a basis for making such a determination. Some teachers must also learn how to administer, score and interpret tests, and how to put the results to good use. All of these experiences and skills can come out of participation by teachers in a measurement programme.

Another way in which measurement contributes to staff improvement is through the construction of tests and other measures for local use. In this activity a teacher must identify objectives of instruction and try to construct instruments which will measure progress toward them. This will direct attention not only to the objectives, but also to methods and materials for attaining them. It will also bring the pupil into the picture, since in constructing tests, the teacher will constantly be thinking of ways in which to measure pupil changes resulting from instruction.

After the results of measurement are known, these will promote professional growth in the teacher by revealing what has worked well in his instruction and what has not. An appraisal of the apparent effectiveness of his methods and materials will cause him to examine these with new insight. Measurement programmes may also help teachers to learn from each other by revealing individual strengths and weaknesses and by encouraging them to exchange ideas much in the same manner as housewives improve their cooking by exchanging recipes.

Educational measurements may also contribute to the professional growth of school staff by giving the teacher better insight into the individual pupil's capacities, interests, achievements, personality problems and needs. Such improvement in understanding will almost certainly make the teacher more useful and effective as a teacher and as a friend and adviser.

Knowledge and use of measuring procedures may contribute to professional growth of the school staff through the development of a better understanding of the problems involved in accurate measurement of human traits and greater appreciation of the efforts of pioneers in this area. Also, such study and investigation by teachers should help to bring about improvement in their own tests and measuring instruments. The better the evaluative procedures used by teachers and counsellors, the more effective will be their teaching and counselling.

Finally, the use of measuring instruments should be helpful to the administrator and supervisor in many ways. Tests may be used to help select personnel for teaching and other positions. Tests of pupil achievement, observations and rating scales will be useful to the supervision in the in-service education of teachers. Various measuring and evaluative devices such as check lists and score cards may also be useful in arriving at sounder judgments concerning physical facilities.

Educational Research

There is some evidence of a growing emphasis on educational research in the schools. In part this has been brought about through the various acts of Congress supporting elementary and secondary education that provide that programmes benefiting from such grants be constantly subjected to evaluation. In part, increased amounts of educational research are the direct result of federal funding of both research projects and training of educational researchers. There can be little question also that the demand by the pubic for more evidence on the efficiency of the schools and on the degree of accomplishment of educational goals has stimulated research designed to provide such evidence. In most such activities measurement plays an active and important role.

In school surveys tests are useful tools for studying such problems as the grade placement of pupils, achievement in basic fundamentals, the relationship of the offerings of the school to the needs of the community, and the degree of success attained in realising the educational goals of the school or of the community. Measuring instruments are not available yet for all of the educational goals a school or community may set for itself, but existing ones are constantly being improved and new and better ones developed. This is true, for example, in the case of educational goals expressed in terms of subject-matter and, to a lesser extent, of such goals as attitudes, desirable habits of work and study, and participation in school and community activities. In other areas such as social adjustment or citizenship it may be necessary to devise original measures. This in itself is a worthwhile type of research activity for teachers, particularly if they have the advice help of specialists.

Tests may also serve research purposes in the schools in conjunction with comparative studies of different methods of teaching. Most teachers are keenly interested in finding the most effective ways of doing things, not only because of the improved efficiency and consequent saving of time and energy, but also because better methods result in better learning or achievement by the pupil. A common type of educational research is to form two equated or equivalent classes or sections and to compare the relative effectiveness of two methods of instruction, one class taught by one method, the other by the other method. If the two groups are equal at the beginning, then any difference at the end may be ascribed to the differences in method—provided, of course, that all other factors that might affect the results are held constant. In all such experiments measurement plays an important part. It is used to measure and equate the status of groups before the experiment is begun, and to measure the results after it is completed.

Bibliography

A. T. Jersild, R. L. Thorndike, B. Goldman, and J. J. Loftus, "An Evaluation of Aspects of the Activity Programme in the New York City Public Elementary Schools," *Journal of Experimental Education,* 8: 166–207 (December 1939).

Alden W. Badal and Edwin P. Larsen, *On Reporting Test Results to Community Groups,* National council on Measurement in Education Special Reports, Vol. 1, No. 4 (May 1970).

Allen L. Edwards and Kathryn C. Kenney, "A Comparison of the Thurstone and Likert Techniques of Attitude Scale Construction," *Journal of Applied Psychology,* 30 : 72–83 (February 1946).

American Psychological Association Committee, *Ethical Standards for Psychologists* (Washington, D.C.: American Psychological Association, 1953), pp. 143-155.

Anne Anastasi, "Some Implications of Cultural Factors for Test Construction," *ibid.*, Chapter 10.

Arno Jewett, J. Dan Hull, *et al.*, *Teaching Rapid and Slow Learners in High School,* U.S. Office of Education Bulletin 1954, No. 5 (Washington, D.C.: Government Printing Office, 1954).

Arthur E. Hamalainen, *An Appraisal of Anecdotal Records,* Contributions to Education, No. 891 (New York: Teachers College, Columbia University, 1943).

Arthur E. Traxler, *The Nature and Use of Anecdotal Records,* Educational Records Bureau Supplementary Bulletin D, Revised (New York: Educational Records Bureau, 1949).

Arthur R. Jensen, "Social Class, Race and Genetics," *American Educational Research Journal,* 5:1–42 (January 1968).

Beeman N. Phillips and Garrett Weathers, "Analysis of Errors Made in Scoring Standardised Tests," *Educational and Psychological Measurement,* 18 : 563–567 (Autumn 1958).

Bernard M. Bass, "Faking by Sales Applicants of a Forced-Choice Personality Inventory," *Journal of Applied Psychology,* 41:403-104 (December 1957).

Byron W. Lindholm, "Changes in Conventional and Deviation I.Q.'s," *Journal of Educational Psychology,* 55: 110–113 (April 1964).

Carl E. Seashore, *et al., Seashore Measures of Musical Talents* (New York: Psychological Corporation, 1919–1960).

Carl W. Pegnato and Jack W. Birch, "Locating Gifted Children in Junior High Schools—A Comparison of Methods," *Exceptional Children,* 25 : 300–304 (March 1959);

Center for the Study of Evaluation, Products For Improving Educational Evaluation. Fifth Annual Report to the U.S. Office of Education. Evaluation Comment; Los Angeles: University of California (September 1970), Vol. 2, No. 3.

David P. Campbell, *Manual, 1969 Supplement, Strong Vocational Interest Blanks* (Stanford, Calif.: Stanford University Press, 1969).

David Wechsler, *The Measurement of Adult Intelligence* (Baltimore: Williams and Wilkins, 1939).

David Wechsler, *Wechsler Adult Intelligence Scale* (New York: Psychological Corporation, 1955).

David Wechsler, *Wechsler Intelligence Scale for Children* (New York: Psychological Corporation, 1949).

David Wechsler, *Wechsler Preschool and Primary Scale of Intelligence* (New York: Psychological Corporation, 1967).

Donald T. Campbell, "Reforms As Experiments," *American Psychologist,* 24 : 409–429 (April 1969).

E. L. Thorndike, *The Measurement of Intelligence* (New York: Teachers College, Columbia University, 1927).

E. L. Thorndike, *The Teacher's Word Book* (New York: Bureau of Publications, Teachers College, Columbia University, 1921).

E. Paul Torrance, *Gifted Children in the Classroom* (New York: The Macmillan Company, 1965).

E. Paul Torrance, *Tests of Creative Thinking* (Princeton, N.J.: Personnel Press, 1966).

Edgar Z. Friedenberg, "The Real Functions of Educational Testing," *Change* (January-February 1970), pp. 43–47.

Edward K. Strong, Jr., *Manual for Vocational Interest Blank for Women* (Stanford, Calif.: Stanford University Press, 1947), p. 14.

Edward L. Thorndike, *Handwriting* (New York: Teachers College, Columbia University, 1910).

Elise H. Martens, *Curriculum Adjustments for Gifted Children,* U.S. Office of Education Bulletin 1946, No. 1 (Washington, D.C.: Government Printing Office, 1946).

Elizabeth M Drews, "The Effectiveness of Homogeneous and Heterogeneous Ability Grouping in 9th Grade English Classes with Sow, Average, and Superior Students Including the Investigation of Attitudes, Self-Concept, and Critical Thinking" (Unpublished manuscript, College of Education, Michigan State University, East Lansing, Michigan, 1961).

Frank N. Freeman, *Handwriting Measuring Scale* (Columbus, Ohio: Zaner-Bloser Company, 1930).

G. Frederic Kuder and M. W. Richardson, "The Theory of the Estimation of Test Reliability," *Psychometrika,* 2:151-260, September, 1937.

G. K. Bennett, H. G. Seashore, and A. G. Wesman. *Differential Aptitude Tests,* 1963 ed.

Gates-MacGinitie Reading Tests (New York: Teachers College, Columbia University, 1965–1968).

Georgia Sachs Adams and John A. Sexson, *California Tests in Social and Related Sciences: Social Sciences* (California Test Bureau, 1955).

Gertrude Hildreth, *Learning the Three R's; A Modern Interpretation,* Second edition (Minneapolis, Minn.: Educational Publishers, Inc., 1947).

Gertrude Hildreth, *Metropolitan Primary Handwriting Scale.* Copyright 1933, copyright renewed 1960 by Harcourt Brace Jovanovich, Inc., New York.

Gordon Personal Profile and *Gordon Personal Inventory.* 1953–63. Harcourt Brace Jovanovich, Inc.

Harry J. Baker and Paul F. Voelker, *Detroit Clerical Aptitudes Examination, Revised* (Indianpolis: The Bobbs-Merrill Company, Inc., 1944).

Helen H. Jennings, *Sociometry in Group Relations* (Washington, D.C.: American Council on Education, 1959).

Henry J. Otto, "Pupil Failure as an Administrative Device in Elementary Education," *Elementary School Journal,* 34 : 576–589 (April 1934).

Horace Mann-Lincoln Institute of School Experimentation, *How to Construct a Sociogram* (New York: Teachers College, Columbia University, 1950).

Irvin A. Keller, "A More Comprehensive and Significant Marking System," *Bulletin of the National Association of Secondary School Principals,* 36 : 70–78 (January 1952).

Irving Lorge, "Difference or Bias in Tests of Intelligence," in *Testing Problems in Perspective* (Washington, D.C.: American Council on Education, 1966), Chapter 10.

J. P. Guilford, "Creativity," *American Psychologist,* 5:444–454 (1950);

see also, J. P. Guilford, *Psychological Bulletin* (1956); *Teachers College Record* (1962); *American Psychologist* (1966).

Jacob L. Moreno, *Who Shall Survive?* (Washington, D.C.: Nervous and Mental Disease Publishing Company, 1934).

Jerome E. Doppelt and George K. Bennett, *Testing Job Applicants from Disadvantaged Groups* (New York: The Psychological Corporation, 1967), Test Service Bulletin, No. 57.

John B. Carroll and Stanley M. Sapon, *Modern Language Aptitude Test*. 1955-58.(New York: Psychological Corporation).

John F. Feldhusen, "Student Perceptions of Frequent Quizzes and Post-Mortem Discussions of Results," *Journal of Educational Measurement,* 1 : 51–54 (June 1964).

John G. Darley, *Testing and Counselling in the High School Guidance Programme* (Chicago: Science Research Associates, Inc., 1943),

pp. 140-141.

John I. Goodlad, "To Promote or Not to Promote," *Childhood Education,* 30 : 212–215 (January 1954).

Joseph Peterson. *Early Conceptions and Tests of Intelligence* (New York: Harcourt Brace Jovanovich, Inc., 1925), pp. 172–174.

Kenneth W. Eells, Allison Davis, Robert J. Havighurst, Virgil E. Herrick, and Ralph Tyler, *Intelligence and Cultural Differences* (Chicago: University of Chicago Press, 1951).

L. L. Thurstone and E. J. Chave, *The Measurement of Attitude* (Chicago: University of Chicago Press, 1929).

Lee J. Cronbach, *Essentials of Psychological Testing,* 3rd ed. (New York: Harper & Row, Publishers, 1970), p. 197.

Leo Goldman, *Using Tests in Counselling* (New York: Appleton-Century-Crofts, Inc., 1961).

Leonard P. Ayres, *Measuring Scale for Handwriting: Gettysburg Edition* (New York: Russell Sage Foundation, 1917).

Lewis M. Terman and Maud A. Merrill, *Measuring Intelligence* (Boston: Houghton Mifflin Company, 1937).

Lewis M. Terman and Maud A. Merrill, *Stanford-Binet Intelligence Scale,* 3rd rev. (Boston: Houghton Mifflin Company, 1960).

M. Vere DeVault, Elizabeth Fennema, K. Allen Neufeld, and Lewis B. Smith, *Wisconsin Contemporary Test of Elementary Mathematics* (Princeton, N.J.: Personnel Press, Inc., 1967).

Margaret Doren, *Doren Diagnostic Reading Test of Word Recognition Skills* (Minneapolis: American Guidance Service, Inc., 1956).

Marion J. Erickson, "Current Trends and Practices in the Education of the Mentally Retarded," *Educational Administration and Supervision,* 44 : 297–308 (September 1958);

Marjorie P. Honzik, Jean MacFarlane, and L. Allen, "The Stability of Mental Test Performance Between Two and Eighteen Years," *Journal of Experimental Education,* 17:309–324 (December 1948).

Maud A. Merrill, *Training Students to Administer the Stanford-Binet Intelligence Scale* (Boston: Houghton Mifflin Company n.d.), Testing Today, No. 2.

Meier Aesthetic Perception Test. 1963. Iowa: Bureau of Educational Research and Service).

Meier Art Judgment Test. 1928–1942. (Iowa City, Iowa: Bureau of Educational Research and Service).

Michael Amrine, ed, "Special Issue: Testing and Public Policy," *American Psychologist,* 20 : 857–993 (November 1965).

Minnesota Paper Form Board, Revised. 1930–48. Grade 9-Adult. Forms AA, BB (hand scored) or MA, MB (machine scored.) (New York: Psychological Corporation).

Miriam L. Goldberg, A. Harry Passow, and Joseph Justman, *The Effects of Ability Grouping* (New York: Teachers College Press, 1966).

Nancy Bayley, "Consistency and Variability in the Growth of Intelligence from Birth to Eighteen," *Journal of Genetic Psychology,* 75:165-1969; 1949.

Ralph F. Berdie, *et al., Testing in Guidance and Counselling* (New York: McGraw-Hill Book Co. Inc., 1963).

Rensis Likert, "A Technique for the Measurement of Attitudes," *Archives of Psychology,* Volume 22, No. 140 (1932).

Robert A. Feldmesser, "Measurement Problems in Performance Contracting," National Council on Measurement in Education *Newsletter,* 14:6-7 (July 1971).

Ross L. Mooney and Leonard V. Gordon. *The Mooney Problem Check Lists* (New York: The Psychological Corporation, 1950).

Ruth B. Ekstrom, *Experimental Studies of Homogeneous Grouping: A Review of the Literature* (Princeton, N.J.: Educational Testing Service, 1961).

S. L. Pressey, *Educational Acceleration: Appraisals and Basic Problems,* Bureau of Educational Research Monograph No. 31 (Columbus, Ohio: Ohio State University, 1949).

S. L. Pressey, *et al., Diagnostic Tests in English Composition* (Indianapolis: The Bobbs-Merrill Company, Inc., 1924).

Stephen M. Corey, "Professed Attitudes and Actual Behaviour," *Journal of Educational Psychology,* 28 : 271–280 (April 1937).

The Grouping of Pupils, Thirty-Fifth Yearbook of the National Society for the Study of Education, Part I (Chicago: The Society [distributed by the University of Chicago Press], 1936), pp. 302-303.

V. S. Ward, *The Gifted Student: A Manual for Programme Improvement* (Atlanta: Southern Regional Education Board, 1962).

Victor H. Noll and Marvin D. Glock, "Functional Courses in Measurement and Evaluation,' *School and Society,* 70 : 339–340 (November 26, 1949).

Victor H. Noll and Walter N. Durost, *Measurement Practices and Preferences of High School Teachers,* Test Service Notebook No. 8 (New York: Harcourt Brace Jovanovich, n.d.).

Victor H. Noll and Walter N. Durost, *Measurement Practices and Preferences of High School Teachers,* Test Service Notebook No. 8 (New York: Harcourt Brace Jovanovich, Inc., n.d.).

Victor H. Noll, "Relation of Scores on *Davis-Eells Games* to Socio-Economic Status, Intelligence Test Results and School Achievement," *Educational and Psychological Measurement,* 20:119–129 (Spring 1960).

Victor H. Noll, "Simulation by College Students of a Prescribed Pattern on a Personality Scale," *Educational and Psychological Measurement,* 11:478–488 (Spring 1951).

Victor H. Noll, "The Effect of Written Tests upon Achievement in College Classes: An Experiment and a Summary of Evidence," *Journal of Educational Research,* 32 : 345–358 (January 1939).

W. S. Miller, "Variation and Significance of Intelligence Quotients Obtained from Group Tests," *Journal of Educational Psychology,* 15:359–366. (September 1924); "Variation of I.Q.'s Obtained from Group Tests," 24: 468–474 (September 1933).

Warren W. Willingham, ed., "Invasion of Privacy in Research and Testing," Supplement to the *Journal of Educational Measurement* (Spring 1967).

Willard C. Olson, *The Measurement of Nervous Habits in Normal Children.* Institute of Child Welfare Monographs, No. 3 (Minneapolis, Minn.: University of Minnesota Press, 1929).

William L. Schmalgemeir and Richard P. Watson, *Michagon Schools. The Organisation and Management of Their Testing Programmes–1970* (Ann Arbor, Mich.: Michigan Bureau of School Services, The University of Michigan, 1970).